BREAKING IN
TO THE MOVIES

BREAKING IN TO THE MOVIES

FILM AND THE CULTURE OF POLITICS

HENRY A. GIROUX

BLACKWELL
Publishers

Copyright © Henry A. Giroux 2002

The right of Henry A. Giroux to be identified as author of this work has been
asserted in accordance with the Copyright, Designs and Patents Act 1988.

First published 2002

2 4 6 8 10 9 7 5 3 1

Blackwell Publishers Inc.
350 Main Street
Malden, Massachusetts 02148
USA

Blackwell Publishers Ltd
108 Cowley Road
Oxford OX4 1JF
UK

Library of Congress Cataloging-in-Publication Data has been applied for

ISBN 0-631-22603-6 (hardback); 0-631-22604-4 (paperback)

British Library Cataloguing in Publication Data

A CIP catalogue record for this book is available from the British Library.

Typeset in Bembo on 11.5pt/13.5pt
by Kolam Information Services Pvt. Ltd, Pondicherry, India

This book is printed on acid-free paper.

To my wonderful Susan whose hand I delight in holding every time we watch a movie together.

Contents

CONTENTS

Acknowledgments

There are many friends who have read these articles and shared their thoughts with me. I am particularly grateful to Susan Searls who engaged in long conversations with me about the ideas in all of these articles, but also brought her incredible editing skills to bear in reading them. Roger Simon has always been an avid supporter of my film work, and I have learned a great deal from him. Ken Saltman has been an invaluable help in both advising me about what films to see and providing a critical reading of my work. Larry Grossberg has been indispensable in providing me with the theoretical tools to think through many of my political, pedagogical, and theoretical ideas about film. Nick Couldry has taught me a great deal about the media. Peter McLaren and Jenny McLaren, my dear friends, taught me something about the joy and social value of sharing films with others. While I was at Boston University, Howard Zinn and I shared a similar joy of films and an equal contempt for much of the ideological junk that Hollywood passed off as serious political film making. My brother Donaldo Macedo doesn't watch many films, but he was kind enough to indulge my writing about them. I also want to thank Stanley Aronowitz who always had an insightful comment about any film in which I expressed an interest. A sincere thanks to my three boys, Chris, Jack, and Brett, who share my love of good movies. Thanks to Eric Weiner for reading and editing all of the essays in this collection. And a heartfelt appreciation to all of my

ACKNOWLEDGMENTS

students who were always a great source of insight and pleasure regarding the films we watched in classes together.

This book would not have been possible without the help of Jayne Fargnoli, who has been my editor over the course of 11 years. She supported this project from the first time I mentioned it, and because of her intelligence and keen insight helped to make the idea a much better book. I also want to thank Annie Lenth at Blackwell for her patience, support, and invaluable help.

Versions of the essays included in this book have appeared in *Jumpcut*, *Cineaste*, *Film Criticism*, *Film Quarterly*, *Journal of Advanced Composition*, *Socialist Review*, *Review of Education/Pedagogy/Cultural Studies*, *Social Identities*, *Third Text*, *New Art Examiner*.

Henry Giroux
May 2001

Breaking in to the Movies: An Introduction

Without a politically guaranteed public realm, freedom lacks the worldly space to make its appearance.

Hannah Arendt[1]

My memories of Hollywood films cannot be separated from the attractions that such films had for me as a young boy growing up in Smith Hill, a working-class neighborhood of Providence, Rhode Island in the 1950s. While we had access to the small screen of black and white television, it held none of the mystery, fascination, and pleasure that we found in the five or six grand movie theaters that populated the downtown section of Providence. Every Saturday afternoon, my friends and I would walk several miles to the business district, all the while making plans to get into the theaters without having to pay. None of us could afford to buy tickets so we had to be inventive about ways to sneak into the theaters without being caught. Sometimes we would simply wait next to the exit doors, and as soon as somebody left the theater we would rush in and bury ourselves in the plush seats, hoping that none of the ushers spotted us. We were not always so lucky. At other times, we would pool our money and have one person buy a ticket, and at the most strategic moment he would open the exit door from the inside and let us in. Generally, we would sit in the balcony so as to avoid being asked for a ticket if the ushers came along and spotted us.

Hollywood film engendered a profound sense of danger and otherness for us. Gaining access to the movies meant we had to engage in illicit behavior, risking criminal charges, if not a beating by an irate owner, if caught. But the fear of getting caught was outweighed by the lure of adventure and joy. Once we got inside the movie theater we were transported into an event. We were able to participate in a public act of viewing that was generally restricted for kids in our neighborhood because films were too expensive, too removed from the daily experiences of kids too poor to use public transportation; we were too restless to sit in a movie theater without talking and laughing, and allegedly too rough to inhabit a public space meant for family entertainment. Silence in the movie theaters was imposed on us by the fear of being noticed. Yet the thrill of adventure and the expectation of what was about to unfold before us was well worth the self-imposed discipline, the contained silence and focus that such viewing demanded. Back on the street, the movies enabled a space of dialogue, criticism, and solidarity for us. Movies were a source of shared joy, entertainment, escape, and, though we were too young to realize it at the time, a source of knowledge – a source of knowledge that, unlike what we were privy to in school, connected pleasure to meaning. Sometimes we saw as many as three double features in one day. When we left the movie theater, the cinematography and narratives that we had viewed filled our conversations and our dreams. We argued, sometimes actually fought, over their meaning and relevance for our lives. Hollywood films took us out of Smith Hill, offered narratives that rubbed against the often rigid identities we inhabited, and offered up objects of desire that both seduced us and left us thinking that the movies were not about reality but fantasies, remote from the burdens and problems that dominated our neighborhoods. Films pointed to a terrain of pseudofreedom located in an inner world of dreams, reinforced by the privatized experience of pleasure and joy offered through the twin seductions of escape and entertainment.

All of these memories of my early exposure to Hollywood films came rushing back to me during a recent visit to Universal Studios in Los Angeles. While I was on one of the tours of the studio lots, the guide attempted to capture the meaning of contemporary films by proclaiming, without hesitation, that the great appeal of movies lies in their capacity to "make people laugh, cry, and sit on the edge of their seats." Surely I believed this as a child, as much as the tourists listening to the guide seemed to believe it almost 40 years later. My first reaction was to dismiss the guide's comments as typical of Hollywood's attempt to commodify experience through simplification and reification, relieving pleasure of the burden of thinking, let alone critique, and positioning the public as passive tourists traveling through the Hollywood dream machine. But there was something about the guide's comments that warranted more than a simple dismissal. While the mythic fantasy and lure of entertainment demands a challenge to the utterly privatized realm of mass-mediated common sense, it also requires more than the arrogance of theory, which often refuses to link the pleasure of film watching with the workings and structures of the public domain. Films do more than entertain, they offer up subject positions, mobilize desires, influence us unconsciously, and help to construct the landscape of American culture. Deeply imbricated within material and symbolic relations of power, movies produce and incorporate ideologies that represent the outcome of struggles marked by the historical realities of power and the deep anxieties of the times; they also deploy power through the important role they play connecting the production of pleasure and meaning with the mechanisms and practices of powerful teaching machines. Put simply, films both entertain and educate.

In the 1970s, I began to understand, though in a limited way, the constitutive and political nature of films, particularly how power is mobilized through their use of images, sounds, gestures, talk, and spectacles in order to create the possibilities for people to be educated about how to act, speak, think, feel, desire, and behave. Films provided me with a pedagogical tool for offering students alternative views of the world. Of course, films not only challenged print culture as the only viable source of knowledge, they were attractive cultural texts for students because they were not entirely contaminated by the logic of formal schooling. As a young high school teacher, I too was attracted to films as a way of challenging the constraints imposed by the rigidity of the text-based curriculum. In opposition to the heavy reliance on the lock-step traditional curriculum, I would rent documentaries from a local Quaker group in order to present students with a critical perspective on the Vietnam War, poverty, youth-oriented issues, the Cold War, and a host of other social concerns. Films now became crucial texts for me, useful as a resource to offset dominant textbook ideologies and invaluable as a pedagogical tool to challenge officially sanctioned knowledge and modes of learning.

The choices I made about what films to show were determined by their overtly educational content. I had not at that point figured out that all films functioned pedagogically in and out of schools. Nor did I ever quite figure out how my students felt about these films. Far removed from the glamor of Hollywood, these documentary narratives were often heavy-handed ideologically, displaying little investment in irony, humor, or self-critique. Certainly my own reception of them was marked by ambivalence. The traditional notion that films were either forms of entertainment, or the more radical argument that dismissed films as one-dimensional commodities, seemed crass to me. One option that I pursued in challenging these deeply held assumptions was to engage films performatively as social practices and events mediated within the give and take of diverse public spheres and lived experiences. My students and I discussed the films we viewed both in terms of the ideologies they disseminated and how they worked to move mass audiences and break the continuity of common sense. In addition, films became important to me as a way of clarifying my role as a critical teacher and to broaden my understanding of critical pedagogy, but there was a price to pay for such an approach. Films no longer seemed to offer me pleasure in as much as my relationship to them was now largely conceived in narrow, instrumental terms. As a subversive resource to enhance my teaching, I focused on films in ways that seemed to ignore how they functioned as sites of affective investment, mobilizing a range of desires while invoking the incidental, visceral, and transitory. Films became for me, though unconsciously, formalized objects of detached academic analysis. I attempted to organize films around important pedagogical issues, but in doing so I did not use theory as a resource to link films to broader aspects of public life – connecting them to audiences, publics, and events within the concrete relations of power that characterized everyday life. I used theory as a way of legitimating film as a social text, rather than as a site where different possibilities of uses and effects intersect. I wanted students to read films critically, but I displayed little concern with what it meant to do more than examine how films as relatively isolated texts were implicated in the production of ideologies. Missing from my approach then was any sustained attempt to address how both documentary and popular films might be used pedagogically to prepare students to function as critical agents capable of engaging those discourses and institutional contexts that closed down democratic public life. In addition, by being overly concerned with how films might be used as alternative educational texts, I failed to understand and impart to my students the powerful role that films now played within a visual culture employing new forms of pedagogy, signaling new forms of literacy, and exemplifying a mode of politics in which "culture [becomes] a crucial site and weapon of power in the modern world."[2]

I am not suggesting, in retrospect, that films are overburdened by theoretical discourses *per se* or that they should be removed from the sphere of engaged textual analysis. But I do want to challenge those versions of textuality and theory that isolate films from those broader social issues and considerations that structure the politics of everyday realities. Drawing upon a distinction made by Lawrence Grossberg, I am more interested in a theorizing politics than in a politics of theory,[3] which suggests less an interest in theory as an academic discourse than as a resource understood and strategically deployed in relation to particular projects, contexts, and practices that both make pressing problems visible and offer the tools to expand the promises of a substantive democracy.

At the same time, as films, particularly Hollywood films, become more commodified, ubiquitous, and increasingly abstracted from serious forms of critical analysis, it is all the more important to engage the varied theoretical discourses around film studies produced by feminists, mass culture theorists, Marxists, and others. These approaches have performed an important theoretical service in enabling us to understand the aesthetic and political significance of film texts, on the one hand, and the specific industrial and economic formations that shape how they are produced and consumed on the other.[4] But while academic film studies dramatically offset the commonplace assumption that films are either simply about entertainment or not worthy of serious academic analysis, such discourses have often become so narrow as to find no way to talk about film as a public pedagogy or to fully engage how film relates to public life. These discourses often treat film in a manner that is overly formalistic and pretentiously scientific, trapped in a jargon that freezes the worldly dimensions of films as public transcripts that link meanings to effects, forged amidst the interconnecting registers of meaning, desire, agency, and power. The refusal to fully engage film as a public medium that, as Gore Vidal points out, provides both a source of joy and knowledge[5] is all the more problematic, especially since film has become so prevalent in popular and global culture as a medium through which people communicate to each other.

The potency and power of the movie industry can be seen in its powerful influence upon the popular imagination and public consciousness. Unlike ordinary consumer items, film produces images, ideas, and ideologies that shape both individual and national identities. The power of its reach and extent of its commodification can be seen as film references are used to sell tee shirts, cups, posters, bumper stickers, and a variety of kitsch. But at the same time, the growing popularity of film as a compelling mode of communication and form of public pedagogy – a visual technology that functions as a powerful teaching machine that intentionally tries to influence the production of meaning, subject positions, identities, and experience – suggests how important it has become as a site of cultural politics. Herman Gray captures this sentiment in arguing that "culture and the struggles over representation that take place there are not just substitutes for some 'real' politics that they inevitably replace or at best delay; they simply represent a different, but no less important site in the contemporary technological and postindustrial society where political struggles take place."[6]

As a form of public pedagogy, film combines entertainment and politics and, as I have attempted to argue, lays claim to public memory, though in contested ways, given the existence of distinctly varied social and cultural formations. Yet, films are more than "vehicles of public memory," mining the twin operations of desire and nostalgia; they are also sites of educated hopes and hypermediated experiences that connect the personal and the social by bridging the contradictory and overlapping relations between private discourses and public life. While films play an important role in placing particular ideologies and values into public conversation, they also provide a pedagogical space that opens up the "possibility of interpretation as intervention."[7] As public pedagogies, they make clear the need for new forms of literacy that address the profoundly political and pedagogical ways in which knowledge is constructed and enters our lives in what Susan Bordo calls "an image saturated culture."[8] For progressive educators and others, this might mean educating students and others to engage the ethical and practical task of analyzing critically how films function as social practices that influence their everyday lives and position them within existing social, cultural, and institutional machineries of power; how the historical and contemporary meanings that films produce align, reproduce, and interrupt broader sets of ideas, discourses, and social configurations at work in the larger society.[9]

How we think about film as a public pedagogy and form of cultural politics is all the more crucial to address as traditional, if not oppositional, public spheres such as religious institutions, schools, trade unions, and social clubs become handmaidens to neoliberal social agendas that turn such noncommodified public spheres into commercial spaces.[10] The decline of public life demands that we use film as a way of raising questions that are increasingly lost to the forces of market relations, commercialization, and privatization. As the opportunities for civic education and public engagement begin to disappear,[11] film may provide one of the few mediums left that enables conversations that connect politics, personal experiences, and public life to larger social issues. Not only does film travel more as a pedagogical form compared to other popular forms such as television and popular music, but film carries a kind of pedagogical weight that other media lack. Films allow their ideologies to play out pedagogically in a way that a three-minute pop song or a 22-minute sitcom cannot do, and by doing so offer a deeper pedagogical register for producing particular narratives, subject positions, and ideologies. In addition, young people inhabit a culture in which watching film demands a certain degree of attention, allowing them to enter into its discourse intertextually in a way that they cannot or often refuse to do with television programs and other electronic media. Often a backdrop for a wide range of social practices, television, video games, and popular music are a kind of distracted media that do not offer the pedagogical possibilities that appear relatively unique to films' mobilization of a shared and public space.

Using films in my classes during the last decade, it became clear to me that film connects to students' experiences in multiple ways that oscillate between the lure of film as entertainment and the provocation of film as a cultural practice. On one hand, many students, feeling powerless and insecure in a society marked by a cut-throat economy, increasing privatization, and a breakdown of all notions of public life, find a sense of relief and escape in the spectacle of film. On the other hand, many students see in the public issues addressed by film culture a connection to public life that revitalizes their sense of agency and resonates well with their sense of the importance of the cultural terrain as both an important source of knowledge and critical dialogue. At best, films offer my students an opportunity to connect the theoretical discourses we engage in classes with a range of social issues represented through the lens of Hollywood movies. Reading about youth seems more compelling when accompanied by a viewing of Larry Clark's film, *Kids*. Theorizing masculinity in American society becomes more meaningful and concrete when taken up within a film such as *Fight Club*, especially since many students identify with the film and only after seeing and talking about it as part of a critical and shared dialogue do they begin to question critically their own investment in the film.

Films no longer merely constitute another method of teaching for me, a view I had held as a high school teacher. They now represent a new form of pedagogical text – not simply reflecting culture but actually constructing it – that signals the need for a radically different perspective on literacy and the relationship between film texts and society. The power and pervasiveness of films not only call into question their status as cultural products, but raise serious questions about how their use of spectorial pleasure and symbolic meaning work to put into play people's attitudes and orientation toward social others and the material circumstances of their own lives. The importance of films as a form of public pedagogy also raises questions about the educational force of the larger culture, and the recognition that to make knowledge meaningful in order to make it critical and transformative, it is necessary to understand, engage, and make accountable those modes of learning that shape students' identities outside of the school. Of course, there is always the risk of using popular cultural forms such as films as a way of policing students' pleasures and in doing so undermining the sense of joy and entertainment that films provided. But, as Margaret Miles points out, it would be an ethical and pedagogical mistake to allow students to believe that films are merely about entertainment, or at the same time to suggest that the pleasure of entertainment is identical to the "learned pleasure of analysis."[12] Scrutinizing the pleasure of entertainment in films, James Snead points out: "[i]t never has been enough to just see a film – and now, more than ever, we need, not just to 'see,' but to 'see through' what we see on the screen."[13] Snead is not denying that students make important affective investments in film, but he wants educators to recognize that such investments often work well to connect people and power through mechanisms of identification and affect that effectively undermine the energies of critical engagement. Snead's comments suggest that students must think seriously about how films not only give meaning to their lives but also mobilize their desires in powerful ways. Seeing through films means, in this sense, developing the critical skills to engage how the ideological and the affective work in combination to offer up particular ways of viewing the world in ways that come to matter to individuals and groups. Films assume a major educational role in shaping the lives of many students, and bell hooks is right in claiming that the pedagogical importance of such films both in terms of what they teach and the role that they can play as objects of pedagogical analysis cannot be underestimated. Her comments about her own use of such films is quite instructive:

> It has only been in the last ten years or so that I began to realize that my students learned more about race, sex, and class from movies than from all the theoretical literature I was urging them to read. Movies

not only provide a narrative for specific discourses of race, sex, and class, they provide a shared experience, a common starting point from which diverse audience can dialogue about these charged issues.[14]

As a teaching form, film often puts into play issues that enter the realm of public discourse, debate, and policy making in diverse and sometimes dramatic ways – whether we are talking about films that deal with racism, challenge homophobia, or provide provocative representations that address the themes of war, violence, masculinity, sexism, and poverty. Uniquely placed between the privatized realm of the home and other public spheres, film provides a distinct space in which a range of contradictory issues and meanings enter public discourse, sometimes in a subversive fashion addressing pressing and urgent issues in American society. As a space of translation, they also bridge the gap between private and public discourses, play an important role in putting particular ideologies and values into public conversation, and offer a pedagogical space for addressing how a society views itself and the public world of power, events, politics, and institutions.

In writing this book, I was not particularly interested in defending film as an art form. Aside from the residue of nostalgia and elitism that guides this position, it is a view that seems particularly out of date, if not irrelevant, given the important role that popular culture, including film, now plays pedagogically and politically in shaping the identities, values, and broader social practices that characterize an increasingly postmodern culture in which the electronic media and visual forms constitute the most powerful educational tools of the new millennium. Similarly, in organizing this book, I was not concerned with analyzing film within the disciplinary strictures of contemporary media and film studies that are designed, in part, to legitimate film as a serious academic subject. Thus, I have chosen not to position my particular approach to discussing film in relation to what is admittedly a vast literature of film theory and viewer response theories. Absent from my analysis is a sustained focus on those specialized film theories that engage films as either self-contained texts or largely focus on film through the narrow lens of specific theoretical approaches such as semiotics, Lacanian psychoanalysis, or feminist theories of pleasure. Film and media studies are bound up within a complex philosophical debate surrounding the meaning and importance of film theory, which I could not do justice to in this book. While this work is enormously important, my aim here is much more modest. I try to address film more broadly as part of a public discourse and cultural pedagogy that participates in a kind of ideological framing and works to structure everyday issues around particular assumptions, values, and social relations. I make no claims suggesting that there is a direct correlation between what people see, hear, and read and how they act; between the representations they are exposed to and the actual events that shape their lives. But I do argue that film as a form of civic engagement and public pedagogy creates a climate that helps to shape individual behavior and public attitudes in multiple ways, whether consciously or unconsciously.

The entertainment industry is the second largest export–second only to military aircraft, and it is estimated that a successful film is seen by 10,000,000 people in theaters, and millions more when it is aired on cable and exported to foreign markets.[15] Moreover, the film industry is controlled by a very limited number of corporations that exercise enormous power in all major facets of movie making – production, distribution, and circulation in the United States and abroad.[16] At the same time, the media is not an unchanging, monolithic bastion of corporate culture and ruling-class power; a critical approach to media and film requires an understanding of film as neither monolithic nor its audiences as passive dupes. Films, like other media, work to gain consent, and operate within limits set by the contexts in which they are taken up. Moreover, as numerous film scholars have indicated, audiences mediate such films rather than simply inhabit their structures of meaning. The audience I hope to address includes educators, students, and others who want to explore film in their classes and other educational sites as part of an interdisciplinary project aimed at linking knowledge to broader social structures, learning to social change, and student experience to the vast array of cultural forms that increasingly shape their identities and values.

While this is not a book about film theory, it is concerned about what it means to situate films within a broader cultural context as well as take up the political and pedagogical implications of films as teaching machines. Theory in this book is used as a resource to study the complex and shifting relations between texts, discourses, everyday life, and structures of power. Rather than reduce it to an academic exercise rooted in a specific theoretical trajectory, I have attempted to analyze films in ways that link texts to contexts, culture to the institutional specificity of power, and pedagogy to the politics of agency and dynamics of social change. By taking up films inter-textually, I have tried to foreground not just questions of meaning and interpretation but also questions of politics, power, agency, and social transformation.

Written over the last 25 years, the mix of old and new essays in this volume represent an ongoing effort to link film as a cultural practice to other public spaces, locations, and conditions, as well as to important social issues. How films derive their meanings and how specific claims are made by different audiences on films is explored in these essays in light of a whole assemblage of other cultural texts, discourses, and institutional formations. Meaning cannot be sutured into a text, closed off from the myriad of contexts in which it is produced, circulated, and renegotiated. On the contrary, films become relevant as public pedagogies to the degree to which they are situated within a broader politics of representation, one that suggests that the struggle over meanings is, in part, defined as the struggle over culture, power, and politics. I have purposely avoided both focusing exclusively on films as isolated texts, and what Doug Kellner refers to as narrowly and one-sidedly ethnographic approaches to audience reception of texts.[17] These approaches are important, but they do not necessarily yield a productive way of dealing with films as a form of public pedagogy. Rather, they often fail to address questions of effects because they do not theorize the relationship of meaning to historical and institutional contexts, and in doing so largely ignore the material and power-saturated relations that structure daily life, which provides the contexts that films both reflect and help to construct. Missing from such analyses are the ways in which films are located along a circuit of power that connects the political economy and regulation of films with how they function as representational systems implicated in processes of identity formation and consumption.[18] The problem of movies is not that they can be understood in multiple ways, but how some meanings have a force that other meanings do not; that is, how some meanings gain a certain legitimacy and become the defining terms of reality because of how well they resonate and align under certain conditions with broader discourses, dominant ideologies, and existing material relations of power.

Throughout these essays, I provide a particular reading of the films I analyze, but in doing so I am not suggesting that my analyses in any way offer interpretations that make a claim to either certainty or finality. My analyses of films are necessarily partial, incomplete, and open to revision and contestation. Rather than closing down student participation, my own interpretations are meant to be strategic and positional, eschewing the notion that any type of closure is endemic to my perspectives on particular films while at the same time using my own position to encourage students to think more critically about their own interpretations as they enter into dialogue about films. Analysis under such circumstances is not replaced or shut down but expanded by encouraging students to enter into dialogue with both the films and the interpretations that frame them, thus engaging the meaning, function, and role of film as a pedagogical, moral, and political practice that can only be understood within a range of theoretically constructed practices and frameworks. Addressing films within a framework that is both defined and problematized, I try to signal to students and others the pedagogical value of taking a position while not standing still.

Films both shape and bear witness to the ethical and political dilemmas that animate the broader social landscape, and they often raise fundamental questions about how we can think about politics in light of such a recognition. Critique, as both a form of self-analysis and as a mode of social criticism, is central to any notion of film analysis that takes seriously the project of understanding just how cultural politics matters in the everyday lives of people and what it might mean to make interventions that are both critical and transformative. All of these essays are guided by the assumption that films can enable people to think more critically about how art can contribute to constructing public spaces that expand the possibilities for both pleasure and political agency, democratic relations, and social justice.

At the same time, the films in this book offer an opportunity for audiences in and out of the academy to examine critically not only how Hollywood films—in spite of their unquestioned fetishization of entertainment, spectacle, and glamor—encourage us to understand (or misunderstand) the wider culture but also how they influence us to live our lives.

All of the films I have chosen for this book were not only widely accessible to the public, they also dealt with complex and provocative subject matter, highlighting a number of important social issues, problems, and values that provoked the public imaginary, and in many cases generated substantial controversy. In addressing film as a form of cultural politics, I have attempted in these essays to stress the pedagogical and political practice of film in ways that render due account of the complexities of film culture itself. At the same time, I attempt to challenge a voyeuristic reception of films by offering students a modicum of the theoretical resources necessary to engage critically how dominant practices of representation work to secure individual desires, organize specific forms of identification, and regulate particular modes of understanding, knowledge, and agency. All of the essays in this book are designed to encourage educators, students, and others to take seriously the importance of films as a vehicle of public pedagogy and to examine how their practices and values embody relations of power and ideological assumptions, admittedly in contradictory ways, that both mirror and construct the interests, fears, longings, and anxieties of the periods in which they were produced. Accordingly, throughout this book I draw upon theory as a resource that sparks political engagement, challenging conventional ways of thinking about film as simply entertainment and simultaneously using film to bridge the gap between the academic discourse of the classroom and those social issues and public concerns that animate the larger society.

As a young boy watching films in Providence, Rhode Island, I believed that movies only provided the diversion of entertainment. I had no idea that they also played an active role in shaping my sense of agency, offering me a moral and political education that largely went unnoticed and uncontested. Films have been a great source of joy throughout my lifetime. Now they not only provide multiple pleasures, but also enable me to think more critically (learned pleasure of analysis) about how power operates within the realm of the cultural and how social relations and identities are forged. All films disseminate ideologies, beckon in sometimes clear and always contradictory ways towards visions of the future, encourage and stultify diverse ways of being in the world. But most importantly, film constitutes a powerful force for shaping public memory, hope, popular consciousness, and social agency and as such invites people into a broader public conversation. As a horizon of "sensory experience and discursive contestation,"[19] films engender a public space in which knowledge and pleasure intersect – no small matter as public life becomes increasingly controlled and regulated, if not militarized.[20] It is in this promise of education and sensuality that films become other, gesturing towards public spheres beyond those spaces offered by the presence of film in which critical dialogue, pleasure, shared interaction, and public participation flourish. Film, in this instance, registers a public dialogue and set of experiences that offer the opportunity to revitalize those democratic public spheres in which the popular intersects with the pedagogical and the political in ways that suggest that film cannot be dismissed simply as a commodity but now becomes crucial to expanding democratic relations, ideologies, and identities.

Notes

1. Hannah Arendt, "What is Freedom?" in *Between Past and Future: Eight Exercises in Political Thought* (New York: Penguin, 1977), p. 149.
2. Lawrence Grossberg, *Bringing It All Back Home: Essays on Cultural Studies* (Durham, NC: Duke University Press, 1997), p. 143.
3. Lawrence Grossberg, "The Cultural Studies' Crossroad Blues." *European Journal of Cultural Studies* 1.1 (1998): 65–82.
4. For a representative example of film studies scholarship see: Joanne Hollows, Peter Hutchings, and Mark Jancovich (eds.) *The Film Studies Reader* (New York: Oxford University Press, 2000); Christine Gledhill and Linda Williams (eds.), *Reinventing Film Studies* (New York: Oxford University Press, 2000); Gilberto Perez, *The Material Ghost* (Baltimore: Johns Hopkins University Press, 1998); Noell Carroll, *Mystifying Movies* (New York: Columbia University Press, 1988); Norman K. Denzin, *The*

Cinematic Society: The Voyeur's Gaze (Thousand Oaks, CA: Sage Publications, 1995). Though not focused on cinema, Durham and Kellner provide a very useful book in which to understand film within the larger body of theoretical work produced around media and cultural studies, see Meenakshi Gigi Durham and Douglas M. Kellner (eds.), *Media and Cultural Studies: Key Works* (Malden, MA: Blackwell, 2001).

5. Gore Vidal, *Screening History* (Cambridge, MA: Harvard University Press, 1992).

6. Herman Gray, *Watching Race: Television and the Struggle for "Blackness"* (Minneapolis: University of Minnesota Press, 1995), p. 6.

7. Gary Olson and Lynn Worsham, "Staging the Politics of Difference: Homi Bhabha's Critical Literacy." *JAC* 18.3 (1999): 29.

8. Susan Bordo, *Twilight Zones: The Hidden Life of Cultural Images from Plato to O.J.* (Stanford: University of California Press, 1997), p. 2.

9. Gray, *Watching Race*, op. cit., p. 132.

10. For some recent analysis of the public sphere, see Mike Hill and Warren Montag (eds.), *Masses, Classes and the Public Sphere* (London: Verso Press, 2000).

11. I take this up in great detail in Henry A. Giroux, *Public Spaces/Private Lives: Beyond the Culture of Cynicism* (Lanham, MD: Rowman and Littlefield, 2001).

12. Margaret Miles, *Seeing and Believing: Religion and Values in the Movies* (Boston: Beacon Press, 1996), p. 14.

13. James Snead, *White Screens/Black Images* (New York: Routledge, 1994), p. 131.

14. bell hooks, *Reel to Real: Race, Sex, and Class in the Movies* (New York: Routledge, 1996), p. 2.

15. Edward Asner, "Foreword" in Gary Crowdus (ed.), *The Political Companion to American Film* (Chicago: Lakeview Press, 1994), p. ix.

16. See, for instance, Robert W. McChesney, *Rich Media, Poor Democracy: Communication Politics in Dubious Times* (New York: The New Press, 2000).

17. Douglas Kellner, *Media Culture* (New York: Routledge, 1995), p. 199.

18. I am drawing here from the "circuit of culture" paradigm that has been developed by Stuart Hall and others in the *Culture, Media, and Identities* series published by Sage. For example, see Stuart Hall (ed.), *Representation: Cultural Representations and Signifying Practices* (Thousand Oaks, CA: Sage, 1997).

19. Mariam Bratu Hansen, "*Schindler's List* is not *Shoah*: The Second Commandment, Popular Modernism, and Public Memory." *Critical Inquiry* 22 (Winter, 1996): 312.

20. I explore this issue in *Public Spaces, Private Lives*, op. cit.

PART I

Reclaiming the Political in Popular Culture

1

Norma Rae: Character, Class, and Culture[1]

The notion of class in America has an elusive quality. In objective and structural terms it is a paramount fact in American society. Yet the complexity and dynamics of class relationships, particularly the dynamics of class struggle, have been treated by mass culture in terms that both depoliticize and flatten the contradictions inherent in such relationships. In other words, the concept of class has been reduced to predictable formulas that represent forms of ideological shorthand. Needless to say, Hollywood has played no small role in dealing with class-based issues in such a way as to strip them of any critical social meaning. This becomes particularly evident when examining how Hollywood has defined working-class life and culture.

With few exceptions Hollywood's treatment of working-class people and events has been characterized by the type of reductionism that functions merely to reinforce those myths and values that provide the ideological bedrock for the existing system of social relations. Both the form and content of Hollywood films about the working class render the latter flat, one-dimensional representations that tell us nothing about the deeper concrete reality of working-class life and struggle. In effect, the portrayal of working-class life and culture is organized around concepts that contribute to its camouflage. Social mobility replaces class struggle in films like *Saturday Night Fever* and *Blood Brothers*. Images of neurosis and feelings of insanity abound in films like *Joe*, *A Woman Under the Influence*, and

Taxi Driver. Masculine adoration and the celebration of racism and sexism provide the characterization in films like *Rocky*, *The Deer Hunter*, and *Blue Collar*. Moreover, while the recent infatuation with the working class may seem refreshing, in reality it is simply a recycled and pale version of the old.

The myths haven't changed and neither has the ideology that informs Hollywood's perception of American society. Freedom is still a personal matter, cast in individualistic terms. Privatism is still the conceptual umbrella that reduces social problems to personal ones, and struggle is still viewed as a solitary rather than a collective endeavor. The point here is that if one views Hollywood as part of an ideological apparatus that functions in the interest of social and cultural reproduction, its treatment of the working class should come as no surprise. Of course, Hollywood's treatment of the working class should not be seen in either mechanistic or conspiratorial terms. Hollywood tycoons are not meeting in small rooms, plotting against the American working class. Such an image is vulgar and absurd. It might be more fruitful to view Hollywood ideology less as a result of conscious lies than as a worldview so closely related to the dominant structures of production that the relationship is not a conscious matter of reflection. In other words, the prevailing ideology that dominates this country is so pervasive and powerful that it goes unquestioned by those who hold power, that is, without carrying this too far we might say that the field and force of ideology becomes particularly powerful when illusion becomes a form of self-delusion. Of course, even in Hollywood there are contradictions, and occasionally decent films will get produced.

Amid such contradictions, films are occasionally produced that capture the real nature of the problems they portray; moreover, this sometimes happens in spite of the writer's or director's intentions. *Norma Rae*, written by Irving Ravetch and Harriet Frank, Jr., and directed by Martin Ritt, may be such a film. *Norma Rae* is a penetrating film about class struggle. It is also a film about unionizing and feminism, but these are subordinate themes, delicately woven into the objective and subjective patterns of working-class culture and everyday life.

The story, based on an actual event, tells how a fast-talking, middle-class union organizer named Reuben Warshovsky (Ron

Liebman) comes to a small southern mill town to organize the textile workers of the O.J. Hanley Plant. In the course of his struggle Reuben meets and enlists the aid of Norma Rae (Sally Field), a tough, southern working-class woman who appears to be caught between a comforting cynicism and the disquieting possibility that there are no other places to go in her life. Trapped between the imperatives of an alienating job, obligations to her two children, and the mixed love–hate relationship she has with her overly protective father (Pat Hingle), Norma Rae has little time to think about the nature or complexity of the social and political forces that shape her life. Under Reuben's continual prodding, however, she finally joins him in organizing the workers in the cotton mill, a struggle which they eventually win. But *Norma Rae* is not just about union organizing; it is more subtly concerned with the specificity of lived experience of class struggle and class solidarity. The film is not meant to provide a false utopian faith in the power of unions as much as it offers viewers an article of faith in the power of men and women to struggle together to overcome the forces that oppress them.

The slowly developing relationship between Reuben and Norma Rae becomes the pivotal force that informs the rest of the film. It is a relationship that is rich in its characterization of the forces that define the nature of each participant's class experience. Most importantly, however, *Norma Rae* is not just about a developing personal relationship between a cosmopolitan labor organizer and a somewhat battered but spirited southern woman; its real force comes from its convincing portrayal of how social, class-based determinants shape the characters' conceptual as well as felt experiences. In short, this means that the film illuminates how the dynamics of class culture and class struggle are reproduced through the lives of two individuals. The contours of this dynamic are seen not only in the relationship between Norma Rae and Reuben, but are also explored through the myriad relationship that they each have to their own work, families, histories, and dreams, and the confusing silences that sometimes awkwardly speak to their frustrations and pain.

If we view the concept of class as not only the objective and structural relationship of a group to the means of production, but also as differing sets of lived experiences, social values, cultural practices, and affective investments shaped through the prism of everyday life and struggle, we will get a better idea of what *Norma Rae* is actually about. The notion of class can be further elaborated if we think about capital as both a material and ideological commodity, as both economic and symbolic. Following Pierre Bourdieu, cultural capital as used here refers to those systems of meanings, understandings, language forms, tastes, and styles that embody specific class interests. Cultural capital points to those combinations of socially inherited and conditioned beliefs and practices that both reproduce as well as challenge existing class (and other dominant) relationships. In other words, each social class has its own contradictory and shifting assemblage of loosely bounded cultural capital, but the dominant classes have the power to foster their own ideas, histories, experiences, and language codes as the most legitimate and valued. For example, the dominant classes not only have the power to distribute goods and services (economic capital), they also use the power to reproduce, through various agencies of socialization and public spheres, forms of cultural capital which legitimate their own power relations while at the same time devaluing the cultural capital of the working class and other groups that present a potential challenge to class domination.

It is within the context of cultural capital that the notion of class becomes concrete, that is, more than a category of political economy. Class now becomes defined, in part, in terms of the received truths and ways of being that characterize different social groups and individuals. Of course, members of the ever-changing and shifting working class are not merely passive receivers of the dominant culture; nor does the existential dimension of language, perception, and style explain their posture toward dominant society. Instead, it is the combination of the existential and the received that gives meaning to the way different social classes view different forms of cultural capital. The power of the dominant culture in all of its diversity is not to be ignored, however, and the way that diverse segments of the working class view its own cultural capital is, in the final analysis, often mediated through the distorted perceptions, representations, meanings, and social relations produced and legitimated by the dominant culture in a wide range of institutions and sites.

In general, working-class cultural capital is seen as crude, in bad taste, and unsophisticated. This perception represents more than a form of elitism and intellectual confusion; it is a piece of raw ideology that is internalized in all of us. Thus, one might say that the class struggle does not simply exist in the contradictions that we have internalized. In one sense it exists as part of the struggle between one's objective and subjective politics. The most subtle dynamic of class struggle exist in the history that we carry around with us and the delimiting and often unconscious effect it has on how we live and act out our subjective politics, the politics to which we often give lip service. This dimension of the class struggle is strikingly portrayed in the character of Reuben and in his interaction with Norma Rae.

Though Reuben appears to be on the progressive side of the political spectrum, one that sympathizes with an exploited working class, he appears to unconsciously carry with him beliefs and experiences that make him very different from the workers with whom he identifies himself. Some critics have noted that the characterization of Reuben is overdrawn. I don't think that is true if you focus on how the stereotypical images function in the service of illuminating his middle-class cultural capital. Reuben's metaphors and language vividly capture the class difference between himself and Norma Rae. She tells him of her first affair, and describes how she lost her virginity in the back seat of a Cadillac, legs hanging out the window. He counters by telling her that he lost his virginity by being seduced by a music teacher under a painting of a Russian icon. She sleeps with traveling salesmen, until she gets married for the second time, and cavorts with her friends in the local bar. He sleeps with a Harvard lawyer, and reads the *New York Times* with her on Sundays. He sprinkles his speech with words like "*mensch*" and makes reference to Dylan Thomas. At one point in the film, Norma calls him to ask him what to do about a racist leaflet the managers have put on the wall in order to incite the workers against the union drive; he first responds by correcting her grammar.

While Norma Rae becomes a tangible character for us, we can only hear Reuben. Norma Rae isn't intimidated by him, however, and Reuben responds positively to her courage and discipline. While Reuben is handing out leaflets to workers entering the cotton plant,

Norma Rae passes him and humorously tells him that he is using too many big words. They begin to learn from each other. Most importantly, one sees in the interaction between this southern mill worker and labor organizer a division of labor that has prevented working-class people and middle-class intellectuals from being able either to understand or communicate with each other. Ordinarily one might expect a Reuben type to use his intellectual skills to manipulate the people he is attempting to organize, not an uncommon practice when one assumes that the people are dumb; but it does not happen in this film. Reuben and Norma Rae appear to listen to each other, an important point in the film. One can see in their growing relationship a possible bridging of the incomplete development that exists among both intellectuals and members of the working class, one voiced by Antonio Gramsci when he said, "The popular element 'knows' but does not always feel."[2] Hence not only do we see remnants of the class struggle exposed in this relationship, but we also see it giving way to a more politically progressive social relationship as Norma Rae and Reuben forge a friendship that moves beyond the sexist, exploitative relationships portrayed between men and women in most Hollywood films. The Hollywood formula of sex, power, and intimacy gives way in this film to a dynamic that demonstrates that men and women can be portrayed in ways that challenge the patriarchical formulas that shape most Hollywood movies. This becomes clear in the nonsexual relationship that Reuben and Norma Rae develop. They talk to each other, sleep in the same room on occasion, and even end up swimming nude together; their attraction is brisk, and energy-filled, but it is an attraction mediated by awareness of its own limits. Norma Rae and Reuben realize that the different cultural capital they carry around leaves little possibility for them to forge an intimate sexual affair. Knowing this, they instead develop a relationship that is nonsexist and mutually respectful.

Moreover, the class divisions that exist between Reuben and Norma Rae are played out against the larger struggle between the workers and the cotton plant executives. Within this scenario, neither the plant workers nor the plant managers are painted in bold lifeless stereotypes. Fortunately, the characteristic propensity of many commercial and documentary films to portray workers as either unadulterated agents of revolutionary change or social puppets tied to a peculiar brand of despair and self-hatred has not been emulated in this film. For instance, many of the characters are convincingly portrayed against the landscape of both their strengths and weaknesses. Norma Rae's father, for example, is viewed as a kindly heavy drinker, who never takes to either Reuben or Norma Rae's unionizing. Security and degradation are the twin pillars of his life, and he doesn't bat an eyelid about refusing to question either the nature of his own life or the experience of his own labor. The frailty and cultural capital of the workers is captured in scenes which portray them coming late to union meetings because they have been at the local gin mill first, or turning their backs on Reuben because they have received a cutback in their hours and wages because of the union drive. How this group of workers think, act, and organize are realistically tied to their work and the basic forces that shape their daily lives. Their days are spent on the job, providing for themselves and for their families. Their pain, struggles, leisure time, and work are all interrelated and provide both the drawbacks and possibilities for social action.

The interrelatedness of the forces that inform working-class life are brought into high relief in the portrayal of the interconnecting roles and forces that affect Norma Rae's life, particularly in the relationship that she has with her second husband Sonny (Beau Bridges). Sonny is a simple man who is sensitive to his wife's needs but does not understand her growing assertiveness, produced by her emerging political consciousness. Thus Norma Rae's union work and her development as a woman are portrayed against the enduring struggles she has with her husband and family, as well as with her friends and herself. The connection between the personal and the political becomes painfully clear as Norma Rae's husband shakes his head and tells Reuben that she isn't the woman he first married; plaintively, he sighs, "Her head's been turned around." Norma Rae's father appears increasingly to distance himself from her; her friends now meet her and talk to her from a different level of experience than they had in the past; some are hospitable and comradely and some have become enemies, as in the case of the sheriff who drags Norma Rae off to jail for refusing to leave the cotton plant when ordered to by the enraged manager.

A portrait of how members of the workforce are pitted and manipulate against each other through the division of labor in the mill is vividly illustrated when the plant manager attempts to quiet Norma Rae by giving her a promotion to quality control checker. She takes the promotion because she needs the money, but she slowly discovers that with her new role comes an estrangement from her former friends. She is now perceived as one of the bosses. Her friends shun her and refuse to talk to her. Even her father complains about her pushing him on the job. Workers in this case are not viewed as automatons simply doing their jobs. They know who the enemy is; they simply don't know how to defeat him. The anger and alienation that the workers exhibit appears to be deeply felt by them, but not quite understood. This is captured in a scene in which Reuben calls a house meeting to give the workers an opportunity to voice their criticisms of the plant. Instead of hearing workers polemically ranting about the evils of global oppression, we hear people faltering, hesitating, and finally speaking about issues that are real to them: women not allowed to sit down when they are having menstrual cramps; workers complaining about plant conditions, speedups, and lousy pay. There is a style, rhythm, and quality about these workers that both dignify them and at the same time reveal their limitations.

But in a larger sense, the people who inhabit the film are seen as social actors, not in the cataclysmic sense that one sees in working-class epics such as *1900* but in the undramatic sense that speaks to concrete struggles and real conflict. In one of the more dramatic scenes in the film, Norma Rae is told to leave the plant. She refuses, runs to her work place, scrawls UNION on a placard, and jumps up on a table. Surrounded by managerial thugs, she holds the sign above her head and the choice for the workers around her becomes dramatically clear. One by one, they turn off their switches and bring the oppressive hum of the cotton machinery to a halt. The scene is simple but powerful and important because it brings home the implicit power workers have; it clearly reveals the source of labor and its relationship to the people who run the plant.

The film has been criticized for not fully developing a number of themes. For instance, the complexity of the struggle to unionize the plant is underplayed. Moreover, it is clear that divisions among the working class – racial, sexual, ideological, and so forth – are blurred. All of these criticisms are true but marginal. The "silences" of the film do less to impair it than to allow it to focus more strongly on the notion of class struggle itself, a struggle personified in this case in the principle characters of the film, Norma Rae and Reuben. This is not meant to suggest that the union struggle, racial issues, sexism, and other forms of oppression are unimportant; it simply suggests that in this instance the register of class struggle has been emphasized at a moment in American history when labor and working-class people are under siege.

There is much in the film that provides room for distance and critical reflection. Ritt is successful here because he does not clutter the film with too many complex themes. I think he has made a wise decision in weaving in references and connections to other issues while at the same time not trying to give them all equal weight. Moreover, by doing so, subordinating and linking a select few of these themes hierarchically, he has provided an important political message. For instance, Norma Rae's developing feminism is linked but subordinate to the social class struggle she is engaged in. Thus the film dramatizes an element of causality that is missed in most working-class films, while pointing to the need to make class analysis critically aware of its own omissions. Norma Rae's feminism, her struggle for independence, is seen as part of a larger social struggle. The struggle for a decent daily existence is linked to overcoming the oppression exercised by the division of labor and power in the plant. The larger issues of global racism and international capitalism linger in the background implied but not explicit. This is a shortcoming but one that does not cancel out the important message or politics of the film.

Beyond the treatment of characters and the portrayal of certain themes, one has to applaud the texture of the script written by Ravetch and Frank, Jr. It sparkles with the rhythm and nuance of working-class dialogue. It is rich, moving, tied to felt experiences, and powerfully supports the concerns of the people it attempts to portray. Moreover, it seems right at home amidst the photography of John A. Alonzo (*Chinatown*). He has photographed this southern mill town in grayish whites and dirt brown tones that convincingly capture an environment filled with a mixture of hope and despair:

the grimy town motel, the peeling paint on the houses, the life-draining atmosphere of the factory. In addition, the background sound in the film does not celebrate the blues; rather, it makes us feel the deafening hum of machines that seem consciously pitted against the people who run them.

Of course there are limitations in this film. The policing power of the state is played down, the union struggle and final victory appear to come too easily, and there are some sexist references that don't quite sit well with the film's overall politics. In the end, however, *Norma Rae* delivers more than one would expect. It provides an insight into the politics of class struggle at the level of everyday life that is both enriching and convincing. In the last analysis, *Norma Rae* extends the definitions and deepens the complexities of the meaning of working-class struggles and culture in a way that has not been matched by other recent Hollywood films on the working class. For this *Norma Rae* should be seen as a reminder of the potential that films have as a pedagogical resource for engaging important critical issues while expanding our social vision.

Notes

1. A version of this essay appeared in *Jumpcut* 22 (May, 1980): 1–7.
2. Antonio Gramsci, *Selections from the Prison Notebooks* (New York: International Publishers, 1971), p. 418.

2

Hollywood Film and the Challenge of Neofascist Culture[1]

Hailed in the American press as "a charming piece of romantic pornography," *The Night Porter* is a thinly disguised fascist propaganda film that glorifies sadism, brutality, and exaggerated machismo. The film's uniqueness lies in its refusal to employ the standard subtle use of technique and content to mask its ideological message. Its barbarism rests not only in its audacity to extoll fascist principles, but also in its attempt to legitimize the death of millions of innocent victims at the hands of the Nazi machine.

The story unfolds around a chance meeting in a Vienna hotel in 1957 between Max (Dirk Bogarde), a former concentration camp SS guard and Lucia (Charlotte Rampling), a female inmate he had met in the camp. Through a series of stylized flashbacks, we learn that the SS guard saved his "little girl" from the death chamber in order to practice on her his own masturbatory sexual fantasies. Guiding her through an elaborate web of sadomasochistic rituals, he successfully unleashes her "repressed" sexual yearnings and turns her into a willing and appreciative sexual apprentice. Responding gleefully and obediently to the superior strength and virtues of her Nazi master, she acts out her masochistic character in a fittingly complementary fashion.

When they meet again, 12 years later, Max, the SS "superman," has been reduced to employment as a night porter in a Vienna hotel. Surrounded by former Nazi friends who hold weekly therapy sessions to bolster their collective ideological purity and reminisce about the "good old days," Max waits patiently for the inexorable rebirth of the old Reich. His former lover/victim has since married a successful American conductor and has, by chance, checked into the hotel where Max is working. In a scene designed to fuse the past with a prophecy for the future, the ex-SS guard successfully persuades his former victim to leave her non-German husband and affirm her link with the past by once again wedding herself to the Nazi virtues of sadomasochistic self-abuse and drooling devotion. This film makes a further dastardly comment when it portrays Max as a weakling for falling in love with this non-Aryan. Max refuses to give up Lucia to his Nazi colleagues who want her silenced for the implicit crime of blood mixing and the explicit threat that she might bring incriminating testimony against all of them. In the stringent tradition of Nazi retribution, Max is forced by his suspicious cohorts to barricade himself into his apartment where he and his girlfriend literally act out the same experiences of torture, starvation, and pain that concentration camp victims all over Europe were forced to suffer at the hands of the Nazi "supermen."

After several weeks on starvation rations, their food supply finally runs out and they are left with no choice but to evacuate their "prison cell" and place themselves at the mercy of their keepers. Intent on surrendering to his fate with the dignity and regality befitting a former member of Hitler's elite corps, Max dresses himself in his old but freshly pressed Nazi uniform. For "his little girl," Max provides a childlike dress reminiscent of the days in the camp when men were men; they then go forth together into the night and are gunned down by Max's former friends.

It is difficult to imagine that only 30 years after Dachau and Auschwitz a film can be made which suggests that the millions of people murdered by the Nazis invited their own destruction by responding favorably to the "virtues" of Nazi sadism and pseudo-strength. Even more disturbing is to see the ideological content of such a film either ignored or overlooked by the mass of critics and the general public. The message of this film is so blatant that it rips across one's sensibilities with hurricane-like force.

Is it possible that the organized consciousness of the present generation of Americans has been locked into one of the most crippling forms of alienation: the inability of a society to develop a critical consciousness capable of testing the present against the past? Such a question poses some problems for understanding the nature of oppression in the postindustrialized West as well as the strategies that are going to be used to fight that oppression. In spite of the writings of a whole generation of thinkers, ranging from Antonio Gramsci to Herbert Marcuse and Paulo Freire, the vast majority of Americans, including leftists, have refused to recognize the importance of cultural domination or "class hegemony" in Western-style nations where the obedience of the population is maintained primarily through ideological means, rather than through the traditional use of force and direct repression, as in many of the Third World countries. John Cammett, a biographer of Antonio Gramsci, the Italian communist who died in Mussolini's prisons in 1937, provides a useful definition of Gramsci's concept of "hegemony":

> . . . hegemony is "an order in which a certain way of life and thought is dominant, in which one concept of reality is diffused throughout society in all its institutional and private manifestations, informing with its spirit all taste, morality, customs, religious and political principles, and all social relations, particularly in their intellectual and moral connotations."[2]

At this point, it must be stressed that the traditional Marxist emphasis on political and economic struggles is not outdated, it simply does not go far enough in establishing a viable strategy for change. Liberation can no longer be defined in purely economic and political terms. Economic exploitation and political oppression in the postindustrial West have been paralleled by psychological forms of domination. The majority of people under class rule in any industrialized state are also the victims of specific forms of oppression on the psychological level. We are not only victims in the political and material sense, but are also tied emotionally and intellectually to the prevailing ruling-class norms and values. There is a dialectical relationship between the subjective and objective forms of oppression which both act upon and reinforce each other.

As André Gorz, the French economist-philosopher, has pointed out:

... a battle which is not from the beginning waged on the cultural, ideological and theoretical fields as well as on the main battleground would be in vain – as vain as a battle fought in the name of an overall alternative but without knowing how to embody it in mediations, without knowing how to link it to immediate struggles and needs.[3]

The methods of ideological manipulation are too well documented to present here. What has often been overlooked is the need for devising a strategy that can operate in the cultural arena while having direct political links with the immediate needs and aspirations of the people who are supposed to be liberated, mainly working-class people. Speaking as one whose roots are in the working class, I want to mention, in the hope of reviving a much-neglected discussion, some shortcomings that have been grossly overlooked in leftist strategy-forming considerations.

Before the left attempts to demystify the destructive myths of the capitalist order, it must clearly come to grips with what the Brazilian educator, Paulo Freire, calls the "pedagogy of oppression."[4] Freire claims that we all carry the "enemy" in our psyches because at one time or another we have internalized "oppressor values." But to liberate ourselves from those values presupposes more than just intellectual liberation. We must recognize that we have been emotionally crippled at our very roots, and that any authentic liberation requires a rebirth that transcends an intellectual awareness. The "oppressor consciousness" reveals itself in many ways on a noncognitive level. It exhibits itself when we reproduce relationships that do not allow people to think for themselves. It exhibits itself when we are patronizing towards the people we are going "to save." The "oppressor consciousness" is revealed less in the content of our speech than in the methodology and procedures we use when dealing with people.

The blatant neofascism of *The Night Porter* and the inability of the public to condemn it stands as a mockery of the idea of the artist/filmmaker as a freely creating individual whose work lies outside moral and political responsibilities. The bourgeois filmmaker, especially in the United States, is caught in a self-indulging fantasy that clings to the empty philosophical notion that art belongs to an ethereal realm whose existence transcends any social demands or obligations. We must bring home as forcefully as possible that the connections between ruling-class interests, values, and beliefs, and the public are not as direct as some vulgar Marxists have claimed. Intellectuals, artists, and specialists function as both mediators and organizers between institutionalized powers and the various spheres of everyday life. The ruling class cannot create culture any more than it can create production, but it certainly can appropriate it by having members of the cultural establishment legitimize and universalize capitalist beliefs and value systems in their plays, books, and films.

While *The Night Porter* represents a high point in social, cultural, and political barbarism, there is a dialectical quality to the film that cannot be overlooked if we are going to move beyond resignation and a static depiction of the film's crimes. If the American public is willing to turn its back on the blatantly fascist content of the film in order to satisfy its needs for compensatory sexual stimulation and a release from the tensions generated by the contradictions of the capitalist system, then we have a positive index of the objective level of psychic and concrete repression existing in this society. The potential for collective mobilization, by the right or the left, is clearly present.

The Night Porter is a film that has shamefacedly exhibited an arrogance and pseudostrength that is nothing more than an attempt to mystify a dying order. The challenge of demystification is ours.

Notes

1. A version of this essay appeared in *Cineaste* (Fall, 1976): 32–41.
2. John M. Cammet, *Antonio Gramsci and the Origins of Italian Communism* (Stanford, CA: Standford University Press, 1967).
3. André Gorz, *Strategy for Labor* (Boston: Beacon Press, 1964).
4. Paulo Freire, *Pedagogy of the Oppressed* (New York: The Seabury Press, 1973).

3

Lina Wertmuller: Film and the Dialectic of Liberation[1]

Lina Wertmuller, the Italian writer-director, has recently gained widespread recognition in this country with the premier of her film, *Swept Away*. Wertmuller's success was slow in developing. Her two previous films, *Love and Anarchy* and *The Seduction of Mimi*, established her reputation primarily among a small minority of politico-filmgoers. *Love and Anarchy* became a cult film and played in major cities for at least a year before its appeal spread to a more general audience. But it was *Swept Away* that brought Wertmuller nationwide recognition. Gene Shallit of the *Today* show has proclaimed to millions that Wertmuller is without a doubt "the best director in the world."

The immediate success of *Swept Away* appears problematic in light of Wertmuller's background and politics. A self-proclaimed leftist and feminist, Wertmuller strongly echoes the influence of the Gramscian-Marxist culture in which she works. In terms that Gene Shallit may have found hard to understand, Wertmuller claimed that politics is the summa of everything, a notion identical to Antonio Gramsci's idea that "everything is political, for everything is based on man's activities within the context of society. Nothing human can happen apart from politics, not even art."

The paradox of Lina Wertmuller rests within the seeming contradiction of her politics and her success among the general public, a contradiction that is heightened because it emerges among one of the most depoliticized populaces in the advanced industrial West. For this is a populace which views culture as entertainment, and a culture in which politics is defined as casting a vote for a presidential candidate. It is within the nature of this paradox that Wertmuller's politics and artistry can be examined. *Swept Away* is a pivotal film in Wertmuller's career, and lends itself to such an analysis.

The film centers around two characters played by Wertmuller's regulars, Giancarlo Giannini and Mariangela Melato. Melato plays a rich, bourgeois woman who charters a yacht on which Giannini plays a hired deck hand. The woman is a biting, haughty, pretentious symbol of her class. She is obsessed with a sense of her own power and importance, and showers the deck hand with a flood of undiluted class invectives. Her monologues are streams of consciousness filled with anticommunist allusions. Her friends gently laugh and tolerate her political diatribes, but the crew, mostly communists, burn beneath her despicable utterances. The yacht becomes a micromodel of the class war that touches the lives of everyone aboard. But it is the deck hand who grates the most under the woman's stinging insults. She soon singles him out and begins to make life miserable for him. She snickers at him because he is from southern Italy, laughs at his politics, and consistently attempts to reveal him as an inept and stupid man. In front of her friends, she chides him because the coffee is not fresh, the spaghetti is overcooked, and because of his smell. After each insult, Giannini retreats to the kitchen and unleashes a barrage of anger on his friends over the way he's being treated by this "rich, bourgeois bitch" whom he would like to kill.

Beneath the humor that shrouds the woman's encounter with the deck hand, there is a glimpse of the class conflict that shapes their lives. Both characters loom much larger than themselves, and amidst the seeming parody of their roles they emerge as embodiments of specific political-social forces. At this point in the film, the deck hand emerges from the conflict as the somber, patient, working-class communist, filled with a class hatred that is held back only with the greatest restraint.

The temper of the film changes when the woman and the deck hand get lost at sea in a small, inflatable dinghy. Cut off from her friends, and dependent upon the deck hand to get her back to the yacht, the woman refuses to suspend her ritualized class war, and unmercifully derides the deck hand, who manages to suppress his anger. He spends hours trying to catch a fish with his hands, and in a gesture of chivalry, offers her his humble catch. She responds with culinary disgust, throwing it back into the sea. His patience is stripped to the bone, and there appears to be no room between them for anything but conflict.

Before long, they land safely on an uninhabited island, and the deck hand realizes that her wealth and power can no longer be brought to bear against him. He graphically tells her to get lost, and proceeds to wander off to gather food and find shelter. Without support from the deck hand, the woman is helpless. She pleads with him to give her some of the fish he has cooked. She offers him $400.00 for it. He begins to wage his own ideological war, telling her that money is worthless to her now and that she will have to work for her food. Since she is incapable of providing for her own needs, the woman is forced to work for the deck hand, who constantly reminds her of how she tormented him on the yacht. He slaps and beats her, insulting her in class terms: " . . . and take that for the high price of cheese!"

He eventually seduces her, and effectively reduces her to the status of a work–sex machine. Between the beatings, seductions, and insults, his character begins to emerge more fully. His displays of sexism make a mockery out of his professed communism. His radical worldview exists in a psyche that is emotionally crippled by a rampant machismo. His call for a redistribution of wealth in Italian society is curiously juxtaposed next to his demand that the woman be his slave because she is a female and "the female is an object of pleasure." She gently asks if that is something he learned from the communist party. But it doesn't take long for her to develop into a full-blown masochist, and eventually she falls in love with her cruel master. They act out their fantasies undisturbed until they are eventually rescued. They finally go back to the real world despite her unwillingness to do so. She has stepped outside of the ritualized confines of her class for a short time, but seems to realize that to go back is to become trapped by them once again. His macho blinds him to the realities of the world, and he demands to go back simply to test how much she really loves him. Once they return to their respective lifestyles, he makes a pathetic attempt to convince her that they should return to the island, where they can be free from the restraints that once again are separating them. She refuses, and the film ends where it began. The two of them, in spite of the emotional changes they have experienced, view each other across class lines that are impenetrable.

While these people appear as caricatures used to parody both the bourgeoisie and the Italian communists there is a deeper and more significant message to Wertmuller's film. It is a message that captures the dialectical properties and complexity of domination and alienation in a way that is unknown to most films. The strength of Wertmuller's analysis is matched by her subtle mode of appeal. Rejecting the stark black and white dichotomies used in many "political" films to highlight the contradictions of capitalism, Wertmuller displays oppression at many different levels and in a multi-dimensional fashion. She abandons the traditional use of serious drama to reveal her point, and uses humor as a vehicle to carry the form, content, and character of her political message. But behind the humor is a dialectical expression of contemporary alienation that baffles and perplexes her critics. The paradox of Wertmuller's work, especially as developed in *Swept Away*, is inextricably related to her sophisticated conception of alienation and her interpretation of the "politics of the unpolitical."

Rejecting the nineteenth century orthodox Marxist notion that identifies alienation with a macroanalysis limited to purely economic and political institutions, Wertmuller focuses in on those forms of alienation produced at the level of everyday life. For Wertmuller, every detail of daily life is saturated with the paralyzing norms of the given society, and herein lies the key to the politics of the unpolitical. For what is often perceived as normal and natural is in effect a political mediation that locks people into the status quo. Wertmuller's keen eye is on those dimensions of alienation that exist at the psychological level and manifest themselves subtly in the behavior and communication patterns of everyday life. Wertmuller's message insists that liberation defined solely in economic and political terms is inadequate. Such a perspective ignores the psychosexual, racist forms of oppression people experience through the mass manipulation of consciousness by the established society's hegemonic control over major socializing institutions.

Wertmuller's leitmotif in *Swept Away* centers around the dichotomy between the deck hand's political beliefs and his reactionary sexism. Wertmuller's portrayal of sexist behavior by both of her characters is not designed to statically depict and reinforce sexism, rather it is designed to illustrate the necessity of merging the political with the personal.

Modern industrial states do not only victimize through the use of force, but also through the use of crippling cultural apparatuses that maim our psyches and character structure in a way that is not easily recognized. Wertmuller's focus is on the day-to-day experiences infused with racism, sexism, and authoritarianism that provide the moral underpinnings of the established order. The characters in *Swept Away* clearly display, in spite of their professed ideological differences, character structures similarly maimed by the oppressive belief and value systems that they have both internalized. But Wertmuller consistently reveals through the characters' dialogue that their subjective feelings have a social basis. Sex and love may be forces that gain their relevance on a personal level, but in the final analysis their content and form are affected by the sociocultural dynamics of the larger society. Though the elements of class and power did not objectively exist on the island on which they lived out their drama, the subjective forces that shaped their behavior were deeply rooted in the sociopolitical system they had inadvertently abandoned.

Some critics have accused Wertmuller of being a Hegelian subjectivist, playing out her ideology in a subjective world that has little bearing on concrete reality. They couldn't be farther from the truth. In the final scene of *Swept Away*, Wertmuller makes it quite clear that in the end the objective realities of class and power are not to be ignored. Love and sex in the real world do not penetrate the barriers established in a class society. Despite the personal failure of her characters, Wertmuller should not be mistaken for one taking a dim vision of the future. The constructiveness of her political vision is portrayed by her willingness to stress the importance of the politics of everyday life and the various modes of consciousness that it is capable of producing. Wertmuller is signaling the way for a redefinition of alienation and liberation, one that is linked to a new understanding of the relationship between politics and culture. Such an insight is infused with optimistic possibilities for creating a constructive strategy to build a new social order.

Wertmuller's artistry is as brilliant as the insightful message she presents. Her method is designed to give the audience room to think, and the emotive elements in her films do not stifle the possibility for critical involvement as much as they help to insure it. The form and content of *Swept Away* represents one facet of the paradox that surrounds Wertmuller's work. Her technical and artistic mastery, and her unconventional use of humor, add a refreshing dimension to the illumination of political questions rooted in the context of common language and events. It is easy to see why the general public has responded to her work in such a positive way. Wertmuller may be open to criticism for distorting her characters in order to make them palpable to the public, but, in effect, her success lies in the use of caricature to attract and educate a public to the substance of their own oppression. There are some on the left who are offended by Wertmuller's technique, but such a criticism may only illustrate the need for these critics to re-examine the multifaceted dimensions of alienation and domination, and the paradox it poses for their own personal political struggle.

Lina Wertmuller has translated to film a message and a foundation for a political strategy that qualifies her as one of the most sophisticated Marxist filmmakers in the West. Beneath the subtle dynamics that flow from her films is a call to "awaken the dreamers from their reified sleep." Therein lies the seed of Wertmuller's talent.

Note

1. A version of this essay appeared in *Film Criticism* (Winter, 1967): 11–20.

4

Looking for Mr. Goodbar: Gender and the Politics of Pleasure[1]

In an age when formalism continues to reduce the politics of culture, specifically film, to questions of technique and style, it seems appropriate *not* to begin an analysis of Richard Brooks's *Looking for Mr. Goodbar* with a comparison of Judith Rossner's bestseller. *Goodbar* has its own center of gravity, reproduces its own images and norms, and it is on that basis that the film will be analyzed.

On the surface, *Goodbar* is about the life of a 28-year-old schoolteacher named Theresa Dunn (played by Diane Keaton) who lives out the tragic/comic contradictions that beset her as she tries to live within the changing social morality of contemporary American society. By day, Terry is a warm, sensitive, dedicated teacher of deaf children. By night, she abandons her public conscience and cruises singles bars, indulging herself in a sex and horror fantasy that eventually leads to her being murdered by an ex-convict she had picked up and taken home.

Goodbar is a perplexing and disturbing film that attempts to analyze the emergence of a new kind of alienation, one that extends Marx's nineteenth-century definition of alienation as simply the dehumanizing of labor. *Goodbar* explores a form of alienation which situates itself in the realm of culture and functions to extend the organization of the workplace to the realms of consumption and leisure as well. Thus the exploitation of labor is mediated by the manipulation of consciousness, a consciousness characterized by feelings of boredom and emptiness. It is the boredom and emptiness that *Goodbar* attempts

40

to deal with. Yet *Goodbar* is perplexing because while it focuses on Theresa Dunn's personal odyssey through the detached and fragmented culture of the "new" morality and sexual freedom, the film never really comes to grips with any of the questions implied in its theme. More importantly, *Goodbar* is disturbing not only for what it does not say, but also because it ends up celebrating the kind of sexist, wooden morality that is, in part, responsible for the very issue it attempts to illuminate.

Director Richard Brooks claims he spoke to 600 women who frequent singles bars. Given the conclusion Brooks brings to the film one can't help but agonize over his petrified ideology. It is difficult to believe that Brooks could not have gleaned one glimmer of insight into the real forces that have shaped the lives of the women he interviewed, regardless of how battered their consciousnesses might have been. Consequently, at its best, *Goodbar* puts into murky relief the problematic of contemporary alienation, that is, the confused, manipulated, and misdirected search for a "meaningful" life. At its worst, the film evokes a pernicious, paralytic morality that is incapable of either explaining or resolving the fundamental problems of contemporary alienation.

Ultimately, the potential of the film's organizing premise is short-circuited by exaggerated dichotomies which characterize the film from beginning to end. Practically every major character, scene, and theme is molded by Brooks in schizophrenic extremes, black and white caricatures. Instead of real-life characters we get a handful of near psychopaths; instead of an acknowledgement of concrete political and social forces we are treated to depthless psychology; instead of portraying confusion, rage, and powerlessness as fundamentally connected to the structure of modern capitalist society, Brooks leads us to believe that these are merely subjective, psychological aberrations; instead of historical analysis, we are served ahistorical amnesia, and so it goes.

Terry Dunn, the main character of the film, is first seen as a young college student whose sexual fantasies turn from the abstract to the concrete when she has an affair with her English professor. It is within the context of this affair that Brooks first presents his simplistic reduction of the complexity of sex, power, and love to an either/or issue. The professor is such a pompous, egocentric figure that he comes off less as a substantive character than as a lurking neurotic, sprung from the demented fears of a member of the John Birch Society. He is married, ejaculates too quickly, hates women, and tantalizes Terry with such verbal bombs as "I can't stand a woman's company after I've fucked her."

Needless to say, if Terry's future portends an attempt to assert her sexuality outside the parameters of love and marriage, Brooks lets us know right off that such behavior must be the result of a neurotic experience in her past. In this case cheap psychology hides Brooks's contempt for an emancipatory sexuality struggling to free itself from the institutionalized sexism of the past. And if Terry's affair with the professor seems unconvincing, Brooks takes up the slack by filling the remainder of the film with a melange of misfits whose lives seem peculiarly disconnected from the socioeconomic system that nourishes them; thus psychology reigns supreme. With the exception of Terry, all of Brooks's characters are portrayed in an ahistorical, insular "here and now" milieu, divorced from social struggles, social justice, and any sense of continuity with earlier generations.

For instance, once Terry leaves home and moves to the city, she encounters an unbroken series of men whose most distinguishing trait is their sexism and their propensity for psychotic violence. Collectively these men strongly reveal Brooks's unconvincing use of overkill to bring his message home. Each of the men in Terry's life appears neurotic enough to have been her murderer. Thus Brooks avoids illuminating the social basis of sexism as well as Terry's self-destruction in order to reinforce instead the simplistic, puritanical notion that indiscriminate sex leads to death. Tony, the singles-bar hood, who is Terry's first lover after the professor, is weakly portrayed as a souped-up Scorsesian maniac. Tony wields fear and dangerous sex as he titillates Terry into fits of self-incriminating laughter and unconvincing orgasmic heights. Brooks's working-class characters, like Scorsese's (specifically Tony and the Arnold Schwarzenegger lookalike who kills Terry in the end), are expressions of a truncated portrayal that views them as neurotic, explosive psychopaths, waging a war against the refined sensibilities of decent middle-class America. Thus, social, political, and economic forces are buried beneath the scapegoating fears of a politically reactionary view of the world.

Brooks outdoes his own pseudo-Freudian psychologizing by having Terry wooed by a sexually incompetent, overly hygenic, ex-seminarian social worker. Terry despises the social worker because he resembles too closely her own father, who is given to pontificating about the virtues of Notre Dame, the family, and the strengths of Irish-Catholic morality. It is within the context of Terry's authoritarian, Irish-Catholic family that Brooks provides a basis for the unfolding of the "new" puritanism. However, his depthless psychology ends up celebrating an illusory freedom, that is, the choice between "healthy" Catholic repression or spiritual/physical death. Moreover, the psychological basis for Brooks's "new" puritanism seems to have been invented in a psychoanalytic institute in which all social and political problems are reduced to the personal and privatized realm of existence. Consequently, Brooks's celebration of the subjective does nothing to provide the kind of rich, complex interplay of subjective and objective forces that could have meaningfully shaped his characters' lives.

Terry's sister fits well into Brooks's morality tale. She is portrayed as a mindless woman whose life is an endless series of disconnected relationships filled with drugs, porno-films, and swinger-style sex; she represents the underside of Brooks's wooden morality coin. The older sister operates in the same world of sexual morality that Terry inhabits, but she moves in a much more familiar scene. Instead of the disco-bar scene, the sister wields her sexual freedom within the broken-down boundaries of monogamous relationships. Her reward for sexual promiscuity is spiritual rather than physical death. The sister stands as a warning to all women that at best impersonal sex results in psychic and moral atrophy. For Brooks it is the extremes that tell the story: repression or death. Consequently, the themes and messages in *Goodbar* reveal themselves statically rather than dialectically.

The static unfolding of *Goodbar* is further represented by an endless montage of flashbacks and fantasy sequences; as Terry travels through Brooks's stylized world of wet-dream porno and disco clubs, the film stretches credibility into farce. Keaton is simply too innocent-looking, too sweet, to portray convincingly the energized desperation and drive that her character suggests. She smiles as men grab her ass; laughs as a petty hoodlum attempts to steal money from a pocketbook at the bar; oozes sugar and honey as her professor makes love to her incompetently in their initial sexual encounter. There is just too little conflict, pain, and struggle in Keaton's role as Terry Dunn. Terry's eventual death, especially her cry for release as she is being stabbed by a psychotic gay, has no substantive, generic validity; the scene is too disconnected from a deeper concrete and abrasive reality. Terry's murder ends up as a cheap piece of sensationalism, one that substitutes drama for analysis. Thus, political and social insight get buried beneath the Hollywood formula of sex and violence.

Not surprisingly, there is nothing sensuous or erotic about *Goodbar*. The boring/neurotic dispositions of the film's characters coupled with Keaton's charming but inappropriate innocence result in sexual scenes which come off like high-gloss, soft-core porn films made for distribution at fashionable country clubs.

In the final analysis, *Goodbar* represents an unsuccessful attempt to examine the nature of contemporary alienation as well as the channeling of the independent sexuality of women into the dead-end anonymity of the singles bars. What Brooks finally gives us is a film which reduces the complexity of important issues to a morality play that stays clear of the real antagonisms and contradictions that shape his characters' lives.

Brooks's "new" puritanism is the ideology of conformism parading in the garb of self-righteousness. Thus histrionics replace logic; and the alienation that fuels modern industrial societies is abstracted from the concrete political and social forces that give it meaning. Hidden behind the glamour of the film's radical facade are what seems to be an endless number of sexist, stunted, scapegoating stereotypes. Brooks refuses to portray women, men, gays, and working-class people dialectically with their strengths and flaws illuminated against the historical and social forces of the times. Instead, he serves us nothing more than flat, one-dimensional caricatures, fundamentally reactionary and unoriginal.

Note

1.   A version of this essay appeared in *Film Quarterly* (Summer, 1978): 52–4.

PART II

Hollywood Film and the War on Youth

5

Slacking Off: Border Youth and Postmodern Education[1]

Postmodernism, if it is about anything, is about the prospect that the promises of the modern age are no longer believable because there is evidence that for the vast majority of people worldwide there is no realistic reason to vest hope in any version of the idea that the world is good and getting better. . . . Postmodernism, therefore, is about a question. What is to be made of the world-concern that preoccupies people outside the cloisters of privilege who believe the world is not what it used to be? . . . [H]ow much of what is called by this name is properly joined to so much of what is said in the wider world of human suffering about how things may have changed.[2]

Introduction

While postmodernism may have been elevated to the height of fashion hype in both academic journals and the popular press in North America during the last 20 years, it is clear that a more sinister and reactionary mood has emerged which constitutes something of a backlash. Of course, postmodernism did become something of a fashion trend, but such events are short-lived and rarely take any subject seriously. But the power of fashion and commodification should not be underestimated in terms of how such practices bestow on an issue a cloudy residue of irrelevance and misunderstanding. But there is more at stake in the recent debates on postmodernism than the effects of fashion and commodification; in fact, the often essentialized terms in which critiques of postmodernism have been framed

47

suggest something more onerous. In the excessive rhetorical flourishes that dismiss postmodernism as reactionary nihilism, fad, or simply a new form of consumerism, there appears a deep-seated anti-intellectualism, one that lends credence to the notion that theory is an academic luxury and has little to do with concrete political practice. Anti-intellectualism aside, the postmodern backlash also points to a crisis in the way in which the project of modernity attempts to appropriate, prescribe, and accommodate issues of difference and indeterminacy.

Much of the criticism that now so blithely dismisses postmodernism appears trapped in what Zygmunt Bauman refers to as modernist "utopias that served as beacons for the long march to the rule of reason [which] visualized a world without margins, leftovers, the unaccounted for – without dissidents and rebels."[3] Against the indeterminacy, fragmentation, and skepticism of the postmodern era, the master narratives of modernism, particularly Marxism and liberalism, have been undermined as oppositional discourses. One consequence is that "a whole generation of postwar intellectuals have experienced an identity crisis. . . . What results is a mood of mourning and melancholia."[4]

The legacy of essentialism and orthodoxy seems to be reasserting itself on the part of left intellectuals who reject postmodernism, along with what they call the "cultural turn" in progressive politics, as a serious mode of social criticism and practical politics.[5] It can also be seen in the refusal on the part of intellectuals to acknowledge the wide-ranging processes of social and cultural transformation taken up in postmodern discourses that are appropriate to grasping the contemporary experiences of youth and the wide-ranging proliferation of forms of diversity within an age of declining authority, economic uncertainty, the expansion of electronically mediated technologies, and the extension of what I call consumer pedagogy into almost every aspect of youth culture.[6]

In what follows, I want to shift the terms of the debate in which postmodernism is usually engaged, especially by its more recent critics. In doing so, I want to argue that postmodernism as a site of "conflicting forces and divergent tendencies"[7] becomes useful pedagogically when it provides elements of an oppositional discourse for understanding and responding to the changing cultural and educational shifts affecting youth in North America. A resistant or political postmodernism seems invaluable to me in helping educators and others address the changing conditions of knowledge production in the context of mass electronic media and the role these new technologies are playing as critical socializing agencies in redefining both the locations and the meaning of pedagogy.

My concern with expanding the way in which educators and cultural workers understand the political reach and power of pedagogy as it positions youth within a postmodern culture suggests that postmodernism is to be neither romanticized nor casually dismissed. On the contrary, I believe that it is a fundamentally important discourse that needs to be mined critically in order to help educators to understand the modernist nature of public schooling in North America.[8] It is also useful for educators to comprehend the changing conditions of identity formation within a virtual economy of visual media and how the latter are producing a new generation of youth who exist between the borders of a modernist world of certainty and order, informed by the culture of the West and its technology of print, and a postmodern world of hybridized identities, mass migrations, local cultural practices, and pluralized public spaces. But before I develop the critical relationship between postmodern discourse and the promise of pedagogy and its relationship to border youth, I want to comment further on the recent backlash against postmodernism and why I believe it reproduces rather than constructively addresses some of the pedagogical and political problems affecting contemporary schools and youth.

Welcome to the Postmodern Backlash

While conservatives such as Daniel Bell and his cohorts may see in postmodernism the worst expression of the radical legacy of the 1960s, an increasing number of radical critics view postmodernism as the cause of a wide range of theoretical excesses and political injustices.[9] For example, criticism from the British cultural critic, John Clarke, argues that the hyper-reality of postmodernism wrongly celebrates and depoliticizes the new informational technologies and encourages metropolitan intellectuals to proclaim the end of everything in order to commit themselves to nothing (especially the materialist problems of the masses).[10] Dean MacCannell goes further and argues that "postmodern writing [is] an expression of soft fascism."[11] Feminist theorist, Susan Bordo, dismisses postmodernism as just another form of "stylish nihilism," and castigates its supporters for constructing a "world in which language swallows up everything."[12] For orthodox left critics such as Todd Gitlin, postmodernism is just another form of identitarian/cultural politics that undermines the possibilities of a unified movement rooted in a materialism based on objective analysis of class.[13] Alan Sokal has made a career arguing that postmodern theorists not only prioritize meaning over reality, but actually deny that reality has any existence outside of language (as opposed to the actual argument that reality cannot be made meaningful outside of language).[14] While some of these criticisms are not without merit (Sokal excluded), the nature of the backlash has become so prevalent in North America that the status of popular criticism and reporting seems to necessitate proclaiming that postmodernism is "dead." Hence, comments ranging from the editorial pages of *The New York Times* to popular texts such as *13th Gen*, to popular academic magazines such as *The Chronicle of Higher Education* alert the general public in no uncertain terms that it is no longer fashionable to utter the "p" word.

Of course, more serious critiques have appeared from the likes of Jurgen Habermas, Perry Anderson, David Harvey, and Linda Nicholson and Steven Seidman, but the current backlash has a different intellectual quality to it, a kind of reductionism that is both disturbing and irresponsible in its refusal to engage postmodernism in any kind of dialogical, theoretical debate.[15] Many of these left critics often assume the moral high ground and muster their theoretical machinery within binary divisions that create postmodern fictions, on the one side, and politically correct, materialist freedom fighters on the other. One consequence is that any attempt to engage the value and importance of postmodern discourses critically is sacrificed to the cold winter winds of orthodoxy and intellectual parochialism. I am not suggesting that all critics of postmodernism fall prey to such a position, nor am I suggesting that concerns about the relationship between modernity and postmodernity, the status of ethics, the crisis of representation and subjectivity, or the political relevance of post-modern discourses should not be problematized. But viewing post-modernism as a terrain to be contested suggests theoretical caution rather than reckless abandonment or casual dismissal.

What is often missing from these contentious critiques is the recognition that since postmodernism does not operate under any absolute sign, it might be more productive to reject any arguments that positions postmodernism within an essentialized politics, an either/or set of strategies. A more productive encounter would attempt, instead, to understand how postmodernism's more central insights illuminate how power is produced and circulated through cultural practices that mobilize multiple relations of subordination.

Rather than proclaiming the end of reason, postmodernism can be critically analyzed for how successfully it interrogates the limits of the project of modernist rationality and its universal claims to progress, happiness, and freedom. Instead of assuming that postmodernism has vacated the terrain of values, it seems more useful to address how it accounts for the way in which values are constructed historically and relationally, and how they might be addressed as the basis or "pre-condition of a politically engaged critique."[16] In a similar fashion, instead of claiming that postmodernism's critique of the essentialist subject denies a theory of subjectivity, it seems more productive to examine how its claims about the contingent character of identity, constructed in a multiplicity of social relations and discourses, re-defines and expands the possibility of critical and political agency. One example of this type of inquiry comes from Judith Butler, who argues that acknowledging that "the subject is constituted is not [the same as claiming] that it is determined; on the contrary, the consti-tuted character of the subject is the very precondition of its agency.[17] The now familiar argument that postmodernism substitutes represen-tations for reality indicates less an insight than a reductionism that refuses to engage critically how postmodern theories of representa-tion work to analyze how meaning is constitutive of and produced by objective forces, or how appeals to the universal, objective, unified, and transcendent often serve to caricaturize, demean, and

51

domesticate difference.[18] Paul Gilroy more recently has argued that postmodern discourses have performed an invaluable theoretical and political service in dismantling those partial and limited narratives that wield their force through an appeal to the universal and transcendent. He writes:

> Universality, reason and progress, modernity and enlightenment: these glorious ideas were once the sturdy cornerstones of an all-conquering Occidental mentality. They have recently registered the shock of the postmodern critique of knowledge, truth, and science. Amid the ruins, more modest activities, both academic and political, have transformed our understanding of the role of intellectuals and helped to specify the character of our times. I would suggest that the critical force of these deliberately postmodern arguments is strongest...where they have addressed the history of the relationship of knowledge to power and domination and converged on the problems of legitimacy that arose where the partial and the particular opted to represent themselves as the totalizing and the transcendent. They have articulated a compelling indictment of those forms of truth seeking which imagined themselves to be eternally and placelessly valid.[19]

A postmodern politics of representation might be better served through an attempt to understand how power is mobilized in cultural terms, how images are used on a global, national and local scale to create a representational politics that is reorienting traditional notions of space and time. A postmodern discourse could also be evaluated through the pedagogical consequences of its call to expand the meaning of literacy by broadening "the range of texts we read, and...the ways in which we read them."[20] The fact of the matter is that mass media, especially popular culture, is where the pedagogy and learning take place for most young people, and as the primary pedagogical medium it cannot be ignored. The issue is not whether such media simply perpetuates dominant power relations–an important question – but how youth and others experience the culture of the media differently, or the ways in which such media are "experienced differently by different individuals."[21] Postmodernism pluralizes the meaning of culture, while modernism firmly situates it theoretically in apparatuses of power. It is precisely in this dialectical interplay between difference and power that postmodernism and modernism inform each other rather than cancel each other out. The dialectical nature of the relationship that postmodernism has to modernism warrants a theoretical moratorium on critiques that affirm or negate postmodernism on the basis of whether it represents a break from modernism. The value of postmodernism lies elsewhere.

Acknowledging both the reactionary and progressive moments in postmodernism, antiessentialist cultural work might take up the challenge of "writing the political back into the postmodern,"[22] while simultaneously radicalizing the political legacy of modernism in order to promote a new vision of radical democracy in a postmodern world. One challenge in the debate over postmodernism is whether its more progressive elements can further our understanding of how power works, how social identities are mediated and struggled over, and how the changing conditions of the global economy and the new informational technologies can be articulated to meet the challenges posed by progressive cultural workers and the new social movements.

One issue that critical educators might consider is appropriating postmodernism as part of a broader pedagogical project which reasserts the primacy of the political while simultaneously engaging the most progressive aspects of modernism. In this context, postmodernism becomes relevant to the extent that it becomes part of a broader political project in which the relationship between modernism and postmodernism becomes dialectical, dialogic, and critical.

In what follows, I want to illuminate and then analyze some of the tensions between schools as modernist institutions and the fractured conditions of a postmodern culture of youth along with the problems they pose for critical educators. First, there is the challenge of understanding the modernist nature of existing schooling and its refusal to relinquish a view of knowledge, culture, and order that undermines the possibility for constructing a radical democratic project in which a shared conception of citizenship simultaneously challenges growing regimes of oppression and struggles for the conditions needed to construct a multiracial and multicultural democracy. Second, there is a need for cultural workers to address the emergence of a new generation of youth who are increasingly constructed within postmodern economic and cultural conditions that are almost entirely ignored by the schools. Third, there is the challenge to critically appropriate those elements of a critical pedagogy that might be useful in educating youth to be the subjects of history in a world that is increasingly diminishing the possibilities for radical democracy and global peace.

Modernist Schools and Postmodern Conditions

A clip from [the film] *War Games*: David Lightman (Matthew Broderick) sees a brochure of a computer company promising a quantum leap in game technology coming this Christmas...breaks into a system and, thinking it's the game company computer, asks to play global thermonuclear war...Sees on TV that for three minutes Strategic Air Command went on full alert thinking there had been a Soviet sneak attack...is arrested and interrogated...breaks back into the system and asks the computer, "Is this a game or is it real?" The computer answers: "What's the difference?"[23]

Wedded to the language of order, certainty, and mastery, public schools are facing a veritable sea change in the demographic, social, and cultural composition of the United States for which they are radically unprepared. As thoroughly modernist institutions, public schools have long relied upon moral, political, and social technologies that legitimate an abiding faith in the Cartesian tradition of rationality, progress, and history. The consequences are well known. Knowledge and authority in the school curricula are organized not to eliminate differences but to regulate them through cultural and social divisions of labor. Class, racial, and gender differences are either ignored in school curricula or subordinated to the imperatives of a history and culture that is often linear and uniform. New accountability schemes and the call for national standards increasingly subordinate the production and value of knowledge to the imperatives of oppressive forms of testing, further disassociating knowledge and pedagogy from the obligations of civic education and political agency.

Within the discourse of modernism, knowledge draws its boundaries almost exclusively from a European model of culture and civilization and connects learning to the mastery of autonomous and specialized bodies of knowledge. Informed by modernist traditions, schooling abets those political and intellectual technologies associated with what Ian Hunter, following Foucault, terms the "governmentalizing" of the social order.[24] The result is a pedagogical apparatus regulated by a practice of ordering that views "contingency as an enemy and order as a task."[25] The practice of licensing, testing, and regulating that structures public schooling is predicated on a fear of difference and indeterminacy. The effects reach deep into the structure of public schooling and include: an epistemic arrogance and faith in certainty that sanctions pedagogical practices and public spheres in which cultural differences are viewed as threatening; knowledge becomes positioned in the curricula as an object of mastery and control; the individual student is privileged as a unique source of agency irrespective of iniquitous relations of power; the technology and culture of the book is treated as the embodiment of modernist high learning and the only legitimate object of pedagogy.

While the logic of public schooling may be utterly modernist, it is neither monolithic nor homogeneous. But at the same time, the dominant features of public schooling are characterized by a modernist project that has increasingly come to rely upon instrumental reason and the standardization of curricula. As mentioned above, this can be seen in the regulation of class, racial, and gender differences through rigid forms of testing, sorting, and tracking. The rule of reason also reveals its Western cultural legacy in a highly centered curriculum that more often than not privileges the histories, experiences, and cultural capital of largely white, middle-class students. Most recently, the instrumentalist nature of modernist schooling can be seen in the growing corporatism of public education and the increasing vocationalism of higher education in the United States. Moreover, as I have implied earlier, the modernist nature of public schooling is evident in the refusal of educators to incorporate popular culture into the curricula or to take account of the new electronically mediated, informational systems in the postmodern age that are generating massively new socializing contexts for contemporary youth.

The emerging conditions of indeterminacy and hybridity that the public schools face, but continue to ignore, can be seen in a number of elements that characterize what I loosely call postmodern culture. First, the United States is experiencing a new wave of immigration which, at the beginning of the 21st century, exceeds in volume and importance the last wave at the turn of the 20th century. Key geographic areas within the country -chiefly large metropolitan regions of the Northeast and Southwest, including California -and major public institutions, especially those of social welfare and education, are grappling with entirely new populations that bring with them new needs. In 1940, 70 percent of immigrants came from Europe, but in 1997 only 15 percent came from Europe while 44 per cent came from Latin America and 37 per cent came from Asia. National identity can no longer be written through the lens of cultural uniformity or enforced through the discourse of assimilation. A new postmodern culture has emerged marked by specificity, difference, plurality, and multiple narratives.

Second, the sense of possibility that has informed the American Dream of material well-being and social mobility is no longer matched by a social order willing to sustain such dreams, especially for those who are considered marginal to such a society. In the last two decades, the American economy has mostly benefitted the rich while real incomes for low and middle-income groups have declined. At the present historical conjuncture, the financial crisis in Asia, Latin America, and Russia suggests that there will be an increase in the expansion of the service economy jobs and an increase in the number of companies that are downsizing and cutting labor costs in order to adapt to the new global downturn.

Not only are full-time jobs drying up, but there has also been a surge in the "number of Americans - perhaps as many as 37 million - [who] are employed in something other than full-time permanent positions."[26]. These so called "contingent workers" are "paid less than full-time workers and often get no health benefits, no pensions and no paid holidays, sick days or vacations."[27] In spite of the economic boom of the 1990s, diminishing expectations have become a way of life for youth all over North America. For most contemporary youth, the promise of economic and social mobility no longer warrants the legitimating claims it held for earlier generations of young people. The signs of despair among this generation are everywhere. Surveys strongly suggest that contemporary youth from diverse classes, races, ethnicities, and cultures "believe it will be much harder for them to get ahead than it was for their parents - and are overwhelmingly pessimistic about the long-term fate of their generation and nation."[28]

Clinging to the modernist script that technological growth necessitates progress, educators refuse to give up the long-held assumption that school credentials provide the best route to economic security and class mobility. While such a truth may have been relevant to the industrializing era, it is no longer sustainable within the post-Fordist economy of the West. New economic conditions call into question the efficacy of mass schooling in providing the "well-trained" labor force that employers required in the past. In light of these shifts, it seems imperative that educators and other cultural workers re-examine the mission of the schools.[29]

Rather than accepting the modernist assumption that schools should train students for specific labor tasks, it makes more sense in the present historical moment to educate students to theorize differently about the meaning of work in a postmodern world. Indeterminacy rather than order should become the guiding principle of a pedagogy in which multiple views, possibilities, and differences are opened up as part of an attempt to read the future contingently rather than from the perspective of a master narrative that assumes rather than problematizes specific notions of work, progress, and agency. Under such circumstances, schools need to redefine curricula within a postmodern conception of culture linked to the diverse and changing global conditions that necessitate new forms of literacy, a vastly expanded understanding of how power works within cultural apparatuses, and a keener sense of how the existing generation of youth are being produced within a society in which mass media plays a decisive if not unparalleled role in constructing multiple and diverse social identities.

As Stanley Aronowitz and I have pointed out elsewhere:

Few efforts are being made to rethink the *entire* curriculum in the light of the new migration and immigration, much less develop entirely different pedagogies. In secondary schools and community colleges for example, students still study "subjects"-social studies, math, science, English and "foreign" languages. Some schools have "added" courses in the history and culture of Asian, Latin American and Caribbean societies, but have little thought of transforming the entire humanities and social studies curricula in the light of the cultural transformations of the school. Nor are serious efforts being made to integrate the sciences with social studies and the humanities; hence, science and math are still being deployed as sorting devices in most schools rather than seen as crucial markers of a genuinely innovative approach to learning.[30]

As modernist institutions, public schools have been unable to open up the possibility of thinking through the indeterminate character of the economy, knowledge, culture, and identity. Hence, it has become difficult, if not impossible, for such institutions to understand how social identities are fashioned and struggled over within political and technological conditions that have produced a crisis in the ways in which culture is organized in the West.

Border Youth and Postmodern Culture

The programmed instability and transitoriness characteristically widespread among a generation of 18 to 25-year-old border youth is inextricably rooted in a larger set of postmodern cultural conditions informed by the following assumptions: a general loss of faith in the modernist narratives of work and emancipation; the recognition that the indeterminacy of the future warrants confronting and living in the immediacy of experience; an acknowledgment that homelessness as a condition of randomness has replaced the security, if not misrepresentation, of home as a source of comfort and security; an experience of time and space as compressed and fragmented within a world of images that increasingly undermine the dialectic of authenticity and universalism. For border youth, plurality and contingency, whether mediated through the media or through the dislocations spurned by the economic system, the rise of new social movements, or the crisis of representation, have resulted in a world with few secure psychological, economic, or intellectual markers. This is a world in which one is condemned to wander across, within, and between multiple borders and spaces marked by excess, otherness, difference, and a dislocating notion of meaning and attention. The modernist world of certainty and order has given way to a planet in which hip hop and rap condenses time and space into what Paul Virilio calls "speed space."[31] No longer belonging to any one place or location, youth increasingly inhabit shifting cultural and social spheres marked by a plurality of languages and cultures.

Communities have been refigured as space and time mutate into multiple and overlapping cyberspace networks. Youth talk to each other over electronic bulletin boards in coffee houses in North Beach, California. Cafes and other public salons, once the refuge of beatniks, hippies, and other cultural radicals, have given way to members of the hacker culture. They reorder their imaginations through connections to virtual reality technologies, and lose themselves in images that wage a war on traditional meaning by reducing all forms of understanding to random access spectacles.

This is not meant to endorse a Frankfurt School dismissal of mass or popular culture in the postmodern age. On the contrary, I believe that the new electronic technologies with their proliferation of multiple stories and open-ended forms of interaction have altered not only the context for the production of subjectivities, but also how people "take in information and entertainment."[32] Values no longer emerge from the modernist pedagogy of foundationalism and universal truths, or from traditional narratives based on fixed identities and with their requisite structure of closure. For many youths, meaning is in rout, media has become a substitute for experience, and what constitutes understanding is grounded in a decentered and diasporic world of difference, displacement, and exchanges. I want to take up the concept of border youth through a general analysis of some recent films that have attempted to portray the plight of young people within the conditions of a changing global culture.[33] I will focus on three films: *River's Edge* (1986), *My Own Private Idaho* (1991), and *Slacker* (1991). While all of these films are now more than a decade old, they occupy an important historical place in which Hollywood films begin to signal some of the economic and social conditions at work in the formation of youth during the next decade, but they often do so within a narrative that combines a politics of despair with a fairly sophisticated depiction of the sensibilities and moods of a generation of youth. The challenge for critical educators is to question how a critical pedagogy might be employed to cancel out the worst dimensions of postmodern cultural criticism while appropriating some of its more radical aspects. At the same time, there is the issue of how a politics and project of pedagogy can be constructed to create the conditions for social agency and institutionalized change among postmodern youth.

For many postmodern youth, showing up for adulthood at the fin de siècle means pulling back on hope and trying to put off the future rather than take up the modernist challenge of trying to shape it. Postmodern cultural criticism has captured much of the ennui among youth and has made clear that "What used to be the pessimism of a radical fringe is now the shared assumption of a generation."[34] Postmodern cultural criticism has helped to alert educators and others to the fault lines marking a generation, regardless of race or class, who seem neither motivated by nostalgia for some lost conservative vision of America nor at home in the new world order paved with the promises of the expanding electronic information highway. For most commentators, youth have become "strange," "alien," and disconnected from the real world. For instance, in Gus Van Sant's film, *My Own Private Idaho*, the main character Mike, who hustles his sexual wares for money, is a dreamer lost in fractured memories of a mother who deserted him as a child. Caught between flashbacks of Mom shown in 8mm color, and the video world of motley street hustlers and their clients, Mike moves through his existence by falling asleep in times of stress only to awake in different geographic and spatial locations. What holds Mike's psychic and geographic travels together is the metaphor of sleep, the dream of escape, and the ultimate realization that even memories cannot fuel hope for the future. Mike becomes a metaphor for an entire generation forced to sell themselves in a world with no hope, a generation that aspires to nothing, works at degrading McJobs, and lives in a world in which chance and randomness rather than struggle, community, and solidarity, drives their fate.

A more disturbing picture of youth can be found in *River's Edge*. Teenage anomie and drugged apathy are given painful expression in the depiction of a group of working-class youth who are casually told by John, one of their friends, that he has strangled his girlfriend, another of the group's members, and left her nude body on the riverbank. The group at different times visit the site to view and probe the dead body of the girl. Seemingly unable to grasp the significance of the event, the youths initially hold off from informing anyone of the murder and with different degrees of concern at first try to protect John, the teenage sociopath, from being caught by the police. The youths in *River's Edge* drift through a world of broken families, blaring rock music, schooling marked by dead time, and a general indifference to life in general. Decentered and fragmented, they view death like life itself as merely a spectacle, a matter of style rather than substance. In one sense, these youth share the quality of being "asleep" that is depicted in *My Own Private Idaho*. But what is more disturbing in *River's Edge* is that lost innocence gives way not merely to teenage myopia, but to a culture in which human life is experienced as a voyeuristic seduction, a video game, good for passing time and diverting oneself from the pain of the moment. Despair and indifference cancel out the language of ethical discriminations and social responsibility while elevating the immediacy of pleasure to the defining moment of agency. In *River's Edge*, history as social memory is reassembled through vignettes of 1960s types portrayed as either burned out bikers or as the ex-radical turned teacher whose moralizing relegates politics to simply cheap opportunism. Exchanges among the young people in *River's Edge* appear like projections of a generation waiting either to fall asleep or to commit suicide. After talking about how he murdered his girlfriend, John blurts out "You do shit, it's done, and then you die." Pleasure, violence, and death, in this case, reasserts how a generation of youth takes seriously the dictum that life imitates art or how life is shaped within a violent culture of images in which, as another character states. "It might be easier being dead." To which her boyfriend, a *Wayne's World* type, replies, "Bullshit, you couldn't get stoned anymore." *River's Edge* and *My Own Private Idaho* reveal the seamy and dark side of a youth culture while employing the Hollywood mixture of fascination and horror to titillate the audiences drawn to these films. Employing the postmodern aesthetic of revulsion, locality, randomness, and senselessness, youth in these films appear to be constructed outside of a broader cultural and economic landscape. Instead, they become visible only through visceral expressions of psychotic behavior or the brooding experience of a self-imposed comatose alienation.

One of the more celebrated youth films of the 1990s is Richard Linklater's *Slacker*. A decidedly low-budget film, *Slacker* attempts in both form and content to capture the sentiments of a 20-something generation of white youth who reject most of the values of the Reagan/Bush era but have a difficult time imagining what an alternative might look like. Distinctly nonlinear in its format, *Slacker* takes place in a 24-hour time frame in the college town of Austin, Texas. Borrowing its antinarrative structure from films such as Luis Bunuel's *Phantom of Liberty* and Max Ophüls's *La Ronde, Slacker* is loosely organized around brief episodes in the lives of a variety of characters, none of whom are connected to each other except that each provides the pretext to lead the audience to the next character in the film.

Sweeping through bookstores, coffee shops, auto-parts yards, bedrooms, and nightclubs, *Slacker* focuses on a disparate group of young people who possess little hope in the future and drift from job to job speaking a hybrid argot of bohemian intensities and new age–pop cult babble. The film portrays a host of young people who randomly move from one place to the next, border crossers with no sense of where they have come from or where they are going. In this world of multiple realities, "schizophrenia emerges as the psychic norm of late capitalism."[35] Characters work in bands with the name "Ultimate Loser," talk about being forcibly put in hospitals by their parents, and one neopunker attempts to sell a Madonna pap smear to two acquaintances she meets in the street: "Check it out, I know it's kind of disgusting, but it's like sort of getting down to the real Madonna." This is a world in which language is wedded to an odd mix of nostalgia, popcorn philosophy, and MTV babble. Talk is organized around comments like: "I don't know... I've traveled... and when you get back you can't tell whether it really happened to you or if you just saw it on TV." Alienation is driven inward and emerges in comments like "I feel stuck." Irony slightly overshadows a refusal to imagine any kind of collective struggle. Reality seems too despairing to care about. This is humorously captured in one instance by a young man who suggests: "You know how the slogan goes, workers of the world, unite? We say workers of the world, relax?" People talk, but appear disconnected from themselves and each other, lives traverse each other with no sense of community or connection.

There is a pronounced sense in *Slacker* of youth caught in the throes of new information technologies that both contain their aspirations while at the same time holding out the promise of some sense of agency. At rare moments in the films, the political paralysis of solipsistic refusal is offset by instances in which some characters recognize the importance of the image as a vehicle for cultural production, as a representational apparatus that can not only make certain experiences available but can also be used to produce alternative realities and social practices. The power of the image is present in the way the camera follows characters throughout the film, at once stalking them and confining them to a gaze that is both constraining and incidental. In one scene, a young man appears in a video apartment surrounded by televisions that he claims he has had on for years. He points out that he has invented a game called "Video Virus" in which through the use of a special technology he can push a button and insert himself onto any screen and perform any one of a number of actions. When asked by another character what this is about, he answers: "Well, we all know the psychic powers of the televised image. But we need to capitalize on it and make it work for us instead of working for it." This theme is taken up in two other scenes. In one short clip, a history graduate student shoots the video camera he is using to film himself, indicating a self-consciousness about the power of the image and the ability to control it at the same time. In another scene, with which the film concludes, a carload of people, each equipped with their Super 8 cameras, drive up to a large hill and throw their cameras into a canyon. The film ends with the images being recorded by the cameras as they cascade to the bottom of the cliff in what suggests a moment of release and liberation.

In many respects, these movies present a culture of white youth who appear overwhelmed by "the danger and wonder of future technologies, the banality of consumption, the thrill of brand names, [and] the difficulty of sex in alienated relationships."[36] The significance of these films rest, in part, in their attempt to capture the sense of powerlessness that increasingly cuts across race, class, and generations. But what is missing from these films along with the various books, articles, and reportage concerning what is often called "the nowhere generation," "generation X," "13th gen," or "Slackers" is any sense of the larger political and social conditions in which youth are being framed. What in fact should be seen as a social commentary about "dead-end capitalism" emerges simply as a celebration of refusal dressed up in a rhetoric of aesthetics, realism, style, fashion, and solipsistic protests. Within this type of commentary, postmodern criticism is useful but limited because of its often theoretical inability to take up the relationship between identity and power, biography and the commodification of everyday life, or the limits of agency in a post-Fordist economy as part of a broader project of possibility linked to issues of history, struggle, and transformation. The contours of this type of criticism are captured in a comment by the late Andrew Kopkind, a keen observer of slacker culture.

> The domestic and economic relationship that have created the new consciousness are not likely to improve in the few years left in this century, or in the years of the next, when the young slackers will be middle-agers. The choices for young people will be increasingly constricted. In a few years, a steady job at a mall outlet or a food chain may be all that's left for the majority of college graduates. Life is more and more like a lottery – is a lottery – with nothing but the luck of the draw determining whether you get a recording contract, get your screenplay produced, or get a job with your M.B.A. Slacking is thus a rational response to casino capitalism, the randomization of success, and the utter arbitrariness of power. If no talent is still enough, why bother to hone your skills? If it is impossible to find a good job, why not slack out and enjoy life?[37]

The pedagogical challenge represented by the emergence of a postmodern generation of youth has not been lost on advertisers and market research analysts. According to a 1992 Roper Organization, Inc. study, the current generation of 18–29 year olds have an annual buying power of 125 billion. Addressing the interests and tastes of this generation, "McDonald's, for instance, has introduced hip hop music and images to promote burgers and fries, ditto Coca-Cola, with its frenetic commercials touting Coca-Cola Classic."[38] Benetton, Reebok, and other companies have followed suit in their attempts to mobilize the desires, identities, and buying patterns of a new generation of youth. What appears as a dire expression of the postmodern condition to some theorists, becomes for others a challenge to invent new market strategies for corporate interests. In this scenario, youth may be experiencing the conditions of postmodernism, but corporate advertisers are attempting to theorize a pedagogy of consumption as part of a new way of appropriating postmodern differences. What educators need to do is to make the pedagogical more political by addressing both the conditions through which they teach and what it means to learn from a generation that is experiencing life in a way that is vastly different from the representations offered in modernist versions of schooling. The emergence of the electronic media coupled with a diminishing faith in the power of human agency has undermined the traditional visions of schooling and the meaning of pedagogy. The language of lesson plans and upward mobility and the forms of teacher authority on which it was based has been radically delegitimated by the recognition that culture and power are central to the authority/knowledge relationship. Modernism's faith in the past has given way to a future for which traditional markers no longer make sense.

Postmodern Education

In this section, I want to develop the assumption that a critical appropriation of certain critical postmodern discourses offers some important resources for alerting educators to a new generation of border youth. Indications of the conditions and characteristics that define such youth are far from uniform or agreed upon. But the daunting fear of essentializing the category of youth should not deter educators and cultural critics from addressing the effects on a current generation of young people who appear hostage to the vicissitudes of a changing economic order with its legacy of diminished hopes, on the one hand, and a world of schizoid images, proliferating public spaces, and an increasing fragmentation, uncertainty, and randomness that structures postmodern daily life on the other. Central to this issue is whether educators are dealing with a new kind of student forged within organizing principles shaped by the intersection of the electronic image, popular culture, and a dire sense of indeterminacy. Differences aside, the concept of border youth represents less a distinct class, membership, or social group than a referent for naming and understanding the emergence of a set of conditions, translations, border crossings, attitudes, and dystopian sensibilities among youth that cuts across race and class and represents a fairly new phenomenon. In this scenario, the experiences of contemporary Western youth in the late modern world are being ordered around coordinates that structure the experience of everyday life outside of the unified principles and maps of certainty that offered up comfortable and secure representations to previous generations. Youth increasingly rely less on the maps of modernism to construct and affirm their identities; instead, they are faced with the task of finding their way through a decentered cultural landscape no longer caught in the grip of a technology of print, closed narrative structures, or the certitude of a secure economic future. The new emerging technologies which construct and position youth represent interactive terrains that cut across "language and culture, without narrative requirements, without character complexities...Narrative complexity [has given] way to design complexity; story [has given] way to a sensory environment."[39]

A critical pedagogy must address the shifting attitudes, representations, and desires of this new generation of youth being produced within the current historical, economic, and cultural juncture. For example, the terms of identity and the production of new maps of meaning and affective investments must be understood within new hybridized cultural practices inscribed in relations of power that intersect differently with race, class, gender, and sexual orientation. But such differences must be understood not only in terms of the context of their struggles but also through a shared language of resistance that points to a project of hope and possibility. This is where the legacy of a critical modernism becomes valuable in that it reminds us of the importance of the language of public life, democratic struggle, and the imperatives of liberty, equality, and justice. This legacy of modernism must be rearticulated within a radical notion of democracy, citizenship, civic education, and public pedagogy.

Educators are increasingly faced with the challenge of addressing how different identities among youth are being produced in spheres generally ignored by schools. Included here would be an analysis of how pedagogy works to produce, circulate, and confirm particular forms of knowledge and desires in those diverse public and popular spheres where sounds, images, print, and electronic culture attempt to harness meaning for and against the possibility of expanding social justice and human dignity. Shopping malls, street communities, video halls, coffee shops, television culture, and other elements of popular culture must become serious objects of school knowledge. But more is at stake here than an ethnography of those public spheres where individual and social identities are constructed are struggled over. More important is the need to fashion a language of ethics and politics that serves to discriminate between relations that do violence and those that promote diverse and democratic public cultures through which youth and others can understand their problems and concerns as part of a larger effort to interrogate and disrupt the dominant narratives of national identity, economic privilege, and individual empowerment.

A critical and public pedagogy must redefine its relationship to modernist forms of culture, privilege, and canonicity, and serve as a vehicle of translation and cross-fertilization. Public pedagogy as a critical cultural practice needs to open up new institutional spaces in which students can experience and define what it means to be cultural producers capable of both reading different texts and producing them, of moving in and out of theoretical discourses but never losing sight of the need to theorize for themselves. Knowledge must be viewed not merely as an act of consumption but as a force for self-production and social change. Moreover, if critical educators are to move beyond the postmodern prophets of hyper-reality, politics must not be exclusively fashioned to plugging into the new electronically mediated community. The struggle for power is not merely about expanding the range of texts that constitute the politics of representation; it is also about struggling within and against those institutions that wield economic, cultural, and economic power.

It is becoming increasingly fashionable to argue for critical pedagogies in which it is important to recognize that "One chief effect of electronic hypertext lies in the way it challenges now conventional assumptions about teachers, learners, and the institutions they inhabit."[40] As important as this concern is for refiguring the nature of the relationship between authority and knowledge and the pedagogical conditions necessary for decentering the curriculum and opening up new pedagogical spaces, it does not go far enough, and runs the risk of degenerating into another hyped-up methodological fix.

Recognizing the importance of a pedagogy that is both public and critical suggests that progressive educators become more sensitive to how teachers and students negotiate the complex and overlapping spaces in which institutions, cultural texts and social identities intersect. Not only does such a recognition make visible the gravity of institutional forces that often shape, limit, and open up particular pedagogical relations, but it equally registers the need for engaging one's own authority, practices, and values within a critical understanding of how pedagogical practices articulate knowledge to effects in ways that enable others to recognize themselves as subjects rather than as objects of history. In other words, to be meaningful, critical, and transformative, a critical pedagogy must address how power is written on, within, and between different groups as part of a broader effort to reimagine schools as democratic public spheres. Authority as a form of autocritique provides one of the essential conditions for pedagogy to assert itself as a political and ethical practice that enables students to become accountable to themselves and others. By making the political and ethical practice of pedagogy primary, educators can define and debate the parameters through which communities of difference located within overlapping and transnational systems of information, exchange, and relations of power can address what it means to be educated as a practice of empowerment. In this instance, schools can be rethought as public spheres, as "borderlands of crossing,"[41] actively engaged in producing new forms of democratic community organized as sites of translation, negotiation, and resistance.

What is also needed by critical educators is a more specific understanding of how affect and ideology mutually construct the knowledge, resistance, and sense of identity that students negotiate as they work through dominant and rupturing narratives attempting in different ways to secure particular forms of authority. Fabienne Worth is right in castigating progressive educators for undervaluing the problematic nature of the relationship between "desire and the critical enterprise."[42] A vibrant, critical pedagogy needs to address how the issue of authority can be linked to democratic processes in the classroom that do not promote pedagogical terrorism and yet still offer representations, histories, and experiences that allow students to critically address the construction of their own subjectivities as they simultaneously engage in an ongoing "process of negotiation between the self and other."[43]

The conditions and problems of contemporary border youth may be postmodern, but they will have to be engaged through a willingness to interrogate the world of public politics while at the same time recognizing the limits of postmodernism's more useful insights. In part, this means rendering postmodernism more political by appropriating modernity's call for a better world while abandoning its linear narratives of Western history, unified culture, disciplinary order, and technological progress. In this case, the pedagogical importance of uncertainty and indeterminacy can be rethought through a modernist notion of the dream-world in which youth and others can shape, without the benefit of master narratives, the conditions for producing new ways of learning, engaging, and positing the possibilities for social struggle and solidarity. Radical educators cannot subscribe either to an apocalyptic emptiness nor to a politics of refusal that celebrates the immediacy of experience over the more profound dynamic of social memory and moral outrage forged within and against conditions of exploitation, oppression, and the abuse of power. Postmodern pedagogy needs to confront history as more than simulacrum, and ethics as something other than the casualty of incommensurable language games. Postmodern educators need to take a stand without standing still, to engage their own politics as public intellectuals without essentializing the ethical referents to address human suffering.

In addition, a postmodern pedagogy needs to go beyond a call for refiguring the curriculum so as to include new informational technologies; instead, it needs to assert a politics that makes the relationship among authority, ethics, and power central to a pedagogy that expands rather than closes down the possibilities of a radical democratic society. Within this discourse, images do not dissolve reality into simply another text; on the contrary, representations become central to revealing the structures of power relations at work in the public, schools, society, and the larger global order. Difference does not succumb to fashion in this logic (another touch of ethnicity); instead, difference becomes a marker of struggle in an ongoing movement towards a shared conception of economic and political justice and a radicalization of the social order. As neoliberalism works to reduce all modes of interaction to exchange relations, youth are being represented within an expanding electronically mediated culture as savvy consumers, while at the same time they are portrayed as indifferent to the world of politics and the imperatives of a democratic public sphere. Poised as being highly individualistic, staunchly competitive, and both chillingly apathetic to the world of ethics, social justice, and public concerns (see CNN ads), youth exemplify the apotheosis, if not perfect expression, of an entrepreneurial spirit that views democracy as merely the freedom to consume and critically engaged politics as the residue of a bygone age. Fortunately, the world that youth inhabit is far more complex than that produced for popular consumption by the corporate controlled media. Moreover, youth both within and outside of the United States are offering opposition to the notion that the only form of citizenship available to them is consumerism. More and more young people are voicing their dissent collectively against a world dominated by conglomerates such as the World Bank, the IMF, and other forces of corporate capital. Demonstrations in Seattle, Quebec, and other locations all over the world have made it clear that young people are more than willing not only to take seriously the promise of a radical democracy but to demonstrate and challenge those economic, political, and social forces that turn democratic communities into shopping malls and public goods into private investments.

Notes

1. A version of this essay appeared in *Journal of Advanced Composition* 14.2 (Fall, 1994).
2. Charles Lemert, *Postmodernism Is Not What You Think* (Cambridge, UK: Blackwell, 1997), pp. xii–xiii.
3. Zygmunt Bauman, *Intimations of Postmodernity* (New York: Routledge, 1992), p. xi.
4. Kobena Mercer "'1968': Periodizing Politics and Identity," in Lawrence Grossberg, Cary Nelson, and Paula Treichler (eds.), *Cultural Studies* (New York: Routledge, 1992), p. 424.
5. See for instance, Todd Gitlin, *Twilight of Our Common Dreams: Why America is Wracked by Culture Wars* (New York: Metropolitan Books, 1995); Michael Tomasky. *Left for Dead: The Life, Death and Possible Resurrection of Progressive Politics in America* (New York: The Free Press, 1996); Jim Sleeper, *The Closest of Strangers* (New York: W. W. Norton, 1990); Barbara Epstein, Richard Flacks, and Marcy Darnovsky (eds.), *Cultural Politics and Social Movements*. (Philadelphia: Temple University Press, 1995).
6. See Henry Giroux, *Channel Surfing: Race Talk and the Destruction of Today's Youth* (New York: Routledge, 1997).
7. Paul Patton, "Giving up the Ghost: Postmodernism and Anti-Nihilism," in Lawrence Grossberg (ed.), *It's a Sin* (Sydney: Power Publications, 1988), p. 89.
8. I have taken this issue up in great detail in Henry Giroux, *Schooling and the Struggle for Public Life* (Minneapolis: University of Minnesota Press, 1988); Henry Giroux, *Border Crossings* (New York: Routledge, 1992); Henry Giroux, *Disturbing Pleasures: Learning Popular Culture* (New York: Routledge, 1994); Henry Giroux, *Channel Surfing*, op. cit.
9. Daniel Bell, *The Cultural Contradictions of Capitalism* (New York: Basic Books, 1976).
10. John Clarke, *New Times and Old Enemies: Essays on Cultural Studies and America* (New York: Harper Collins, 1991), especially chapter 2. Clarke's analysis has less to do with a complex reading of postmodernism than with

a defensive reaction of his own refusal to take seriously a postmodern critique of the modernist elements in Marxist theories.

11. Dean MacCannell, *Empty Meeting* (New York: Routledge, 1992), p. 187.

12. Susan Bordo, *Unbearable Weight: Feminism, Western Culture, and the Body* (Berkeley: University of California Press, 1993), p. 291.

13. Gitlin, *Twilight of Our Common Dreams*, op. cit.

14. See Alan Sokal and Jean Bricmont, *Fashionable Nonsense: Postmodern Intellectuals' Abuse of Science* (New York: Picador, 1998).

15. Jurgen Habermas, *The Philosophical Discourse of Modernity* (Cambridge, MA: MIT Press, 1978); Perry Anderson, "Modernity and Revolution." *New Left Review* 144 (1984): 96–113; David Harvey, *The Conditions of Postmodernity* (Cambridge, MA: Blackwell, 1989);
Linda Nicholson and Steven Seidman (eds.), *Social Postmodernism* (New York: Routledge, 1995). Needless to say, one can find a great deal of theoretical material that refuses to dismiss postmodern discourses so easily and in doing so performs a theoretical service in unraveling its progressive from its reactionary tendencies. Early examples of this work can be found in Hal Foster (ed.), *Postmodern Culture* (London: Pluto Press, 1985); Dick Hebdige, *Hiding in the Light* (New York: Routledge, 1988); Gianni Vattimo, *The Transparent Society* (Baltimore: The Johns Hopkins University Press, 1992); Andrew Ross (ed.). *Universal Abandon? The Politics of Postmodernism* (Minneapolis: University of Minnesota Press, 1988); Linda Hutcheon, *The Poetics of Postmodernism* (New York: Routledge, 1988); Jim Collins, *Uncommon Cultures* (New York: Routledge, 1989); Steven Connor, *Postmodernist Culture* (Cambridge, MA: Blackwell, 1989). Also see Linda Nicholson (ed.), *Feminism/Postmodernism* (New York: Routledge, 1990); Scott Lasch, *Sociology of Postmodernism* (New York: Routledge, 1990); Iain Chambers. *Border Dialogues,* (New York: Routledge, 1990); Stanley Aronowitz and Henry A. Giroux *Postmodern Education* (Minneapolis: University of Minnesota Press, 1991); Stephen Best and Douglas Kellner, *Postmodern Theory* (New York: Guilford Press, 1990); Norman Denzin, *Images of a Postmodern Society* (Newbury Park, CA: Sage, 1991); Nancy Fraser, *Justice Interruptus: Critical Reflections on the "Postsocialist" Condition* (New York: Routledge, 1997).

16. Judith Butler, "Contingent Foundations: Feminism and the Question of Postmodernism," in Judith Butler and Joan Scott (eds.), *Feminists Theorize the Political* (New York: Routledge, 1991), pp. 6–7.

17. Ibid., p. 13.

18. See Judith Butler, "Merely Cultural." *Social Text* 52–3 (Fall/Winter, 1997): 266–77.

19. Paul Gilroy, *Against Race: Imagining Political Culture Beyond the Color Line* (Cambridge, MA: Harvard University Press, 2000), pp. 68–9.

20. Michael Berube, "Exigencies of Value." *The Minnesota Review* 39 (1992/93): 75.

21. John Tomlinson, *Cultural Imperialism* (Baltimore: The Johns Hopkins University Press, 1991), p. 40.

22. Teresa Ebert, "Writing in the Political: Resistance (Post)modernism." *Legal Studies Forum* 15.4 (1991): 291.

23. Walter Parkes, "Random Access, Remote Control: The Evolution of Story Telling." *Omni* (January, 1994): 48.

24. Ian Hunter, *Culture and Government: The Emergence of Literary Education* (London: Macmillan, 1988).

25. Bauman, *Intimations of Postmodernity* op. cit., p. xi.

26. Kenneth Jost, "Downward Mobility." *Congressional Quarterly Researcher* 27.3 (July 23, 1993): 633.

27. Ibid., p. 628.

28. Neil Howe and Bill Strauss, *13th Gen: Abort, Retry, Ignore, Fail?* (New York: Vantage Books, 1993), p. 16.

29. Stanley Aronowitz and William Defazio, *The Jobless Future* (Minneapolis: University of Minnesota Press, 1994).

30. Stanley Aronowitz and Henry A. Giroux, *Education Still Under Siege* (Westport, CT: Bergin and Garvey, 1993), p. 6.

31. Paul Virilio, *Lost Dimension*, trans. Daniel Moshenberg (New York: Semiotext(e), 1991).

32. Parkes, "Random Access, Remote Control," op. cit., p. 54.

33. On this issue, see Zygmunt Bauman, *Work, Consumerism, and the New Poor* (Philadelphia: Open University Press, 1999).

34. Carol Anshaw, "Days of Whine and Poses." *The Village Voice* 10 (November, 1992): 27.

35. Dick Hebdige, *Hiding in the Light* (New York: Routledge, 1988), p. 88.

36. Andrew Kopkind, "Slacking Toward Bethlehem." *Grand Street* 44 (1992): 183.

37. Ibid., p. 187.

38. Pierce Hollingsworth, "The New Generation Gaps: Graying Boomers, Golden Agers, and Generation X." *Food Technology* 47 (October, 1993): 30.

39. Parkes, "Random Access, Remote Control" op. cit., p. 50

40. George Landow, *Hypertext: The Convergence of Contemporary Critical Theory and Technology* (Baltimore: The Johns Hopkins University Press, 1992), p. 120.

41. Iain Chambers, *Border Dialogues*, op. cit., p. 134.

42. Fabienne Worth, "Postmodern Pedagogy in the Multicultural Classroom: For Inappropriate Teachers and Imperfect Strangers." *Cultural Critique* 25 (Fall, 1993): 8.

43. Ibid., p. 26.

6

Culture, Class, and Pedagogy in
Dead Poets Society

We live in an age in which the new conservatism that has reigned in
the United States for the last two decades has consistently struggled to
depoliticize politics while simultaneously attempting to politicize
popular culture and the institutions that make up daily life. The
depoliticizing of politics is evident, in part, in the ways in which the
new conservative formations use the electronic technologies of image,
sound, and text not only to alter traditional systems of time, space, and
history, but also to displace serious political issues to the realm of the
aesthetic and the personal.[1] In this context, discourses of style, form,
and authenticity are employed to replace questions concerning how
power is mobilized by diverse dominant groups to oppress, marginal-
ize, and exploit large portions of the American population. Understood in ideological terms, the depoliticizing of politics is about the
attempt to construct citizens who believe that they have little or no
control over their lives: that issues of identity, culture, and agency bear
no relationship to or "acknowledgment of mediations: material, historical, social, psychological, and ideological."[2] Hence, the depoliticizing of the political represents a complex, though incomplete, effort
by the new conservatism to secure a politics of representation that
attempts to render the workings of its own ideology indiscernible.
That is, dominant groups seize upon the dynamics of cultural power to
secure their own interests while simultaneously attempting to make
the political context and ideological sources of such power invisible.

In the current historical conjuncture there is an ongoing attempt by the forces of the new right to replace the practice of substantive democracy with a democracy of images. At the same time, the discourse of responsible citizenship is subordinated to the market-place imperatives of choice, consumption, and standardization. This is particularly true with respect to public schools. The Reagan/Bush administrations drastically cut financial support for public school programs, systematically attempted to reprivatize the public school sector by sponsoring legislation that would allow public money to be used to support private schooling, and linked educational reforms to the needs of big business.[3] Moreover, the new conservatives have made schooling an intense site of struggle in their efforts to eliminate noncanonical and subordinate cultures as serious objects of knowledge.[4] Education is now defined as a private rather than public good, and multicultural curricula are viewed as either "racist" or incompatible with the imperatives of the new accountability and standards movement.

The struggle over the economic and political apparatuses of the state has been extended principally by new conservative formations to the sphere of culture.[5] Contrary to the conventional left thinking, as Laclau and Mouffe have pointed out, the greatest challenge to the right and its power may be lodged not in the mobilization of universal agents such as the working class or some other oppressed group, but in a cultural struggle in which almost every facet of daily life takes on a degree of undecidability and thus becomes unsettled and open to broader collective dialogue and multiple struggles.

What has become important to recognize is that the new conservative bloc, while firmly controlling the state and its major apparatuses, turned its attention during the Reagan/Bush era towards the wider terrain of culture and identified as visible targets higher education, public schooling, the art world, and rock music.[6] This is evident in the right-wing blitz organized around issues such as pornography, political correctness, and multiculturalism, and testifies to a new level of hegemonic struggle over the institutions and discourses through which a politics of representation is directly linked to the production of mobile fields of knowledge, shifting and multiple social identities, and new cultural formations. The war being waged by the new

conservative bloc is not simply over profit or the securing of traditional forms of authority; it is over the emergence of decentered and
diverse oppositional discourses, such as feminism, postmodernism,
and postcolonialism, that have begun to call into question all of the
grand narratives of modernism with its unfettered conviction in
science and technology as the engine of progress, its unflinching
belief in the humanist subject as the unified agent of history, and its
adamant insistence that Western culture is synonymous with the very
notion of civilization itself. What is interesting regarding these
struggles is that they not only pose an emerging threat to the dominant order, but they also offer a new set of discourses and strategies that
are being taken very seriously by the new right. The dominant
conservative formations in the United States appear haunted and
besieged by the emergence of the discourses and cultures of difference that refuse to remain silent or confined to the margins of history,
power, and politics. This new politics of cultural difference has
important implications for redefining the notions of hegemony,
resistance, and struggles over forms of self and social representation.[7]

Within the paradox of the reality of depoliticization, the politiciza-
tion of culture, and the emerging politics of difference, hegemony
has to be read as always fractured, contradictory, and decentered.
Moreover, domination does not present itself as a universal practice,
exhausting those it oppresses. In actuality, hegemonic power can only
be understood in its specificity, in its constant attempt to restructure
and refigure its strengths and weaknesses, and in its continual attempt
to recuperate forms of resistance that are as ongoing as they are
different. I believe that new opportunities present themselves for
deepening the pedagogical as a form of cultural politics by recognizing that within the fractured and contradictory struggles that constitute oppressive social practices, institutions, and movements, there are
always opportunities for resistance and struggle, however weak they
sometimes may appear to be.

In what follows, I want to examine how the pedagogical can be
taken up as a form of cultural production that reworks the relationship between cultural texts, teachers, and students. On the one hand,
this means developing a theoretical case for using popular cultural
texts such as film, television, advertisements, music videos, and mass

77

circulation magazines as serious objects of knowledge related to the power of self-definition and the struggle for social justice. Equally important is the necessity to refuse to take up popular culture within a liberal pedagogical model that reduces its use to a discourse of relevance or the narrow, methodological imperative to teach the conflicts.[8] On the other hand, I want to reassert the importance of critical pedagogy as a form of cultural practice which does not simply tell the student how to think or what to believe, but provides the conditions for a set of ideological and social relations which engender diverse possibilities for students to produce rather than simply acquire knowledge, to be self-critical about both the positions they describe and the locations from which they speak, and to make explicit the values that inform their relations with others as part of a broader attempt to produce the conditions necessary for either the existing society or a new and more democratic social order.[9]

As part of examining the relationship between popular culture and critical pedagogy, I want to avoid using a binary framework that locates schooling in a context which focuses either on how schools monolithically reproduce the dominant social order through particular forms of social and cultural reproduction or how students contest the dominant society through various forms of resistance. Instead, I want to analyze radical pedagogy as a theoretical discourse that helps to illuminate how cultural texts can be understood as part of a complex and often contradictory set of ideological and material processes through which the transformation of knowledge, identities, and values takes place. Such texts, like schools, in this sense, produce narratives, desires, and subjectivities that are far from homogeneous and in turn encounter students whose own subjectivities are constructed in multiple, complex, and contradictory ways.

Central to such a task are at least three important issues. First, there is the task of redefining teachers as cultural workers, that is, as educators committed to a political project and normatively based discourse that expands the possibility for radical democracy; second, there is the issue of reclaiming, without romanticizing, popular culture as a complex terrain of pedagogical struggle; third, pedagogy must be viewed as the deliberate attempt to produce knowledge, forms of ethical address, and social identities.[10] More specifically, a pedagogy

of the popular would take as its objective the interrogation of traditional positivist and modernist notions of the curriculum and canonicity, the rupturing of the universalized view of identity as a
privatized consciousness, and the elimination of the view that cultural
difference is a threat to civic democratic culture. I will attempt to
take up some of these issues by analyzing a class I taught on education
and the politics of identity, focusing primarily on the use of the film,
Dead Poets Society.

Popular cultural texts such as *Dead Poets Society* can be analyzed
within the discourse of political economy and transnational capitalism
in order to gain a better understanding of how such forces produce
dominant social reading formations that often limit the range of
meanings that can be taken up by readers in addressing films and
other media texts. As Michael Parenti points out, the dominant
media, including the Hollywood studio system, has a deep interest
in inscribing a number of prevalent myths into its films. Audiences
are consistently bombarded with messages that suggest that one
function of such films is to entertain rather than educate. Touted as
an art form, Hollywood films largely organize their plots and narrative structures around a range of what appears to be commonsensical
myths. Some of the more prevailing myths include assumptions such
as: "Individual effort is preferable to collective action; free enterprise
is the best economic system in the world; the ills of society are caused
by individual malefactors and not by anything in the socioeconomic
system; women and ethnic minorities are not really as capable,
effective, or interesting as White males,"[11] and so on. Such films
must be analyzed as both public pedagogies and as commodities that
both entertain and educate, that offer both enjoyment and put into
place modes of desire, subject positions, and forms of identification
that offer the possibility of critique even as they position us to
become complicit with the norms and practices of the dominant
society. But most importantly for my purposes, films such as *Dead
Poets Society* are neither the bearers of monolithic themes, nor should
they be read simply as sites of conflicting ideologies. On the contrary,
rather than reducing such a text to the reified terrain of relevance and
teaching the conflicts, it should be posited as a site of struggle over
how representations mean differently and what the consequences of

such differences might be if they are to matter as part of a wider theoretical, ethical, and political discourse. Second, *Dead Poets Society* can be engaged not only to deconstruct how it represents a particular view of the political, but also how it functions to secure specific forms of affective investments. What is it in films such as *Dead Poets Society*, for instance, that mobilizes specific desires, identifications, and needs? And finally, how might students engage this film critically as part of a broader discourse of ethics and politics that promotes a deeper understanding of the historical and cultural locations from which they might speak, act, and struggle?

Pedagogy, Resistance, and Celluloid Culture

During the Fall of 1991, I taught an undergraduate class for teachers in training on curriculum and secondary education. The class consisted of mostly white, middle-and upper-middle-class students. Most of the work we had been analyzing in the class consisted largely of exposing the role that schools play in the process of social and cultural reproduction. I wanted to go beyond this type of analysis by introducing students to films and other texts in which both teachers and students exhibited forms of resistance in the classroom. One assignment consisted of having the students choose a popular cultural form which addressed the issue of pedagogy and schooling. At issue here was having the students analyze the relationship between their own experiences in schools and those portrayed in popular cultural forms. The class largely decided to focus on Hollywood films, and finally choose to view two films, *Dead Poets Society* and *Stand and Deliver*.

In one sense *Dead Poets Society* was an exemplary film to use pedagogically because it had been suggested by some students as a text which embodied much of what was perceived as the political and pedagogical principles encouraged in the course. That is, the film was comprehended as "living out" the perceived requirements and practices of critical teaching. What became apparent to me was that my students' initial motivations in choosing the film had less to do with an analytical reading of the text than it did with an investment in the film that was largely affective. According to my students, *Dead Poets Society* was valuable as an exemplary model of critical pedagogy because it staked out a terrain of hope, and offered subject positions from within which they could project an image of themselves as future teachers; an image that encouraged them to identify themselves as agents rather than as mere technicians. As some students pointed out, the film made them feel good about themselves as teachers in the making.

In my view, the film presented a model of liberal pedagogy, in part, by mobilizing popular sentiment through what Larry Grossberg has called an "affective epidemic."[12] That is, even though the film takes as its central narrative the issue of resistance, its structure undermined a critical reading of its own codes by establishing a strong emotional affinity between the viewers and the progressive teacher portrayed in this film.

The pedagogical challenge presented by *Dead Poets Society* was grounded in making clear the multiple and often contradictory ways in which it ruptured and supported dominant codes regarding issues of knowledge, pedagogy, and resistance. Deconstructing this film was not meant as a pedagogical exercise in canceling the affective and meaning-making investments students brought to it. Nor was my pedagogical approach meant as an attempt to provide a definitive ideological reading of the film. On the contrary, I wanted to address how the mobilization of meaning and affective investments within the film's form and content functioned as part of a broader cultural and pedagogical practice that was neither innocent nor politically neutral. What has to be recognized here is a central dilemma faced by educators who engage the popular as part of a broader pedagogical project. The dilemma is constituted by the need to challenge the structures of meaning and affect without delegitimating the importance of the varied investments mobilized within the students' response to the film. Hence, I wanted to take up the film as a cultural form which produced knowledge in the service of particular forms of authority, proffered conditions for agency which privileged some groups over others, and revealed contradictory and partial insights regarding how oppression works through various aspects of schooling.

Canonicity, Pedagogy, and Resistance in *Dead Poets Society*

Dead Poets Society (1989), directed by Peter Weir and written by Tom Schulman, is set in a boys boarding school, Welton Academy. The opening shots of the film portray Welton Academy as an exclusive prep school, situated in a picture postcard setting that tries hard to emulate the beauty and peacefulness of the English countryside. The school itself has all the aesthetic trappings of an Ivy League college. The architecture of the school is monumentalist and Gothic. The students, teachers, and parents are from the ruling class. The parents and students move easily within a cultural capital that signifies privilege, wealth, and power. Social identities in this film are constructed within an unspoken yet legitimating discourse that privileges whiteness, patriarchy, and heterosexuality as the universalizing norms of identity. Precisely because it exists outside of the context of racial difference, whiteness as a basis of privilege in *Dead Poets Society* becomes "invisible" because there is no context to render it visible as a dominant racial category, as a mark of power and identity that refuses to call attention to itself.[13] The film is set in 1959 and the "whiteness" of the faculty and students is a historically accurate representation; however, *Dead Poets Society* suspends the dynamics of historical contingency and specificity within a reactionary nostalgia. An aura of universality radiates through this film which expresses its cultural and political narratives within a mythical, timeless age when the messy relations of democracy, cultural difference, and social struggle were kept in place, or at least out of sight; when aesthetics took precedence over politics, and students (of privilege) were safely cushioned within monastic borders removed from the potentially antagonistic relations of everyday life. The politics and aesthetics of nostalgia in this film mobilize affective identifications and investments in order to secure the authority of a particular history, "that story which institutionally seeks to legitimate a continuum of sense, which as [Walter] Benjamin insisted, has to be blasted apart."[14]

In the opening address to the parents and students of Welton, the headmaster celebrates Welton's record of academic achievement, pointing out that over 75 percent of its graduates go on to attend Ivy League schools. There is no pretense here. Welton is less concerned about teaching its students how to think than it is in preparing them to assume positions of power. Within this context, pedagogy defines itself through a ruthless instrumentalism removed from the progressive goals of creating the conditions for critical agency, ethical accountability, and the obligations of democratic public life. As the film shifts to portray the dynamics of classroom life, it becomes clear that the curriculum is a no frills version of high-culture canonicity, and the pedagogy used by the all-white male teachers emphasizes a numbing combination of discipline and transmission as the prevailing pedagogical practices.

Initially, the students appear to fully embrace this anesthetized reactionary environment. For instance, on the first day of school they trade stories about having gone to summer school in order to get the edge over their classmates; the routinization and authoritarianism of the school appears to shape every aspect of their lives unproblematically; they appear to be academic zombies living out the projections and wishes of their successful fathers. Moreover, every other older male figure at this school who figures prominently as a surrogate father reinforces the same unproblematic relation to the competitive milieu. It's hardly surprising then, that before the semester classes even begin a number of boys decide to form a study group that will meet that very evening. (The film critic, Tania Modleski, has suggested a potential, though repressed, homosexual bond between men and boys in this film; it is not, however, liberatory as realized by Weir.) An unsettling of sorts occurs with the appearance at Welton of a new English teacher named Mr. Keating, played by Robin Williams. Framed against the deadening pedagogy of his peers, Keating appears to be witty, unconventional, and courageous. In his first meetings with the class, he ruptures traditional pedagogical standards by having them rip out the introduction to their poetry book, which equates reading poetry to the same logic one would use to measure the heights of trees. This is not merely deconstruction, this is a textual assault that attempts to relocate poetry within the interests and voices the students actually bring to the class. Keating doesn't simply want them to read poetry, he wants them to undertake it as a form of cultural production. According to him, poetry is about the relationship between passion and beauty. He tell his students "The powerful play goes on and you may contribute a verse." For Keating, poetry offers the basis not for social-empowerment but self empowerment. Keating wants to resurrect the humanist subject within an aesthetic of resistance, and eschews any notion of resistance which calls into question how the operations of power work to promote human suffering, and social injustice, and exploitation. Keating's invocation to his students "*Carpe diem*, lads! Seize the day! Make your lives extraordinary" is expressed in forms of pedagogical resistance that celebrate the privatized ego of ruling-class boys without any reference or analysis of how dominant social forms work subjectively to make these students complicit with the hierarchies of domination that inform the organization of the school, the curriculum, and the social formations that influence a wider society, to which Keating never alludes.

Resistance in Keating's pedagogy suggests a strangely empty quality. He has students stand on their desks so they can see the world from another position. Looking at the room from the top of their desks has an ironic twist to it since most of these students will be looking at the world when they leave school from the pinnacle of power rather than from the horizontal spaces that most people occupy at the bottom of the social and economic pyramid. On another occasion, Keating takes his students to the school courtyard and asks them to march in different strides. The pedagogical lesson taught in this case is that they must learn how to swim against the stream, to find "their own walk." In one celebrated scene in the film, Keating makes a particularly shy student get up before the class, asks him to close his eyes and free associate on a phrase from Whitman, "I sound my barbaric Yawp over the roofs of the world." The boy stutters, Keating whirls the student around and encourages him to speak to the metaphor. The boy finally attempts to articulate a poem and his classmates respond with resounding applause. In this instance, the audience is positioned to see Keating as a sensitive, caring teacher, who creates a space for the student that is metaphorically safe for the student *and* the audience.

In *Dead Poets Society*, resistance demands no sacrifices, no risks, no attempt to deconstruct the relationship between the margins and the centers of power. On the contrary, resistance in Keating's pedagogy serves to depoliticize and decontextualize, since it is only developed within a romanticized aesthetic. In fact, even Keating doesn't appear to understand how he is complicitous with dominant relations of power. If he does possess such recognition, it is likely couched in a conventional bourgeois resignation guided by the conviction that poverty and suffering will always be with us; in fact, they may even be good for the soul. He appears to represent the classic modernist teacher whose pedagogical sensibilities have been spawned by Enlightenment thinking, with its narratives of unending progress, faith in a unified social world, and the power of an unencumbered individualism. Keating wants to be loved but is incapable of recognizing that resistance is less the production of a vapid and aesthetic individualism rooted in the traditions of British high culture than it is a call for solidarity and collective action. This is largely due to the aesthetics surrounding his epistemology and his particular "style" of coming to know something that obscures deeper political and social issues. In fact, as soon as Keating's unorthodox teaching methods appear to threaten the legitimating ideology of the school, he resorts to the discourse of accommodation rather than resistance. For example, when Keating is blamed for the suicide of one of his students, he refuses to challenge the trumped-up charges on the part of the headmaster, Mr. Knowland, and accepts his fate passively by simply leaving the school. As soon as politics crosses over into the realm of power and politics, Keating presents himself as incapable of acting on his own behalf. His pedagogical call to make one's life extraordinary reveals itself as rhetoric that limits rather than expands the capacity for human agency and struggle. There is nothing extraordinary in Keating's failure to resist at the end of this film.

Another major subtext of the film centers around the influence that Keating has on a group of students in his English class who discover that, as a former student of Welton Academy, Keating founded the Dead Poets Society. The students immediately query Keating about the society and what it meant and are told that Keating and a group of friends found a cave off campus and read the poetry of the Romantics in order to "suck the marrow out of life [while] letting poetry drip from our tongue." With the sensitive Neil Perry as their leader, a group of Keating's admirers proceed to recuperate the Dead Poets Society. It is here that the boys begin their own journey of resistance. They violate school rules by meeting in a cave off campus. Initially, they meet to read the Romantic poets; they then resort to reading their own poetry, smoking, playing musical instruments while emulating beat poetry, and bringing some girls to the cave. In one of the final cave scenes, a member of the group proclaims that he wants to be called Nuwanda, and in a striking display of colonialism takes on the identity of the Other as the province of the primitive, exotic, and romanticized warrior. Other acts of resistance that inform the boys' behavior unfold when Neil Perry defies the wishes of a particularly stern father for him to concentrate on his course work by taking a role in a local play; another student, Knox Overstreet, boldly pursues a public high school cheerleader at the risk of being beaten up by her boyfriend; and Charlie Dalton puts a notice in the school newspaper signed by the Dead Poets Society calling for the admission of women to Welton Academy.

The dynamics of power and student resistance collide around two issues. In the first instance, Dalton is berated and paddled by Mr. Knowland, the headmaster, for standing up at a school assembly and mocking him by announcing that the headmaster has a call from God. Dalton, who is from a wealthy family, takes his punishment but refuses to give the headmaster the names of other members of the Dead Poets Society. Neil Perry, a pivotal character in the film, is torn between the individualism encouraged by Keating and the tyrannical demands imposed on him by his father. Finally, when his father discovers him acting in the school play, he pulls Neil out of Welton and threatens to send him off to a military school the next day. Neil leaves Welton and shortly afterwards commits suicide. There is a curious twist here. Neil Perry comes from a family that is lower middle class; his father constantly justifies his own imperious manner by arguing that he wants Neil to have the education and social status he never had the chance to experience. Neil in this context becomes the Other, the class-specific misfit who lacks the wealth and privilege to take risks, to move easily within the demands and imperatives of ruling-class culture. The message of *Dead Poets Society* seems clear in this case. Resistance for members of this class of "climbers" is not only out of place, it ultimately leads to self-destruction. On the other hand, Charlie Dalton challenges the authority of the headmaster, gets expelled from Welton, and yet there is no doubt that, because of his wealth and family position, his life will not be altered drastically. He belongs to the culture of the winners; resistance is simply harmless play, in which one can afford to engage when one moves in circles of privilege. In this context, risk translates into an aesthetic, an inconvenience or maybe an interesting story to be repeated later by an adult recalling his own resistance as simply part of a rite of passage engaged in within the hallowed traditions of an oppressive but pragmatic form of schooling. As played out in *Dead Poets Society*, resistance is more often than not an emotional breach of convention and received social realities; it has more to do with a particular change in personal disposition towards an event than changing the structural conditions of events themselves. Resistance here is used as a form of cultural negotiation rather than social transformation.[15]

Following Neil Perry's suicide, the headmaster, in an attempt to ward off any negative publicity for the school, uses Keating as a scapegoat. In the investigation that follows, the group of boys who idolize Keating are obliged to sign statements indicating that he forced them into resurrecting the Dead Poets Society, filled their heads with heretical thoughts, and was directly responsible for Neil's decision to appear in the school play, disobey his father, and thus commit suicide. With the exception of one member of the group all of the boys sign the statement, rat on their teacher, and continue with their lives at Welton as if nothing had happened. In the final scene of the film, Keating comes back to his office to collect his personal belongings. He has to pass through his English class which is now being taught by Knowland, the headmaster. As he is about to exit, some of the boys in the class as a gesture of nonconformity stand up on their respective desks as a show of support for Keating. He smiles at them and says "Thank you boys." Hence, in the end, resistance, betrayal, and repressive authority are reworked and reconciled in a discourse of politeness which cancels out dominating relations of power and those who are complicitous with it. Keating remains the well-mannered man until the end, confirming the idea that resistance does not permanently change the world but merely interrupts it only to return us to the canonical past in which tradition, patriarchy, and Eurocentricism continue to provide a sense of order and continuity. The relationship between power and knowledge in Keating's pedagogy of resistance betrays itself by claiming that the alternative to stuffy textbooks is British and American Romanticism of the 19th century -not the socially engaged literature of the day.[16]

One of the most pernicious subtext in the film is organized around the construction of gendered subject positions in which women are represented in terms that are misogynist and demeaning.[17] Understood in these terms, *Dead Poets Society* does more than ignore structured inequalities in the wider society, depoliticize resistance, and naturalize how the canon is used to produce racist and class-specific practices. It also legitimates gendered social practices through various images and representations in which sexual identity is inscribed in various forms of sexist domination. This is most obviously evidenced in the relegation of women in this film to either trophies or appendages of male power. In one glaring example, Keating tells the "boys" that one of the central purposes of poetry is to "woo women." In this case, resistance as a form of "hip" pedagogical posturing is structured through the legitimation of sexist social relations. This lesson is certainly not lost on Keating's boys. While meeting in the cave, one of the boys reads a poem that is written on the back of a *Playboy* centerfold. Resistance for Keating's boys appears to support rather than rupture their own patriarchal identities. On another occasion, the girls who are brought to the cave are treated as if they are too dumb to recognize or understand the poetry of the Romantics. Following a similar logic, Knox's courtship with the public school cheerleader serves to reduce her to a reified object of desire and pleasure. Even the call by Keating's "resisters" to admit girls to Welton Academy transparently reveals itself as an opportunity for the boys to get more dates, to offset their academic work with sexual pleasure. In the end, resistance, knowledge, and pedagogy come together in *Dead Poets Society* to harness identity and power to the misogynist interests and fortunes of patriarchy. Within this coming-of-age narrative, whiteness reasserts itself through the logic of cultural racism, class discrimination, and the objectification of women. This is not merely a foreshortened view of gender relations within prep school culture, it is an active assertion, a politics of representation, in which resistance is incorporated as a pedagogical practice that actively produces sexism as part of its own legacy of power and domination.

Pedagogical Authority and the Politics of the Popular

In order to structure a position from which students might understand how their own subject positions are partly constructed within a dominant Eurocentric assemblage of liberal humanism mobilized within configurations of meaning and desire, I used the presentation of *Dead Poets Society* to raise important questions about the ideological interests at work in forms of textual authority that foster particular reading practices. In taking up this issue I framed my discussion of the film with my students around a number of important pedagogical concerns. These included: how are readers' choices defined and limited by the range of readings made available through the representations mobilized by particular forms of textual authority? How do power and authority articulate between the wider society and the classroom so as to create the conditions at work in constructing particular discourses in the reading of this film? The tension I had to confront was how to address the power of hope and agency provided by the discourse of liberal humanism without destroying a sense of pedagogical possibility.

For me the pedagogical challenge presented itself in trying to engage the film as a form of writing, which took the form of allowing the students to make the "text" mean differently by reorganizing the systems of intertextual, ideological, and cultural references in which it was constructed historically and semiotically, and in relation to wider social events. In the first instance, this meant giving students the opportunity to analyze the plurality of meanings that informed the film. This was done by having students view the film from the perspective of their own experiences and histories by writing short, critical papers, which they then duplicated and shared with the rest of the class for dialogue and comment. It was at this point that the students' initial affective investments in the film were mediated critically by other texts, presented, and dialogically voiced and challenged. As well, I introduced magazine and newspaper reviews along with my own written commentary on the film. The pedagogical issue here centered on both having the teachers' voice heard, but at the same time providing the conditions for such a voice to be engaged and challenged. Roger Simon has referred to this pedagogical moment as the reaffirmation of both critical authority and the struggle over the sign. He notes that such a struggle has to be ongoing, because if it stops, learning itself stops.

Once students analyzed how the film can be read differently to mobilize different forms of affect and meaning, and diverse points of identification, they were given the opportunity to analyze how *Dead Poets Society* might be understood within the larger framework that informed the course. This suggested analyzing how the film mobilized particular, if not contradictory, relations of domination and possibility, and how such relations articulate with some of the conservative educational reform policies advocated by the Bush administration. Within this frame, a number of students addressed how *Dead Poets Society* could be understood within some of the current problems regarding issues of race, class, and gender. For instance, students discussed how the film might be taught as part of an antiracist pedagogy and how the film both excludes cultural differences and erases whiteness as a privileged racial category. The class also discussed how the film reproduced patriarchal relations and how it might be read from a variety of feminist discourses. Of course, there were students whose positions did not change, and who actively argued from a liberal humanist discourse. These students were able to affirm and defend their positions, without being subjected to forms of pedagogical pressure which would put their identities on trial.

Finally, the class took up the related issues of identity, class, and cultural differences by watching *Stand and Deliver* (directed by Roman Menendez), which portrays a math teacher, Jamie Escalante (Edward James Olmos), similarly engaged in an act of resistance. Here, however, the setting is a contemporary public school in the barrio in East Los Angeles. Fighting the lethal conditions of overcrowding, lack of resources, and institutional inertia (read as racism), Escalante wages a one-man war against the system in order to "save the barrio kids." Escalante combines a form of pedagogical wizardry and authoritarianism in challenging both the students and the school. He speaks to his students in both Spanish and English, and he affirms their cultural capital while extending their expectations of success and possibility. Inspiring them to reach beyond the inequities and discrimination that routinely structure their daily school experiences and aspirations, he introduces them to the alien world of calculus, which signifies high academic status and is the mark of a privileged cultural currency in the school curriculum. As the film unfolds, Escalante's notion of resistance translates into getting the students to study hard, pass the Advanced Placement Test in calculus, and hopefully get a chance to go on to college.

I think *Stand and Deliver* is ultimately a very conservative film. That is, it appropriates elements of a progressive pedagogy to affirm the problematic goal of teaching for the test and legitimizing canonical knowledge rather than getting "students to think critically about their place in relation to the knowledge they gain and to transform their world view fundamentally by taking the politics of knowledge seriously."[18] On the other hand, *Stand and Deliver* does spark serious questions about racial discrimination, the specificity of the cultural context of teaching, and the importance of teachers and students engaging in the process of negotiation and translation in order to engage both beyond it as part of a broader attempt at self and social empowerment. But like *Dead Poets Society*, the film does not link resistance to recognizing the "materiality of conflict, of privilege, and of domination."[19] Resistance in both films provides a trace of what it means to push against authority, but neither film takes up adequately what it might mean to name and struggle against institutional practices within rather than outside of history, politics, and power. While the students response to *Stand and Deliver* was taken up more critically because of its concerns with race, class, and identity, it raised once again the crucial issue of how desire is mobilized by film narratives.

In engaging these two films, it became clear to me that the binarism that often structures the relationship between meaning and pleasure was ruptured. Those students who initially took up either of the films in terms of a desired images of themselves as a future teacher reworked that particular image not by canceling out the importance of desire, but by extending its possibilities by developing a trans- formed sense of agency and power.

Reclaiming the Popular

Any attempt to reclaim the popular in the service of a critical pedagogical practice runs the risk of at least three serious reactionary interventions. First, the popular or everyday is often used by main- stream and liberal educators merely to reaffirm the textual authority of canonical texts. Second, humanistic discourses sometimes use the popular as if it were an unproblematic mode of discourse and style; as if student voices in and of themselves lend authority that needs no further discussion or analysis. Third, there is the risk of colonizing the popular in the interests of subordinating it to the discourse of peda- gogical techniques.[20]

The political currency of popular culture is not to be determined within a binarism that simply reverses its relationship to high culture. Popular culture is not important because it appears to occupy some place on the margin of cultural politics or because it challenges the elitist authority of what is legitimated as high culture. Popular culture is important because it is a crucial sphere in which symbolic and material transaction take place at the level of everyday life in shaping the meaning and ethical substance people give to their lives. It is the space where agency is often made manifest through the educational force of a culture that structures investments of meaning and pleasure as particular practices of teaching and learning. It is also a sphere where knowledge offers up the possibilities for expanding or restrict- ing the political and practical activities that bear down on our capacities to be social agents, to understand and participate in the various social and institutional forms that shape everyday life. As such, popular culture is crucial for rethinking the role that intellec- tuals and other cultural workers might play in addressing how the issue of political agency is defined through the cultural representations and resources that are largely enacted in the social formations that constitute everyday life.

The category of cultural worker used throughout this chapter refigures the role of educators within a discourse that takes a subject position, a standpoint that argues that without a political project there can be no ground on which to engage questions of power, domination, and the possibilities of collective struggle. This suggests a political project that goes beyond merely discursive struggles. Such a project also attempts to transform nondiscursive and institutional relations of power by connecting educational struggles with broader struggles for the democratization, pluralization, and reconstruction of public life. With all apologies to the new conservativism, this is not an endorsement of that strange "species" of discourse popularly known as political correctness but a refusal to erase the political as an essential sphere of pedagogical practice.

If the popular is not to be used to reassert the validity of dominant texts and power relations, it must be viewed as part of a broader process of cultural production that is inextricably linked to issues of power, struggle, and identity. In this case, the popular does not derive its importance as an exotic text brought in from the margins of everyday life. On the contrary, it is used to raise questions about how its exclusion from the centers of power serve to secure specific forms of authority. The more important task for cultural workers is to reconstruct the very problematic that informs the high vs. popular culture distinction in order to understand more specifically how cultural production works within and outside of the margins of power in texts actively engaged in the production of institutional structures, social identities, and horizons of possibility. For example, educators might use films, videos, or television within an English class so as to draw attention to the relevance of certain canonical works for everyday life. This approach does not challenge canonicity, it merely serves to make it appear more relevant.

Another use of the popular rests with the assumption that the use of rock music, popular films, and current novels represent a discourse of authenticity that resonates with the "real" experiences that constitute student voices. This position not only wrongly posits experience as something that is unriddled with contradictions but also treats students' voices as texts whose authenticity dispenses with the need to make them the object of critical interrogation, mediation, and theoretical inquiry. Paul Smith captures this sentiment well:

> Deriving from the liberal-progressivist educational tradition which reached its acme (or nadir) with the call to relevance in the late 1960s, whatever increased interest there is in [such texts] often leads teachers to use them to facilitate students in expressing or assessing their own experiences. The logic is that the nearest access that most students have to culture is through and in mass culture and that their interest and participation in that realm can be turned toward self-expression and self-consciousness. In this process, so the argument goes, students will see their own experiences reflected and thus be more satisfied with the classroom experience than if they were taught canonical texts.[21]

What Smith is rightly criticizing is not only a prevailing form of anti-intellectualism, but also a view of pedagogy that romanticizes student experience by removing it from the historical, institutional, and discursive forces which shape it in multiple and contradictory ways. Moreover, such a discourse locates experience within an individualist ethos that renders its social grounds and collective obligations invisible. In this case, relativism overrides the concerns of social justice, and individual views outweigh the consequences of the actions that follow from them on the broader public sphere. Finally, it is important to resist the pedagogical practice of treating the cultural text solely as an ever-expanding site of meanings, interpretations, and translations. While the reading of any cultural text can be reduced to the bad faith of textual essentialism or the one right meaning, which must be avoided, it is imperative to recognize that popular texts must be read differently and politically; the readings of cultural texts must be understood within the larger dynamics of historical and social formations that struggle over such texts as sites of meaning and possibility.[22] Similarly, both cultural texts and the readings that circulate within, above, and against them must be examined as part of a broader discourse that takes up the circuits of power that constitute the ideological and material dynamics of capitalism (or any other social and economic system).

Conclusion

Rather than assuming that the popular is simply out there beyond the margins of disciplinary knowledge, ensconced in the play of everyday life waiting to be rescued as a serious object of knowledge, I want to conclude by addressing more directly the relationship between pedagogical authority and the appropriation of popular texts such as Hollywood films. Put another way, how can a notion of pedagogical authority be used to justify engaging what is problematically constituted as the popular in the first place? To be sure, it is important for cultural workers to use pedagogical authority in an emancipatory fashion to engage popular culture, to question and unlearn the benefits of privilege, and to allow those who have generally not been allowed to speak to narrate themselves, to speak from the specificity of their own voices. At the same time, it is in the service of reactionary interests for teachers and students to redefine authority as a legitimating discourse that opens up dialogue around the terrain of popular culture, but in doing so fails to interrogate how the dynamics of race, class, and gender, in particular, structure pedagogical projects in which everyday life is appropriated as part of a wider politics of containment. Needless to say, this does not always happen without struggle or resistance, but the issue here is how does one locate oneself as a cultural worker or educator within a notion of authority that legitimates engaging particular forms of popular texts without committing at the same time a form of pedagogical terrorism. How does one legitimate a notion of pedagogical authority that does not justify forms of voyeurism, looking, and appropriation that mimic the legacy of colonialism?

Raising this postcolonial caveat is not meant to suggest that progressive and left cultural workers who take up a directive notion of authority locate themselves by default in the discourse and practice of authoritarianism. On the contrary, authority needs to be reworked and struggled over as part of a wider effort to develop the pedagogical conditions necessary to make the invisible visible, expose how power is mobilized in the interests of oppression, and challenge the very terms of dominant representations. This suggests a notion of authority, popular culture, and pedagogical practice that combines a discourse of hope with forms of self-and social criticism while reclaiming a politics of location that recognizes how power, history, and ethics position, limit, and enable the cultural practices we engage in as educators. At issue here is an emancipatory notion of authority that should be fashioned in pedagogical practices rewritten in terms that articulate the importance of creating the conditions for students to take up subject positions consistent with the principles of equality, justice, and freedom rather than with interests and practices supportive of hierarchies, oppression, and exploitation. Central to this notion of authority is the need for critical educators to develop those spaces and practices that engage but don't erase the identities, compassion, or willingness of students to challenge the discourses of authority. The legitimation for such authority is as self-critical as it is deeply political, multiaccentual as it is committed to working within and across cultural and social differences to produce the basis for diverse critical public cultures that expand rather than restrict a democratic society.

To reclaim the popular within a committed view of authority is not meant to smother students under the weight of a suffocating form of political correctness. On the contrary, it is to engage the popular within a broader circuit of power relations that range from considerations about production, to textual analysis, to issues of reception. A critical pedagogy of popular culture also suggests that as critical educators and cultural workers we address how multiple subject positions are produced within dominant cultural practices but without erasing the crucial issue of agency; at the same time, a pedagogy of popular culture points to the necessity for expanding the possibilities for reading texts differently while making visible how representations work within different contexts mediated by dominant discourses and relations of power. In addition, there is the need for cultural workers to expand the boundaries of historical and semiotic analyses by making the pedagogical more political by addressing and transforming the conditions that will undermine relations of domination while simultaneously creating spaces of resistance, hope, and collective struggle. Hollywood films constitute one terrain of popular culture and as such can be viewed as a sphere of struggle infused with practices that are both pedagogical and political. Since consent has to be won for popular forms to be integrated in the dominant culture, films such as *Dead Poet's Society* are never free from the ideologies and practices of pedagogy. Such films function less as sutured texts than as practices actively engaged in the mobilization of desires, meanings, identifications, and values. A pedagogy that takes popular culture as an object of study must work to both engage and disrupt such meanings so as to break into their commonsense assumptions while simultaneously challenging the lived experiences and social relations that they produce as part of a broader attempt to construct particular notions of literacy, national identity, and political agency. The crisis of democracy is not only about the crisis of politics but also about the crisis of civic education, and film along with other media play a central role pedagogically in fostering this crisis. What is at stake is not simply the ability of individuals to be critically literate when it comes to reading the media, but understanding the crucial role the media now play in constituting the very conditions pedagogically and politically for individuals to define the terms of citizenship, justice, and democracy as more than merely the spectacle of commodification.

Notes

1. For a theoretical analysis of the depoliticizing nature of aesthetic discourse, principally as it has been used by Marxists, see Tony Bennett, "Really Useless 'Knowledge': A Political Critique of Aesthetics." *Theses Eleven* 12 (1985): 28–51; Tony Bennett, *Outside Literature* (New York: Routledge, 1990). For an analysis of the depoliticizing of politics, see Lawrence Grossberg, *We Gotta Get Out of This Place: Popular Conservatism and Post-modern Culture* (New York: Routledge, 1992).
2. Abigail Solomon-Godeau, *Photography at the Dock: Essays on Photographic History, Institutions, and Practices* (Minneapolis: University of Minnesota Press, 1991), p. xxviii.
3. I have taken this issue up in Henry A. Giroux, *Border Crossings: Cultural Workers and the Politics of Education* (New York: Routledge, 1992).
4. This issue is taken up in great detail in Stanley Aronowitz and Henry A. Giroux, *Postmodern Education: Politics, Culture, and Social Criticism* (Minneapolis: University of Minnesota Press, 1991).

5. This issue is explored from a variety of contexts in Russell Ferguson, "Introduction: Invisible Center," in Russell Ferguson et al. (eds.), *Out There: Marginalization and Contemporary Culture* (Cambridge, MA.: MIT Press, 1991), pp. 9–14. For an analysis of the relationship between culture and politics as part of the new hegemonic thrust in the UK, see Stuart Hall, *The Hard Road to Renewal: Thatcherism and the Crisis of the Left* (London: Verso, 1989).

6. For a critical analysis of the conservative assault on education and the arts in the United States see Henry A. Giroux and David Trend, "Cultural Workers, Pedagogy, and the Politics of Difference: Beyond Cultural Conservatism." *Cultural Studies* 6.1 (January, 1992): 51–72.

7. For three excellent collections that address these issues in feminist, post-modern, and postcolonial terms, see Lawrence Grossberg, Cary Nelson, and Paula Treichler (eds.), *Cultural Studies* (New York: Routledge, 1991); Jonathan Rutherford (ed.), *Identity, Community, Culture, Difference* (London: Lawrence and Wishart, 1990); Ferguson, "Introduction: Invisible Center," op. cit.

8. The chief proponent of this position is Gerald Graff, "Teach the Conflicts." *South Atlantic Quarterly* 89.1 (1990): 51–68. As Bruce Henricksen points out, Graff does not sufficiently "contextualize his model as a class and power-allocating activity"; nor does he move beyond the relativism of a dialogic model in which there is "no firm ground, nothing to believe in but the conversation itself." See Bruce Henricksen, "Teaching Against the Grain," in Bruce Henricksen and Thais E. Morgan (eds.), *Reorientations: Critical Theories and Pedagogies* (Urbana: University of Illinois Press, 1990), pp. 31, 35.

9. The theoretical rationale and specifics of this type of critical pedagogy, one which is linked to the imperatives of defining teachers as transformative intellectuals, and pedagogy as a broader exercise in the creation of critical citizens can be found in Henry A. Giroux, *Schooling and the Struggle for Public Life* (Minneapolis: University of Minnesota Press, 1988).

10. For an exemplary analysis of critical pedagogy as a form of cultural politics, see Roger I. Simon, *Teaching Against the Grain* (New York: Bergin and Garvey, 1992).

11. Michael Parenti, *Make Believe Media* (New York: St. Martin's Press, 1992), pp. 2–3.

12. Grossberg, *We Gotta Get Out of This Place*, op. cit.

13. On the radical need to engage "whiteness" as a central racial category in the construction of moral power and political/cultural domination, see Richard Dyer, "White." *Screen* 29.4 (1988): 44–64; Cornel West, "The New Cultural Politics of Difference." *October* 53 (Summer, 1990): 93–

109; Ferguson et al. (eds.), *Out There: Marginalization and Contemporary Culture*, op. cit.

14. Iain Chambers, *Border Dialogues: Journeys into Postmodernity* (New York: Routledge, 1990), p. 78.

15. For another analysis of the relationship between critical pedagogy and the issue of resistance in *Dead Poets Society*, see Peter Mclaren, "Critical Pedagogy: Constructing an Arch of Social Dreaming and a Doorway to Hope." *Journal of Education* 173.1 (1991): 9–34.

16. There is a curious "structuring silence" in Keating's refusal to engage or indicate any evidence of the "beat" literature of the 1950s, which appropriated *"carpe diem"* as a countercultural text. Given Keating's hip, iconoclastic pedagogy, it seems inconceivable that a "free thinking" English teacher would not be aware of the works of "beat" poets and novelist such as Jack Kerouac, William Burroughs, Gregory Corso, Allen Ginsberg, and others.

17. I would like to thank Hilary Radner for her comments about gender relations in this film.

18. Chandra T. Mohanty, "On Race and Voice: Challenges for Liberal Education in the 1990s." *Cultural Critique* 14 (Winter, 1989/90): 192.

19. Ibid., p. 206.

20. I have taken up this issue particularly with respect to the appropriation of Paulo Freire's work and the pedagogy of the popular. See Henry A. Giroux, "Paulo Freire and the Politics of Post-Colonialism." *Journal of Advanced Composition* 12.1 (1992): 15–26; Henry A. Giroux and Roger I. Simon (eds.), *Popular Culture, Schooling, and Everyday Life* (New York: Bergin and Garvey, 1989).

21. Paul Smith, "Pedagogy and the Popular-Cultural-Commodity-Text," in Henry A. Giroux and Roger Simon (eds.), *Popular Culture, Schooling and Everyday Life* (New York: Bergin and Garvey, 1989), p. 33.

22. For an excellent analysis of the politics of reading formations, see Bennett, *Outside Literature*, (op. cit., 1990).

7

Children's Culture and Disney's Animated Films[1]

The Politics of Children's Culture

As a single father of three young boys, I found myself somewhat reluctantly being introduced to the world of Hollywood animation films, and in particular those produced by Disney. Before becoming an observer of this form of children's culture, I accepted the largely unquestioned assumption that animated films stimulate imagination and fantasy, create a feeling of innocence and healthy adventure and, in general, are "good" for kids. In other words, such films appeared to be wholesome vehicles of amusement, a highly regarded and sought after source of fun and joy for children. However, within a very short period of time, it became clear to me that these films do more than entertain.[2] They also tell stories that influence children's experiences, desires, and pleasures. Needless to say, animated films operate on many registers, but one of the most persuasive is the role they play as the new "teaching machines." I soon found that for my children, and I suspect for many others, these films possess at least as much cultural authority and legitimacy for teaching specific roles, values, and ideals as more traditional sites of learning such as the public schools, religious institutions, and the family. Disney films combine an ideology of enchantment and aura of innocence in narrating stories that help children understand who they are, what societies are about, and what it means to construct a world of play and fantasy in an adult environment. The authority and power of such films, in part, stems from their unique form of representation and their ever-growing presence within and outside of the United States. But such authority is also produced and secured within the predominance of an expanding global media apparatus equipped with dazzling technology, sound effects, and imagery packaged as entertainment, spin-off commercial products, and "huggable" stories.

The significance of Disney's animated films as a site of learning is heightened by the widespread recognition that schools and other public sites are increasingly beset by a crisis of vision, purpose, and motivation. The mass media, especially the world of Hollywood films, constructs a dream-like world of security, coherence, and childhood innocence where kids find a place to situate themselves in their emotional lives. Unlike the often hard-nosed, joyless reality of schooling, children's films provide a high tech visual space where adventure and pleasure meet in a fantasy world of possibilities and a commercial sphere of consumerism and commodification. The educational relevance of animated films became especially clear to me as my kids experienced the vast entertainment and teaching machine embodied by Disney. Increasingly as I watched a number of Disney films, first in the movie theater and then on video, I became aware of how necessary it was to move beyond treating these films as transparent entertainment and to question the diverse messages that constitute Disney's conservative view of the world.

Trademarking Innocence

I recognize that any attempt to take up Disney films critically rubs against the grain of American popular opinion. But kids learn from them, and maybe it's time parents and educators paid closer attention to what these films are saying. I realize that this is heresy, especially at a time when kids are being subjected to an increasing glut of violence in Hollywood blockbusters, video games, and through other commercial forms of entertainment. And while these films do not promote the shameless violence that has become central to many other forms of popular and mass culture, they do carry cultural and social messages that need to be carefully scrutinized. After all, "the happiest place on earth" has traditionally gained its popularity in part through a self-proclaimed image of trademark innocence that has largely protected it from the interrogating gaze of critics. Left criticism of Disney is often completely ignored by the popular press. Yet, the charge a few years ago by conservative Southern Baptists that Disney films promote a seditious, anti-Christian ideology received enormous publicity in the mainstream media. The catch is that such criticism appeared so extreme as to be comical and therefore safe for the media to cover. More liberal critiques often ignore entirely the racist, sexist, and antidemocratic ethos that permeates Disney films. For instance, *New York Times* critic, Michiko Kakutani, has argued that if anything is wrong with Disney's animated films it is that the characters of late are too preachy and promote "wholesome messages" that "only an ogre or bigot could hate."[3] One can't help but wonder what is "wholesome" about Disney's overt racism toward Arabs displayed in *Aladdin*, the retrograde gender roles at work in *The Little Mermaid*, *Beauty and the Beast*, *Pocahontas*, and *Mulan* or the undisguised cele-bration of antidemocratic governments and racism (remember the hyenas sounding like poor blacks and Hispanics) evident in *The Lion King* (I will discuss some of these films in detail later on in this chapter).

There is more at work here than a successful public relations campaign intent on promoting Disney's claim to fabled goodness and uncompromising morality. There is also the reality of a powerful economic and political empire that in 1999 made over $23.4 billion in revenues from all of its divisions.[4] Disney is more than a corporate giant, it is also a cultural institution and dominant story teller that fiercely struggles to protect its mythical status as a purveyor of American innocence and moral virtue.

Quick to mobilize its monolith of legal representatives, public relations spokespersons, and professional cultural critics to safeguard the borders of its "magic kingdom," Disney has aggressively pros-ecuted violations of its copyrights and has a legendary reputation for bullying authors who use the Disney archives and refuse to allow Disney to approve their prepublished work.[5] For example, in its zeal to protect its image and extend its profits, Disney has gone so far as to threaten legal action against three South Florida day-care centers for using Disney cartoon characters on their exterior walls. In this instance, Disney's role as an aggressive defender of conservative family values was undermined through its aggressive endorsement of property rights. While Disney's reputation as an undisputed moral authority on United States' values has taken a beating in the last few years, the power of Disney's mythological status cannot be overestimated.

Once again, it is worth noting that Disney's image of itself as an icon of American culture is consistently reinforced through the penetration of the Disney empire into every aspect of social life. Operating as a $23 billion empire, Disney shapes children's experiences through a maze of representations and products found in box office movies, home videos, theme parks, hotels, sports teams, retail stores, classroom instructional films, CDs, radio programs, television shows, Internet servers, and family restaurants.[6] Through the widespread use of public visual space, Disney inserts itself into a network of power relations that promotes the construction of an all-encompassing world of enchantment allegedly free from the dynamics of ideology, politics, and power.[7] At the same time, Disney goes to great lengths to boost its civic image. Defining itself as a vehicle for education and civic responsibility, Disney has sponsored "Teacher of the Year Awards," provided "Doer and Dreamer" scholarships to students, and offered financial aid, internships, and other learning opportunities to disadvantaged urban youth through a number of educational and work programs, such as its ice skating program called "Goals." Intent on defining itself as a purveyor of ideas rather than commodities, Disney is aggressively developing its image as a public service industry.[8] For example, in what can be seen as an extraordinary venture, Disney has become a copartner in a business school venture in Celebration, Florida. No longer content to spread its values through the world of media entertainment and theme parks, Disney now wants to insert itself within the growing lucrative market of the public school system.

What is interesting here is that Disney no longer simply dispenses the fantasies through which childhood innocence and adventure are produced, experienced, and affirmed. Disney now provides model prototypes for families, schools, and communities. From the seedy urban haunts of New York City to the spatial monuments of consumption-shaping Florida, Disney takes full advantage of refiguring the social and cultural landscape while spreading its corporate ideology through the inventive practices of its Disney imagineers. For instance, not only has Disney transformed large sections of West 42nd Street in New York City into an advertisement for a cleaned up Disney version of America, it has also created the town Celebration in Florida, which, according to Disney executives, is designed after the "main streets of small-town America and reminiscent of Norman Rockwell images."[9] What Disney leaves out of its upbeat promotional literature is the rather tenuous notion of democracy that informs its view of municipal government, since the model of Celebration is "premised upon citizens not having control over the people who plan for them and administer the policies of the city."[10] But Disney does more than provide prototypes for up-scale communities; it also makes a claim on the future through its nostalgic view of the past and its construction of public memory as a metonym for the magical kingdom. French theorist Jean Baudrillard provides an interesting theoretical twist on the scope and power of Disney's influence by arguing that Disneyland is more "real" than fantasy because it now provides the image on which America constructs itself. For Baudrillard, Disneyland functions as a "deterrent" designed to "rejuvenate in reverse the fiction of the real."

> Disneyland is there to conceal the fact that it is the "real" country, all of "real" America, which is Disneyland (just as prisons are there to conceal the fact that it is the social in its entirety, in its banal omnipresence, which is carceral). Disneyland is presented as imaginary in order to make us believe that the rest is real, when in fact all of Los Angeles and the America surrounding it are no longer real but of the order of the hyperreal and of simulation.[11]

At the risk of taking Baudrillard too literally, examples of the Disnification of America abound. For instance, Houston airport models its monorail after the one at Disneyland. Small towns throughout America appropriate a piece of nostalgia by imitating the Victorian architecture of Disneyland's Main Street USA. Moreover, throughout America, shopping malls imitate Disney's approach to retailing so "that shopping takes place in themed environments."[12] It seems that the real policy makers are not those that reside in Washington, D.C. but in California, calling themselves the Disney imagineers. The boundaries between entertainment, education, and commercialization collapse through the sheer omnipotence of Disney's reach into diverse spheres of everyday life. The scope of the Disney empire reveals both shrewd business practices as well as a sharp eye for providing dreams and products through forms of popular culture in which kids are willing to invest materially and emotionally.

Popular audiences tend to reject any link between ideology and the prolific entertainment world of Disney. And yet Disney's pretense to innocence appears to some critics as little more than a promotional mask that covers over its aggressive marketing techniques and influence in educating children to the virtues of becoming active consumers. Eric Smooden, editor of *Disney Discourse*, a book critical of Disney's role in American culture, argues that "Disney constructs childhood so as to make it entirely compatible with consumerism."[13] Even more disturbing is the widespread belief that Disney's trademarked innocence renders it unaccountable for the diverse ways in which it shapes the sense of reality it provides for children as they take up specific and often sanitized notions of identity, difference, and history in the seemingly apolitical, cultural universe of "the Magic Kingdom." For example, Jon Wiener argues that Disneyland's version of Main Street USA harkens back to an "image of small towns characterized by cheerful commerce, with barbershop quartets and ice cream sundaes and glorious parades." For Wiener this view not only fictionalizes and trivializes the history of real Main Streets at the turn of the 20th century, it also represents an appropriation of the past to legitimate a present that portrays a world "without tenements or poverty or urban class conflict. . . . it's a native white Protestant dream of a world without blacks or immigrants."[14]

Animated Pedagogy

I want to venture into the contradictory world of Disney through an analysis of some of its more recent animated films. These films, all produced since 1989, are important because they have received enormous praise from the dominant press and have achieved blockbuster status. For many children they represent an entrance into the world of Disney. Moreover, the financial success and popularity of these films, rivaling many adult features, do not engender the critical analyses often rendered on adult films. In short, popular audiences are more willing to suspend critical judgment about such children's films.[15] Animated fantasy and entertainment appear to fall outside of the world of values, meaning, and knowledge often associated with more pronounced educational forms such as documentaries, art films, or even wide circulation adult films. Bell et al. capture this sentiment: "Disney audiences . . . legal institutions, film theorists, cultural critics, and popular audiences all guard the borders of Disney film as 'off limits' to the critical enterprise, constructing Disney as a metonym for 'America' – clean, decent, industrious – 'the happiest place on earth.'"[16]

Given the influence that the Disney ideology has on children, it is imperative for parents, teachers, and other adults to understand how such films attract the attention and influence the values of the children who view and buy them. As a producer of children's culture, Disney should not be given an easy pardon because it is defined as a universal citadel of fun and good cheer. On the contrary, as one of the primary institutions constructing childhood culture in the United States, it warrants healthy suspicion and critical debate. Such a debate should not be limited to the home, but should be a central feature of the school and other critical public sites of learning.

In what follows, I will argue that it is important to address Disney's animated films without simply condemning Disney as an ideological reactionary corporation deceptively promoting a conservative worldview under the guise of entertainment. It is also important not to celebrate Disney as the Hollywood version of Mr. Rogers doing nothing more than providing sources of joy and happiness to children all over the world.[17] Disney does both. The productive side of Disney lies in its ability to offer children visual stimulation and joyful pleasure. Dramatic thunderstorms, kaleidoscopic musical numbers, and the magical ability to transform real life issues into wondrous fanciful spectacles are a trademark of Disney's brilliance in making animated films. Disney's films offer opportunities for children to experience pleasure and to locate themselves in a world that resonates with their desires and interests. Pleasure becomes one of the defining principle of what Disney produces, and children are the serious subjects and objects of Disney's project. Hence, rather than simply being dismissed, Disney's animated films have to be interrogated and mined as an important site for the production of children's culture. Similarly, such films are often filled with contradictory messages. At the same time, Disney's influence and power must be situated within the broader understanding of the company's role as a corporate giant intent on spreading the conservative and commercial values that erode civil society while proclaiming to restructure it.

The role that Disney plays in shaping individual identities and controlling the fields of social meaning through which children negotiate the world is far too complex to be simply set aside as a form of reactionary politics. If educators and other cultural workers are to include the culture of children as an important site of contestation and struggle then it becomes imperative to analyze how Disney's animated films powerfully influence the way America's cultural landscape is imagined. Disney's scripted view of childhood and society needs to be engaged and challenged as "a historically specific matter of social analysis and intervention." This is particularly important since Disney's animated films work to provoke and inform children's imaginations, desires, roles, and dreams while simultaneously sedimenting affect and meaning.[18]

The wide distribution and popular appeal of Disney's animated films provides diverse audiences the opportunity for critical viewing. Critically analyzing how Disney films work to construct meanings, induce pleasures, and reproduce ideologically loaded fantasies is not meant to promote a particular exercise in film criticism. Like that of any educational institution, Disney's view of the world needs to be taken up in terms of how it narrates children's culture and how it can be held accountable for what it does as a significant cultural public sphere – a space in which ideas, values, audiences, markets, and opinions serve to create different publics and social formations. Of course, Disney's self-proclaimed innocence, inflexibility in dealing with social criticism, and paranoid attitude towards justifying what it does, is now legendary, and suggests all the more reason why Disney should be both challenged and engaged critically. Moreover, as a multibillion dollar company, Disney's corporate and cultural influence is too enormous and far-reaching to allow it to define itself exclusively within the imaginary discourse of innocence, civic pride, and entertainment.[19]

The question of whether Disney's animated films are good for kids has no easy answers and resists simple analysis within the traditional and allegedly nonideological registers of fun and entertainment. Disney's most recent films, which include *The Little Mermaid* (1989), *Beauty and the Beast* (1991), *Aladdin* (1992), *The Lion King* (1994) *Pocahontas* (1995), *The Hunchback of Notre Dame* (1996), *Hercules* (1997), and *Mulan* (1998) provide ample opportunity to address how Disney constructs a culture of joy and innocence for children out of the intersection of entertainment, advocacy, pleasure, and consumerism.[20] All of these films have been high profile releases catering to massive audiences. Moreover, their commercial success is not limited to box office profits. Successfully connecting the rituals of consumption and moviegoing, Disney's animated films provide a "marketplace of culture," a launching pad for an endless number of products and merchandise that include videocassettes, sound track albums, children's clothing, furniture, stuffed toys, and new rides at the theme parks.[21] For example, in the video market, *Little Mermaid* and *Beauty and the Beast* have combined sales of over 34 million videocassettes. *Aladdin* has earned over "$1 billion from box-offices income, video sales and such ancillary baubles as Princess Jasmine dresses and Genie cookie jars."[22] Moreover, produced as a video interactive game, *Aladdin* had sold over three million copies in 1993. Similar sales are expected for the video and interactive game version of the film, *The Lion King*, which grossed $253.5 million in profits as of August 24, 1994.[23] In fact, the first few weeks after *The Lion King* videocassette was released, it had sales of over 20 million, and Disney's stock soared by $2.25 a share based on first-week revenues of $350 million. It was ranked as one of the most profitable films every made. Jessica J. Reiff, an analyst at Oppenheimer & Company, said, "the movie will represent $1 billion in profits for Disney over two or three years."[24]

At the launch of *The Hunchback of Notre Dame*, Disney Records shipped two million Sing Along home videos and seven types of *Hunchback* audio products, including the soundtrack CD and cassette and a toddler-targeted My First Read-Along. Tie-promotions for the film included Burger King, Payless Shoes, Nestlé, and Mattel.[25] While *The Hunchback of Notre Dame* did not fare well at the box office, generating a disappointing $99 million in North American revenue, it is expected, according to *Adweek* magazine, "to generate $500 million in profit (not just revenues), after the other revenues streams are taken into account."[26] Similarly, Disney characters such as Mickey Mouse, Snow White, Jasmine, Aladdin, and Pocahontas become prototypes for numerous toys, logos, games, and rides that fill department stores all over the world. Disney theme parks, which made over $4.0 billion in revenues in 1997, produced a sizable portion of their profits through the merchandising of toys based on characters from the animated films. *The Lion King* has been one of Disney's biggest commercial successes and provided a model for marketing its future animated films, including the more recent *Hercules* (with its blatant pitch commercialism built into the movie itself) and *Mulan*. *The Lion King* produced a staggering $1 billion in merchandizing profits in 1994 alone – the year of its release – not to mention the profits made from spinoff products from the movie. For example, when *The Lion King* was first released Disney shipped over three million copies of the soundtrack.[27] Disney's culture of commercialism is big business and the toys modeled after Disney's animated films provide goods for over 728 Disney Stores worldwide. As a commentator in *Newsweek* recently pointed out, "The merchandise – Mermaid dolls, Aladdin undies, and collectibles like a sculpture of Bambi's Field Mouse – account for a stunning 20 percent of Disney's operating income."[28]

One of Disney's biggest promotion campaigns was put into effect with the summer 1995 release of *Pocahontas*. A record line-up of tie-in merchandise included Pocahontas stuffed animals, sheets, pillowcases, toothbrushes, games, moccasins, and over "40 different picture and activity books."[29] A consortium of corporations spent an estimated $125 millon on cross-marketing *Pocahontas*. Two well-known examples included Burger King, which was converted into an advertisement for the film and gave away an estimated 50 million

Pocahontas figurines, and the Mattel Corporation which marketed over 50 different dolls and toys.

But Disney's attempt to turn children into consumers and construct commodification as a defining principle of children's culture should not suggest a parallel vulgarity in its willingness to experiment aesthetically with popular forms of representation. Disney has shown enormous inventiveness in its attempts to reconstruct the very grounds on which popular culture is defined and shaped. By defining popular culture as a hybridized sphere that combines genres, forms, and often collapses the boundary between high and low culture, Disney has pushed against the grain of aesthetic form and cultural legitimacy. For instance, when *Fantasia* appeared in the 1930s it drew the wrath of music critics, who, holding to an elite view of classical music, were outraged that the musical score of the film drew from the canon of high culture. By combining high and low culture in the form of the animated film, Disney opened up new cultural spaces and possibilities for artists and audiences alike. Moreover, as sites of entertainment, Disney's films "work" because they put both children and adults in touch with joy and adventure. They present themselves as places to experience pleasure, even when we have to buy it.

And yet, Disney's brilliant use of aesthetic forms, musical scores, and inviting characters can only be "read" in light of the broader conceptions of reality and predispositions shaped by specific Disney films within a wider system of dominant representations about gender roles, race, and agency that are endlessly repeated in the visual worlds of television, Hollywood film, and videocassettes.

A number of the films mentioned draw upon the talents of song writers Howard Ashman and/or Alan Menken, whose skillful arrangements provide the emotional glue of the animation experience. The rousing calypso number, "Under the Sea," in *The Little Mermaid*, and the "Be Our Guest," Busby Berkeley-inspired musical sequence in *Beauty and the Beast*, are indicative of the musical talent at work in Disney's animated films. Fantasy abounds as Disney's animated films produce a host of exotic and stereotypical villains, and heroes. The Beast's enchanted castle in *Beauty and the Beast* becomes magical as household objects are transformed into dancing teacups, a talking teapot, and dancing silverware. And yet, tied to the magical fantasy and lighthearted musical scores, are representations and themes that emulate the repetitive stereotypes that are characteristic of Disney's view of the childhood culture. For example, while Ursula, the large oozing, black and purple squid in *The Little Mermaid* gushes with evil and irony, the mermaid, Ariel, appears as a cross between a typical rebellious teenager and a Southern California fashion model. Disney's representations of evil and good women appear to have been fashioned in the editorial office of *Vogue*. The wolf-like monster in *Beauty and the Beast* evokes a rare combination of macho terror and Disney-inspired gentleness, while Scar, the suave feline in *The Lion King*, masterfully embraces a scheming sense of evil and betrayal. Disney's evocation of war and battle are expansive and provocative in *Mulan*. The array of animated objects and animals in these films is of the highest artistic standards, but they do not exist in some ideologically free comfort zone. Their characters are tied to larger narratives about freedom, rites of passage, intolerance, choices, greed, and the brutalities of male chauvinism. These are just some of the many themes explored in Disney's animated films. But enchantment comes with a high price if one of its effects is to seduce its audience into suspending critical judgment of the dominant ideological messages produced by such films. Even though these messages can be read from a variety of viewpoints shaped within different contexts of reception, the dominant assumptions that structure these films carry enormous weight in restricting the number of cultural meanings that can be brought to bear on these films, especially when the intended audience is mostly children.

This should not suggests that the role of the critic in dealing with Disney's animated films is to simply assign them a particular ideological reading. On the contrary, the challenge of such films is to analyze the various themes and assumptions that inform them both within and outside of the dominant institutional and ideological formations that attempt to shape and constrain how they might be taken up. This allows educators and other to try to understand how such films can become sites of contestation, translation, and exchange in order to be read differently. But there is more at stake here than recognizing the plurality of readings such films might animate; there is also the pedagogical task of provoking audiences to reflect upon the ways in which Disney's themes function as part of a broader public discourse, privileging some definitions or interpretations over others. The conservative values that Disney's films promote assume a force that others do not because of the company's power and ability to produce, distribute, and promote its goods so as to virtually place them in every conceivable public and commercial space. Adults and young people grow up with Disney products and images, which in many instances resonate very powerfully with already inscribed dominant perceptions and meanings. Yet, it must be stressed that Disney does not crudely impose its belief system on children and others. On the contrary, its pedagogical power and influence is rooted in a historical legacy and ongoing ability to produce and circulate an environment of images that become a commonsensical part of the public imagination and people's everyday lives. Through a process of accumulation and accretion, these images begin to slowly influence and shape how children come to know themselves and their relationship to the larger social order. Pedagogically, this suggests the need for educators, parents, and others to analyze critically how privileged dominant readings of Disney's animated films work to generate and affirm particular pleasures, desires, and subject positions that define for children specific notions of agency and its possibilities in society.

Contexts mold interpretations; but political, economic, and ideological contexts also produce the texts to be read. Focusing on films must be supplemented with analyzing the institutional practices and social structures that work to shape such texts. This type of analysis does not mean that cultural workers should subscribe to a form of determinism in which cultural texts can be assigned a singular meaning, as much as it should suggest pedagogical strategies for understanding how dominant regimes of power work to severely limit the range of views that children might bring to reading Disney's animated films. By making the relationship between power and knowledge visible, while simultaneously referencing what is often taken for granted, teachers and critics can incorporate Disney's animated films pedagogically for students and others to read such films within, against, and outside of the dominant codes that inform them. There is a double pedagogical movement here. First, there is the need to read Disney's films in relation to their articulation with other dominant texts in order to assess their similarities in legitimating particular ideologies. Second, there is the need on the part of parents and others to use Disney's thematization of America and America's thematization of Disney as a referent to make visible and disrupt dominant codings, but to do so in a space that invites dialogue, debate, and alternative readings. For instance, one major pedagogical challenge would be to assess how dominant ideas that are repeated over time in these films and reinforced through other popular cultural texts can be taken up as a referent for engaging how children define themselves within such representations. The task here is to provide readings of such films that serve as a pedagogical referent for engaging them in the context in which they are shaped, understood, or might be seen.[30]

But providing a particular ideological reading of these films should not suggest this is the only possible reading. On the contrary, by providing a theoretical referent for engaging Disney films, it becomes possible to explore pedagogically how children, students, and adults both construct and defend the readings they actually bring to such films. Such a position provides an opportunity to expand the dialogue regarding what Disney's films mean while simultaneously challenging the taken-for-granted assumptions that often surround dominant readings of such films. Taking a position on Disney's films should not degenerate into a doctrinaire reading or legitimate a form of political or pedagogical indoctrination with children or anybody else. Rather, such an approach should address how any reading of these films is ideological and should be engaged in terms of the context that produces a particular reading, its content, and what it suggests about the values and social relations it endorses as part of a broader discourse. Moreover, engaging such films politically and ideologically provides the pedagogical basis for making such films problematic and thus open to dialogue rather than treating them uncritically as mere entertainment.

Reading Disney

The construction of gender identity for girls and women represents one of the most controversial issues in Disney's animated films.[31] In both *The Little Mermaid* and *The Lion King* the female characters are constructed within narrowly defined gender roles. All of the female characters in these films are ultimately subordinate to males, and define their sense of power and desire almost exclusively in terms of dominant male narratives. For instance, modeled after a slightly anorexic Barbie doll, Ariel, the woman-mermaid in *The Little Mermaid*, at first glance appears to be engaged in a struggle against parental control, motivated by the desire to explore the human world and willing to take a risk in defining the subject and object of her desires. But in the end, the struggle to gain independence from her father, Triton, and the sense of desperate striving that motivates her, dissolves when Ariel makes a Mephisrophelean pact with the sea witch, Ursula. In this trade, Ariel gives away her voice to gain a pair of legs so that she can pursue the handsome Prince Eric. While children might be delighted by Ariel's teenage rebelliousness, they are strongly positioned to believe, in the end, that desire, choice, and empowerment are closely linked to catching and loving a handsome prince. Bonnie Leadbeater and Gloria Lodato Wilson explore succinctly the pedagogical message at work in the film with their comment:

> The 20th-century innocent and appealing video presents a high-spirited role for adolescent girls, but an ultimately subservient role for adult women. Disney's "Little Mermaid" has been granted her wish to be part of the new world of men, but she is still flipping her fins and is not going too far. She stands to explore the world of men. She exhibits her new-found sexual desires. But the sexual ordering of women's roles is unchanged.[32]

Ariel in this film becomes a metaphor for the traditional housewife-in-the-making narrative. When the sea-witch Ursula tells Ariel that taking away her voice is not so bad because men don't like women who talk, the message is dramatized when the prince attempts to bestow the kiss of true love on Ariel even though she has never spoken to him. Within this rigidly defined narrative, womanhood offers Ariel the reward of marrying the right man and renouncing her former life under the sea as a telling cultural model for the universe of female choices and decision-making in Disney's world-view. The forging of rigid gender roles in *The Little Mermaid* does not represent an isolated moment in Disney's filmic universe; on the contrary, the power that informs Disney's reproduction of negative stereotypes about women and girls gains force, in part, through the consistent way in which similar messages are circulated and reproduced, in varying degrees, in all of Disney's animated films. In fact, one of the distinguishing features of Disney's animated films over the years is how little the representations and images of females change. In both animal and human form, Disney portrays young girls as highly sexualized, with small waists and big breasts; all of these characters are coquettish—fluttering eyelashes-and exhibiting seductive behavior. Moreover, all of Disney's female protagonists, regardless of how strong they might appear, cannot live out their lives without being rescued by men.

For example, in *Aladdin* the issue of agency and power is centered primarily on the role of the young street tramp, Aladdin. Jasmine, the princess he falls in love with, is simply an object of his immediate desire as well as a social stepping stone. Jasmine's life is almost completely defined by men, and, in the end, her happiness is insured by Aladdin, who finally is given permission to marry her.

Catering to a more complicated notion of femininity, Disney's gender theme becomes a bit more complicated in *Beauty and the Beast*, *Pocahontas*, and *Mulan*. Belle, the lead character of *Beauty and the Beast*, is portrayed as an independent woman stuck in a provincial village in 18th century France. Seen as odd because she always has her nose in a book, she is pursued by Gaston, the ultimate vain, macho male typical of Hollywood films of the 1980s. To Belle's credit she rejects him, but in the end she gives her love to the Beast, who holds her captive, hoping she will fall in love with him and break the evil spell cast upon him as a young man. Belle not only falls in love with the Beast, she "civilizes" him by instructing him on how to eat properly, control his temper, and dance. Belle becomes a model of etiquette and style as she turns this narcissistic, muscle-bound tyrant into a "new" man, one who is sensitive, caring, and loving. Some critics have labeled Belle a Disney feminist because she rejects and vilifies Gaston, the ultimate macho man. Less obviously, *Beauty and the Beast* also can be read as a rejection of hypermasculinity and a struggle between the macho sensibilities of Gaston and the reformed sexist, the Beast. In this reading, Belle is less the focus of the film than a prop or "mechanism for solving the Beast's dilemma."[33] Whatever subversive qualities Belle personifies in the film, they seem to dissolve when focused on humbling male vanity. In the end, Belle simply becomes another woman whose life is valued for solving a man's problems. But there is a more sinister message in *Beauty and the Beast* that needs to be told. Dr. Carolyn Newberger, a psychologist at the Harvard Medical School, argues that if you examine *Beauty and the Beast* through the lens of family violence, the abuses that are graphically represented in the film are horrific, especially as a teaching message for young girls. In making this claim, Newberger underscores the manner in which the Beast screams at Belle, imprisons her, throws her father out of the house, and takes her family away from her. The Beast's behavior is violent and, as she argues "horrifically abusive." Yet, the central message of the story is that Belle succumbs to him, interprets his rage and anger as simply expressions of a bad temper, and in turn discovers beneath his horrible abuse a personality that is tender and vulnerable; she then proceeds to fall in love with him. The pedagogical terrorism that takes place here is hard to miss. The message to young girls and boys is that they should overlook the abuse and violence, and that such displays of rage are really a cover for tenderness and that women who are abused should just stick with it because in the end, as Newberger points out, "there is a tender prince lurking within and it is [the young girl's job] to kiss the beast and bring it out."[34]

Disney's next femme fatale, Pocahontas, appears to both challenge and reproduce some of these stereotypes. Rather than being portrayed as a young adolescent, Pocahontas is made over historically to resemble a shapely, animated, contemporary, high-fashion supermodel. Represented as a woman who is bright, courageous, literate, and politically progressive, she is a far cry from the traditional negative stereotypes of Native Americans portrayed in Hollywood films. But like many of Disney's female protagonists, Pocahontas's character is drawn primarily in relation to the men that surround her. Initially, her identity is defined in resistance to her father's attempts to marry her off to one of the bravest warriors in the tribe. But her coming-of-age identity crisis is largely defined by her love affair with John Smith, a colonialist who happens to be blond and looks like he belongs in a Southern California pin-up magazine of male surfers. Pocahontas's character is drawn primarily through her struggle to save her colonial lover, John Smith, from being executed by her father. Pocahontas exudes a kind of soppy romanticism that not only saves John Smith's life, but convinces the crew of the British ship to turn on its greedy captain and return to England. Of course, this is a Hollywood rewrite of history that bleaches colonialism of its genocidal legacy. No mention is made of the fact that John Smith's countrymen would ultimately ruin Pocahontas's land, bring disease, murder, and poverty to her people, and eventually destroy their religion, economic livelihood, and way of life. In the Disney version of history, colonialism never happened, and the meeting between the old and new worlds simply becomes fodder for reproducing a "love conquers all" narrative. One wonders how this film would have been taken up in the public mind if it had been a film about a Jewish woman who falls in love with a blond Aryan Nazi, while ignoring any references to the Holocaust.

The issue of female subordination returns with a vengeance in *The Lion King*. All of the rulers of the kingdom are male, reinforcing the assumption that independence and leadership are tied to patriarchal entitlement and high social standing. The dependency that the beloved lion king, Mufasa, engenders from the females of Pride Rock is unaltered after his death when the evil Scar assumes control of the kingdom. Lacking any sense of outrage, independence, or resistance, the female felines hang around to do his bidding.

The gender stereotyping is somewhat modified in *Mulan* (1998). The lead character of the same name is presented as a bold female warrior who challenges traditional gender stereotypes of young women, but for all of her independence, in the end, the film is, as Janet Maslin points out, "still enough of a fairy tale to need a Mr. Right."[35] Mulan may be an independent strong-willed young woman, but the ultimate payoff of her own bravery comes in the form of catching the handsome son of a general. And if the point is missed, when Mulan's grandmother first sees the young man as he enters her granddaughter's house, she affirms what she (the audience?) sees as Mulan's real victory, which is catching a man, and yells out: "Sign me up for the next war!" But there is an equally disturbing side to Mulan's alleged makeover as a strong woman. Rather than defining herself against the patriarchal celebration of war, violence, and militarism, Mulan is transformed into a cross-dresser who proves that when it comes to war she can perform as well as any male. By embracing a disturbing masculine view of war, Mulan cancels out any pretense of rupturing traditional gender roles by becoming one of the boys. But unless the fantasy be taken too far, Disney reminds us at the conclusion of the film that she is still just a girl in search of a man, and as in so many other Disney animated films, Mulan becomes an exoticized version of the all-American girl who manages to catch the most handsome boy on the block, square jaw and all. *Mulan*, the film, also continues the long legacy of orientalism that is endemic to Hollywood representations of Asians. History is ignored, complexity rendered meaningless, and racial stereotyping becomes the motivating force in producing the "entertaining" spectacle of exoticizing the "other."

Given Disney's purported obsession with family values, especially as a consuming unit, it is curious that, with the exception of *Mulan*, there are no strong mothers or fathers in these films.[36] Not only are powerful mothers absent, but with the exception of the fathers of Pocahontas and Mulan, all of the father figures in these films are portrayed as either weak or stupid. Only the mermaid has a domineering father; Jasmine's father is outwitted by his aides; and Belle has an airhead for a father.

Jack Zipes, a leading theorist on fairy tales, claims that Disney's animated films celebrate a masculine type of power, but more importantly he believes that they reproduce "a type of gender stereotyping... that has an adverse effect on children in contrast to what parents think.... Parents think they're essentially harmless – and they're not harmless."[37] Disney films are seen by enormous numbers of children in both the United States and abroad. As far as the issue of gender is concerned, Disney's view of female agency and empowerment is not simply limited, it borders on being overtly reactionary.

Racial stereotyping is another major issue that surfaces in many of the recent Disney animated films. But the legacy of racism does not begin with the films produced since 1989; on the contrary, there is a long history of racism associated with Disney. This history can be traced back to denigrating images of people of color in films such as *Song of the South*, released in 1946, and *The Jungle Book*, which appeared in 1967.[38] Moreover, racist representations of native Americans as violent "redskins" were featured in Frontierland in the 1950s.[39] In addition, the main restaurant in Frontierland featured the real life figure of a former slave, Aunt Jemima, who would sign autographs for the tourists outside of her "Pancake House." Eventually the exhibits and the native Americans running them were eliminated by Disney executives because the "Indian" canoe guides wanted to unionize. They were displaced by robotic dancing bears. Complaints from civil rights groups got rid of the degrading Aunt Jemima spectacle.[40]

One of the most controversial examples of racist stereotyping facing the Disney publicity machine occurred with the release of *Aladdin* in 1989, although such stereotyping reappeared in full force in 1994 with the release of *The Lion King*. *Aladdin* represents a particularly important example because it was a high profile release, the winner of two academy awards, and one of the most successful Disney films ever produced. Playing to massive audiences of children, the film's opening song, "Arabian Nights," begins its depiction of Arab culture with a decidedly racist tone. The lyrics of the offending stanza states: "Oh I come from a land/From a faraway place/Where the caravan camels roam./Where they cut off your ear/If they don't like your face./It's barbaric, but hey, it's home." In this characterization, a politics of identity and place associated with Arab culture magnifies popular stereotypes already primed by the media through its portrayal of the Gulf War. Such racist representations are further reproduced in a host of supporting characters who are portrayed as grotesque, violent, and cruel. Yousef Salem, a former spokesperson for the South Bay Islamic Association, characterized the film in the following way:

All of the bad guys have beards and large, bulbous noses, sinister eyes and heavy accents, and they're wielding swords constantly. Aladdin doesn't have a big nose; he has a small nose. He doesn't have a beard or a turban. He doesn't have an accent. What makes him nice is they've given him this American character. . . . I have a daughter who says she's ashamed to call herself an Arab, and it's because of things like this.[41]

Jack Shaheen, a professor of broadcast journalism at Southern Illinois University of Edwardsville, along with radio personality, Casey Kasem, mobilized a public relations campaign protesting the anti-Arab themes in *Aladdin*. At first, the Disney executives ignored the protest, but due to the rising tide of public outrage agreed to change one line of the stanza in the subsequent videocassette and worldwide film release; it is worth noting that Disney did not change the lyrics on its popular CD release of *Aladdin*.[42] It appears that Disney executives were not unaware of the racist implications of the lyrics when they were first proposed. Howard Ashman, who wrote the main title song, submitted an alternative set of lyrics when he delivered the original verse. The alternative set of lyrics, "Where it's flat and immense/And the heat is intense" eventually replaced the original verse, "Where they cut of your ear/If they don't like your face." Though the new lyrics appeared in the videocassette release of *Aladdin*, many Arab groups were disappointed because the verse "It's barbaric, but hey it's home" was not altered. More importantly, the mispronunciation of Arab names in the film, the racial coding of accents, and the use of nonsensical scrawl as a substitute for an actual written Arabic language were not removed.[43]

Racism in Disney's animated films does not simply appear in negative imagery, it is also reproduced through racially coded language and accents. For example, *Aladdin* portrays the "bad" Arabs with thick, foreign accents, while the Anglicized Jasmine and Aladdin speak in standard Americanized English. A hint of the racism that informs this depiction is provided by Peter Schneider, president of feature animation at Disney at the time, who points out that Aladdin was modeled after Tom Cruise. Racially coded representations and language are also evident in *The Lion King*. Scar, who is the icon of evil, is portrayed as darker than the good lions. Moreover, racially coded language is evident as all of the members of the royal family speak with posh British accents while Shenzi and Banzai, the despicable hyena storm troopers, speak through the voices of Whoopi Goldberg and Cheech Marin in jive accents that take on the nuances of the discourse of a decidedly urban, black and Hispanic youth. Disney falls back upon the same racialized formula in *Mulan*. Not far removed from the Amos 'n' Andy crows in *Dumbo*, *Mulan* resurrects the racialized low-comedy figure in the form of Mushu, a tiny red dragon with a black voice (Eddie Murphy). Mushu takes on the role of a servile and boastful clown that seems less suited to a mythic fable about China than it does to the craven stereotype of the backward, Southern, chitlin-circuit character that appears to feed the popular racist imagination. The use of racially coded language is not new in Disney's films and can be found in an early version of *The Three Little Pigs*, as well as in *Song of the South*, and *The Jungle Book*.[44] What is astonishing in these films is that they produce a host of representations and codes in which children are taught that cultural differences that do not bear the imprint of white, middle-class ethnicity are deviant, inferior, unintelligent, and a threat to be overcome. The racism in these films is defined by both the presence of racist representations in which people of color are portrayed as gorillas, as jive-talking hyenas, or as shuffling buffoons; or, as in the latest Disney version of *Tarzan*, are actually removed from the very land they inhabit while a white man fills in the only force able to conquer the "dangers" of Africa.

At the same time, whiteness is universalized through the privileged representation of middle-class social relations, values, and linguistic practices. Moreover, the representational rendering of history, progress, and Western culture bears a colonial legacy that seems perfectly captured by Edward Said's notion of orientalism and its dependency on new images of centrality and sanctioned narratives.[45] Cultural differences in Disney's recent films are expressed through a "naturalized" racial hierarchy, one that is antithetical to a viable democratic society. There is nothing innocent in what kids learn about race as portrayed in the "magical world" of Disney. Even in a film such as *Pocahontas*, where cultural difference are portrayed more positively, there is the suggestion in the end that racial identities must remain separate. *Pocahontas* is one of the few love stories in Disney's animated series in which the lovers do not live together happily ever after. It is also one of the few love stories that brings lovers from different races together.

In what follows, I want to comment on another central feature common to many of Disney's recently animated films, that is, the celebration of deeply, antidemocratic social relations. Nature and the animal kingdom provide the mechanism for presenting and legitimating caste, royalty, and structural inequality as part of the natural order. The seemingly benign presentation of celluloid dramas in which men rule, strict discipline is imposed through social hierarchies, and leadership is a function of one's social status, suggests a yearning for a return to a more rigidly stratified society, one modeled after the British monarchy of the 18th and 19th centuries. Within Disney's animated films, nature provides a metaphor where "harmony is bought at the price of domination. . . . no power or authority is implied except for the natural ordering mechanisms [of nature]."[46] For children, the messages offered in Disney's animated films suggest that social problems such as the history of racism, the genocide of Native Americans, the prevalence of sexism, and crisis of democracy are simply willed through the laws of nature.

Cultural Pedagogy and Children's Culture

Given the corporate reach, cultural influence, and political power that Disney exercises over multiple levels of children's culture, Disney's animated films should be neither ignored nor censored by those who dismiss the conservative ideologies they produce and circulate. I think there are a number of issues to be taken up regarding the forging of a pedagogy and politics responsive to Disney's shaping of children's culture. In what follows, I want to provide in schematic form some suggestions regarding how cultural workers, educators, and parents might critically engage Disney's influence in shaping the "symbolic environment into which our children are born and in which we all live out our lives."[47]

First, it is crucial that the realm of popular culture that Disney increasingly uses to teach values and sell goods be taken seriously as a site of learning and contestation, especially for children. This means, at the very least, that those cultural texts that dominate children's culture, including Disney's animated films, should be incorporated into schools as serious objects of social knowledge and critical analysis. This would entail a reconsideration of what counts as really useful knowledge in public schools, while offering a new theoretical register for addressing how popular media aimed at shaping children's culture are implicated in a range of power/knowledge relationships. This is not simply a call for making media literacy an essential part of what kids learn in schools (as crucial as such a pedagogy is),[48] but a reconsideration of the meaning, range, and possibilities of what counts as school knowledge itself. In simple terms, this means making popular culture an essential object of social analysis in schools.

Second, parents, community groups, educators, and other concerned individuals must be attentive to the multiple and diverse messages in Disney films in order to both criticize them when necessary and, more importantly, to reclaim them for more productive ends. At the very least, we must be attentive to the processes whereby meanings are produced in these films and how they work to secure particular forms of authority and social relations. At stake pedagogically is the issue of paying "close attention to the ways in which [such films] invite (or indeed seek to prevent) particular meanings and pleasures."[49] In fact, Disney's films appear to assign, quite unapologetically, rigid roles to women and people of color. Similarly, such films generally produce a narrow view of family values coupled with a nostalgic and conservative view of history that should be challenged and transformed. Educators need to take seriously Disney's attempt to shape collective memory, particularly when such attempts are unabashedly defined by one of Disney's imagineers in the following terms: "What we create is a sort of 'Disney realism,' sort of Utopian in nature, where we carefully program out all the negative, unwanted elements and program in the positive elements."[50] Needless to say, Disney's rendering of entertainment and spectacle, whether expressed in Frontierland, Main Street USA, or in its endless video and film productions, does not merely represent an edited, sanitary, and nostalgic view of history, one that is free of poverty, class differences, and urban decay. Disney's writing of public memory also aggressively constructs a monolithic notion of national identity that treats subordinate groups as either exotic or irrelevant to American history, while simultaneously marketing cultural differences within "histories that corporations can live with."[51] Disney's version of United States history is neither innocent, nor can it be dismissed as simply entertainment.

Disney's celluloid view of children's culture often works to strip the past, present, and future of diverse narratives and multiple possibilities. But it is precisely such a rendering that needs to be revealed as a historically specific and politically constructed cultural "landscape of power." Positing and revealing the ideological nature of Disney's world of children's films opens up further opportunities for educators and others to critically engage such texts in order to make them mean differently. Rustom Bharacuha puts it well in arguing that "the consumption of . . . images . . . can be subverted through a particular use in which we are compelled to think through images rather than respond to them with a hallucinatory delight." [52] One interpretation of the call to "think through images" is for educators and cultural workers to demonstrate pedagogically and politically that history and its rendering of national identity have to be contested and engaged, even when images parade as innocent film entertainment for children. The images that pervade Disney's production of children's culture along with their claim to public memory need to be challenged and rewritten, "moved about in different ways," and read differently as part of the script of democratic empowerment.[53] Issues regarding the construction of gender, race, class, caste, and other aspects of self and collective identity are defining principles of Disney's films for children. It is within the drama of animated storytelling that children are often positioned pedagogically to learn what subject positions are open to them as citizens and what positions aren't. Hence, the struggle over children's culture should be considered as part of a struggle over the related discourses of citizenship, national identity, and democracy itself.

Third, if Disney's films are to be viewed as more than narratives of fantasy and escape, becoming sites of reclamation and imagination, which affirm rather than deny the long-standing relationship between entertainment and pedagogy, it is important to consider how we might insert the political and pedagogical back into the discourse of entertainment. In part, this points to analyzing how entertainment can be addressed as a subject of intellectual engagement rather than a series of sights and sounds that wash over us. This suggests a pedagogical approach to popular culture that engages how a politics of the popular works to mobilize desire, stimulate imagination, and produce forms of identification that can become objects of dialogue and critical investigation. At one level, this suggests addressing the utopian possibilities in which children often find representations of their hopes and dreams. The pedagogical value of such an approach is that it alerts educators to taking the needs, desires, languages, and experience of children seriously. But this is not meant to merely affirm the necessity for relevance in the curriculum as much as it means recognizing the pedagogical importance of what kids bring with them to the classroom or any other site of learning as crucial to decentering power in the classroom and expanding the possibility for teaching students multiple literacies as part of a broader strategy in expanding their capacities to read the world critically.

It appears crucial that parents, educators and others pay attention to how these Disney films and visual media are used and understood differently by diverse groups of kids. Not only does this provide the opportunity for parents and others to talk to children about popular culture, it also creates the basis for better understanding how young people identify with these films, what issues are raised within such cultural forms that need to be addressed, and how such discussions would open up a language of pleasure and criticism rather than simply foreclose one. This suggests that we develop new ways of critically understanding and reading electronically produced visual media. Teaching and learning the culture of the book is no longer the staple of what it means to be literate.

Children learn from exposure to popular cultural forms, providing a new cultural register to what it means to be literate. Educators and cultural workers must not only be attentive to the production of popular art forms in the schools. On one level this suggests a cultural pedagogy rooted in cultural practices that utilizes students' knowledge and experience through their use of popular cultural forms. As I have stressed previously, students should not merely be taught to critically analyze the messages produced by the vast range of electronically mediated popular culture, they must also be able to master the skills and technology to produce it in its various forms. Put another way, students should gain experience in making films, videos, music, and other forms of cultural production, thus giving students more power over the conditions for the production of knowledge.

But a cultural pedagogy also involves the struggle for more resources for schools and other sites of learning. Providing the conditions for students and others to become the subject and not simply the object of pedagogical work by asserting their role as cultural producers is crucial if students are to become attentive to the workings of power, solidarity, and difference as part of a more comprehensive project for democratic empowerment.

Fourth, Disney's all-encompassing reach into the spheres of economics, consumption, and culture suggest that we analyze Disney within a broad and complex range of relations of power. Eric Smoodin argues that the American public needs to "gain a new sense of Disney's importance, because of the manner in which his work in film and television is connected to other projects in urban planning, ecological politics, product merchandising, United States domestic and global policy formation, technological innovation, and constructions of national character."[54] This suggests undertaking new analyses of Disney which connect rather than separate the various social and cultural formations in which the company actively engages. Clearly, such a dialectical practice not only provides a more theoretically accurate understanding of the reach and influence of Disney's power; it also contributes to forms of analysis that rupture the notion that Disney is primarily about the pedagogy of entertainment.

Questions of ownership, control, and the possibility of public participation in making decisions about how cultural resources are used, to what extent, and for what effect, should become a central issue in addressing the world of Disney and other corporate conglomerates that shape cultural policy. In part, teachers, students, and others should situate the control, production, and distribution of such films as part of a wider circuit of power. Such an approach provides concerned parents and public citizens with relevant information for understanding and addressing how Disney, Inc. exercises its power and influence within the context of a larger cultural strategy and public policy initiative. In this context, Disney's influence in the shaping of children's culture cannot be reduced to critically interpreting the ideas and values promoted in films and other forms of representation. Any viable analysis of Disney must also confront the institutional and political power Disney exercises through its massive control over diverse sectors of what Mark Crispin Miller has called the "National Entertainment State."[55] This form of analysis would combine research about Disney's reach and influence in the world and offer knowledge and strategies that address how the issue of cultural power and the shaping of children's culture could be taken up as a matter of public policy on both a national and transnational level.

The availability, influence, and cultural power of Disney's children's films demand that they become part of a broader political discourse regarding who makes cultural policy. As such, issues regarding how and what children learn could be addressed through broader public debates about how cultural and economic resources can be distributed and controlled to insure that children are exposed to a variety of alternative narratives, stories, and representations about themselves and the larger society. When the issue of children's culture is taken up and shaped in the schools, it is assumed that this is a commonplace matter of public policy and intervention, but when it is shaped in the commercial public sphere the discourse of public intervention gets lost in abstract appeals to the imperatives of the market and free speech. Free speech is only as good as the democratic framework that makes possible the extension of its benefits to a wider range of individuals, groups, and public spheres. Treating Disney as part of a media sphere that needs to be democratized and held accountable for the ways in which it sells power and manufactures social identities needs to be taken up as part of the discourse of pedagogical analysis and public policy intervention. This type of analysis and intervention is perfectly suited for cultural theorists and community activists across a wide number of sites who are willing to employ an interdisciplinary approach to such an undertaking, address popular culture as an object of serious analysis, make the pedagogical a defining principle of such work, and insert the political into the center of such projects.[56]

This suggests that cultural workers need to readdress the varied interrelations that define both a politics of representation and a discourse of political economy as a new form of cultural work that rejects the material/cultural divide. The result would be a renewed understanding of how such modalities mutually inform each other within different contexts and across national boundaries. It is particularly important for cultural workers to understand how Disney films work within a broad network of production and distribution as teaching machines within and across different public cultures and social formations. Within this type of discourse, the messages, forms of emotional investment, and ideologies produced by Disney can be traced through the various circuits of power that both legitimate and insert "the culture of the Magic Kingdom" into multiple and overlapping public spheres. Moreover, such films need to be analyzed not only for what they say, but also for how they are used and taken up by adult audiences and groups of children within diverse national and international contexts. That is, cultural workers need to study these films intertextually and from a transnational perspective. Disney does not represent a cultural monolith ignorant of different contexts; on the contrary, its power, in part, rests with its ability to address different contexts and to be read differently by transnational formations and audiences. Disney engenders what Inderpal Grewal and Caren Kaplan have called "scattered hegemonies."[57] It is precisely by addressing how these hegemonies operate in particular spaces of power, specific localities, and differentiated transnational locations that progressives will be able to understand more fully the specific agendas and politics at work as Disney is both constructed for and read by different audiences.

While it is indisputable that Disney provides both children and adults with the pleasure of being entertained, Disney's public responsibility does not end there. Rather than being viewed as a commercial public sphere innocently distributing pleasure to young people, the Disney empire must be seen as a pedagogical and policy-making enterprise actively engaged in the cultural landscaping of national identity and the "schooling" of the minds of young children. This is not to suggest that there is something sinister behind what Disney does, as much as it points to the need to address the role of fantasy, desire, and innocence in securing particular ideological interests, legitimating specific social relations, and making a distinct claim on the meaning of public memory. Disney needs to be held accountable not just at the box office, but also in political and ethical terms. If such accountability is to be impressed upon the "Magic Kingdom" then parents, educators, and others will have to challenge and disrupt both the institutional power and the images, representations, and values offered by Disney's teaching machine. The stakes are too high to ignore such a challenge and struggle, even if it means reading Disney's animated films critically.

Notes

1. A version of this essay appeared in *Socialist Review* 24.3 (1995): 23–55.
2. This is not to suggest that I believed that the world of fantasy, amusement, and entertainment could be abstracted from ideology. On the contrary, I simply did not address such ideologies as serious objects of analysis. For a critical engagement of commercialization, popular culture, and children's culture, see Marsha Kinder, *Playing With Power in Movies, Television, and Video Games* (Berkeley: University of California Press, 1991); Doug Kellner, *Media Culture* (New York: Routledge, 1995); David Buckingham and Julian Sefton-Green, *Cultural Studies Goes to School* (London: Taylor and Francis, 1994).
3. Cited in Michiko Kakutani, "This Mouse Once Roared." *The New York Times Magazine* (January 4, 1998): 8. Compare Kakutani's analysis with Matt Roth, "A Short History of Disney-Fascism." *Jumpcut* 40 (1996): 15–20.
4. See Michael D. Eisner, "Letter to Shareholders," in *The Walt Disney Company 1999 Annual Report* (Burbank, CA: The Walt Disney Company, 1999), p. 2.
5. There is an ever-growing list of authors who have been pressured by Disney either through the refusal to allow copyrighted materials to be used or through Disney's reputation for influencing publishers not to publish certain work. Examples can be found in Jon Wiener, "In the Belly of the Mouse: The Dyspeptic Disney Archives." *Lingua France* (July/August, 1994): 69–72; Jon Wiener, "Murdered Ink." *The Nation* (May 31, 1993): 743–50. One typical example occurred in a book in which one of my own essays on Disney appears. While in the process of editing a book critical of Disney, Laura Sells, Lynda Haas, and Elizabeth

Bell requested permission from Disney executives to use the archives. In response, the editors received a letter from one of Disney's legal assistants asking to approve the book. The editors declined and Disney forbade the use of their name in the title of the book, and threatened to sue if the Disney name was used. Indiana University Press argued that it did not have the resources to fight Disney and the title of the book was changed from *Doing Disney* to *From Mouse to Mermaid*. In another instance, Routledge Publishing decided to omit an essay by David Kunzle on the imperialist messages in Disney's foreign comics in a book entitled *Disney Discourse*. Fearing that Disney would not provide permission for illustrations from the Disney archives, Routledge decided they could not publish the essay without illustrations. Discouraged, Kunzle told Jon Wiener that "I've given up. I'm not doing any more work on Disney. I don't think any university press would take the risk. The problem is not the likelihood of Disney winning in court, it's the threat of having to bear the cost of fighting them" (Kunzle cited in Wiener, "In the Belly of the Mouse," op. cit., p. 72).

6. As Eisner points out, in describing Disney's empire:

> We now have seven theme parks (with four more in the works), 27 hotels with 36,888 rooms, two cruise ships, 728 Disney Stores, one broadcast network, 10 TV stations, nine international Disney Channels, 42 radio stations, an Internet portal, five major Internet web sites, interests in nine U.S. cable networks, and in the past decade, we have enhanced our library with 17 animated films, 265 live-action films, 1252 animated television episodes and 6,505 live-action television episodes. (In Eisner, "Letter to Shareholders," op. cit., p. 2.)

7. The mutually determining relationship of culture and economic power as a dynamic hegemonic process is beautifully captured by Sharon Zukin's work on Disney. She writes:

> The domestication of fantasy in visual consumption is inseparable from centralized structures of economic power. Just as the earlier power of the state illuminated public space – the streets – by artificial lamplight, so the economic power of CBS, Sony, and the Disney Company illuminates private space at home by electronic images. With the means of production so concentrated and the means of consumption so diffused, communication of these images becomes a way of controlling both knowledge and imagination, a form of corporate social control over technology and symbolic expressions of power. (In Sharon Zukin, *Landscapes of Power: From Detroit to Disney World* (Berkeley: University of California Press, 1991), p. 221.)

8. For a listing of various public service programs that Disney has initiated, see Jennifer J. Laabs, "Disney Helps Keep Kids in School." *Personnel Journal* (November, 1992): 58–68.
9. Cited in Mark Walsh, "Disney Holds up School as Model for next Century." *Education Week* XIII. 39 (June 22, 1994): 1.
10. Tom Vanderbilt, "Mickey Goes to Town(s)." *The Nation* 261.6 (August 28/September 4, 1995): 199.
11. Jean Baudrillard, *Simulations* (New York: Semiotext(e), 1983), p. 25. Also, see Jean Baudrillard, "Consumer Society," in Mark Poster (ed.), *Jean Baudrillard: Selected Works* (Stanford, CA: Stanford University Press, 1988), pp. 29–56.
12. Alan Bryman, *Disney and His Worlds* (New York: Routledge, 1995), p. 26.
13. Eric Smoodin, "How to Read Walt Disney," in *Disney Discourse: Producing the Magic Kingdom* (New York: Routledge, 1994), p. 18.
14. Jon Wiener, "Tall Tales and True." *The Nation* (January 31, 1994): 134.
15. Actually, Disney's animated film *The Lion King* may be the most financially successful film ever made. Disney's animated films released since 1990 have all been included in the top 10 grossing films. For example *Lion King* ranked no.1 with $253.5 million; *Aladdin* ranked second with $217.4 million; and *Beauty and the Beast* ranked seventh grossing $145.9 million. See Thomas King, "Creative but Unpolished Top Executive for Hire," *The Wall Street Journal* (August 26, 1994): B1.
16. Elizabeth Bell, Lynda Haas, Laura Sells, "Walt's in the Movies," in Elizabeth Bell et. al. (eds.), *From Mouse to Mermaid* (Bloomington: Indiana University Press, 1995), p. 3.
17. The celebrations of Walt Disney are too numerous to mention in any great detail. But an early example would be Bob Thomas, *Walt Disney: An American Original* (New York: Simon and Schuster, 1976). Thomas's book followed on the heels of a scathing attack on Disney by Richard Schickel, *The Disney Version* (New York: Simon and Schuster, 1968). A more recent version of the no-holds-barred critique of Disney can be found in Carl Hiassen, *Team Rodent: How Disney Devours the World* (New York: Ballantine Publishing, 1998). The more moderate position can be found in Steven Watts, *The Magic Kingdom* (New York: Houghton Mifflin, 1997). Disregarding the alleged virtues of balance, I think Schickel's book ranks as one of the best critiques of Disney.
18. Barbara Foley, "Subversion and Oppositionality in the Academy," in Maria-Regina Kecht (ed.), *Pedagogy is Politics: Literary Theory and Critical Teaching* (Urbana: University of Illinois Press, 1992), p. 79. See also,

Roger I. Simon, "Forms of Insurgency in the Production of Popular Memories." *Cultural Studies* 1.1 (1993): 73–88.

19. A number of recent authors address Disney's imagined landscape as a place of economic and cultural power. See, for example, Zukin, *Landscapes of Power*, op. cit.; Michael Sorkin, "Disney World: The Power of Facade/ the Facade of Power," in Michael Sorkin (ed.), *Variations on a Theme Park* (New York: The Noonday Press, 1992); and see the especially impressive Stephen M. Fjellman, *Vinyl Leaves: Walt Disney World and America* (Boulder, CO: Westview Press, 1992).

20. Norman Klein argues in his brilliant book, *7 Minutes: The Life and Death of the American Animated Cartoon* that Disney actually constructed his expanded cartoons as a form of animated consumer memory. As Klein puts it:

> The atmospheric lighting of Disney epic cartoons is very similar to the reverie of shopping, to shopping arcades, even to the permanent dusk of a room illuminated by television. It takes us more to the expanded shopping mall than a planned suburb, to a civilization based on consumer memories more than urban (or suburban) locations. . . . Disney showed us how to stop thinking of a city as residential or commercial, but rather as airbrushed streets in our mind's eye, a shopper's nonscape. If we can make a city remind us of animated consumer memory, it removes the alienation of changing cities, and replaces it with a cloud of imaginary store windows. (In Norman M. Klein, *7 Minutes: The Life and Death of the American Animated Cartoon* (London: Verso, 1993, reprinted 1998), p. 144.)

21. The term "marketplace of culture" comes from Richard de Cordova, "The Mickey in Macy's Window: Childhood Consumerism and Disney Animation," in Eric Smoodin (ed.), *Disney Discourse*, op. cit., p. 209. It is worth noting that Disney was one of the first companies to tie the selling of toys to consuming of movies. Challenging the assumption that toy consumption was limited to seasonal sales, Disney actively pursued creating Mickey Mouse Clubs, advertising its toys in storefront windows, and linking its movies directly to the distribution of children's toys.

22. Cited in Richard Corliss, "The Mouse that Roars." *Time* (June 20, 1994): 59.

23. Cited in Richard Turner, "Walt Disney Presents: Forward to the Future." *The Wall Street Journal*, Marketplace Section (August 26, 1994): B1.

24. Cited in Sallie Hofmeister, "In the Realm of Marketing, the 'Lion King' Rules." *The New York Times* (July 12, 1994): D1.

25. Moira McCormick, "'Hunchback' Soundtrack Tie-Ins Abound," *Billboard* (May 25, 1996): 10.

26. Cited in Robert W. McChesney, *Corporate Media and the Threat to Democracy* (New York: Seven Stories Press, 1997), pp. 20–1.

27. For an amazing summation of the merchandizing avalanche that accompanied the movie theater version of *The Lion King*, see Sallie Hofmeister, "In the Realm of Marketing," op. cit., pp. D1, D17.

28. Cited in Karen Schoemer, "An Endless Stream of Magic and Moola." *Newsweek* (September 5, 1994): 47.

29. Tom McNichol, "Pushing 'Pocahontas.'" *USA Weekend* (June 9–11, 1995): 4.

30. Tony Bennett touches on this issue through an explication of his rendering of the concept of reading formation. He argues:

> the concept of reading formation is an attempt to think context as a set of discursive and inter-textual determinations, operating on material and institutional supports, which bear in upon a text not just externally, from the outside in, but internally, shaping it – in the historically concrete forms in which it is available as a text-to-be-read -from the inside out. (In Tony Bennett, "Texts in History: The Determinations of Readings and Their Texts," in Derek Atridge et al. (eds.), *Poststructuralism and the Question of History* (Cambridge, UK: Cambridge University Press, 1987), p. 72.)

31. Critiques of Disney's portrayal of girls and women can be found in: Elizabeth Bell et al. (eds.), *From Mouse to Mermaid*, op. cit.; also see Susan White, "Split Skins: Female Agency and Bodily Mutilation in *The Little Mermaid*," in Jim Collins, Hilary Radner, and Ava Preacher Collins (eds.), *Film Theory Goes to the Movies* (New York: Routledge, 1993), pp. 182–95.

32. Bonnie J. Leadbeater and Gloria Lodato Wilson, "Flipping Their Fins for a Place to Stand: 19th-and 20th-Century Mermaids." *Youth and Society* 27.4 (June 1993): 466–86.

33. Susan Jefford develops this reading of *Beauty and the Beast* in *Hard Bodies: Hollywood Masculinity in the Reagan Era* (New Brunswick NJ: Rutgers University Press, 1994), p. 150.

34. All of these quotes and the analysis of this position are taken from the video, *Mickey Mouse Monopoly*, produced by the Media Education Foundation (2001).

35. Janet Maslin, "Disney Turns to a Warrior of the East in 'Mulan.'" *The New York Times* (June 19, 1998): B10.

36. I would like to thank Valerie Janesick for this insight.

37. Cited in June Casagrande, "The Disney Agenda." *Creative Loafing* (March 17–23, 1994): 6–7.

38. Upon its release in 1946, *Song of the South* was condemned by the NAACP for its racist representations.

39. For a historical context in which to understand Frontierland, see Fjellman, *Vinyl Leaves*, op. cit.

40. These racist episodes are highlighted in Jon Wiener, "Tall Tales and True." *The Nation* (January 31, 1994): 133–5.

41. Yousef Salem cited in Richard Scheinin, "Angry Over 'Aladdin.'" *The Washington Post* (January 10, 1993): G5.

42. Howard Green, a Disney spokesperson, dismissed the charges of racism as irrelevant claiming that such criticisms were coming from a small minority and that "most people were happy with [the film]." Cited in Richard Scheinin, "Angry Over Aladdin," op. cit., p. G1.

43. I have taken this criticism from Jack Shaheen, "Animated Racism." *Cineaste* 20:1 (1993): 49.

44. See Susan Miller and Greg Rode, who do a rhetorical analysis of *The Jungle Book* and *Song of the South* in their chapter, "The Movie You See, The Movie You Don't: How Disney Do's That Old Time Derision," in Elizabeth Bell et al. (eds.), *From Mouse to Mermaid*, op. cit.

45. Edward Said, *Culture and Imperialism* (New York: Alfred A. Knopf, Inc. 1993).

46. Susan Willis brilliantly explores this theme in "Fantasia: Walt Disney's Los Angeles Suite." *Diacritics* 17 (Summer, 1987): 83–96.

47. George Gerbner, Larry Gross, Michael Borgan, and Nancy Signorielli, "Growing Up with Television: The Cultivation Perspective," in Jennings Bryant and Dolf Zillmann (eds.), *Media Effects: Advances in Theory and Research* (Hillsdale, NJ: Lawrence Erlbaum, 1995), p. 17.

48. See, for instance, Andrew Hart (ed.), *Teaching the Media: International Perspectives* (Hillsdale, NJ: Lawrence Erlbaum, 1998).

49. David Buckingham, "Conclusion: Re-Reading Audiences," in David Buckingham (ed.), *Reading Audiences: Young People and the Media* (Manchester, UK: Manchester University Press, 1993), p. 211.

50. Cited in Sharon Zukin, *Landscapes of Power*, op. cit, p. 222. While this quote refers to Disney's view of its theme parks, it represents an ideological view of history that strongly shapes all of Disney's cultural productions. For a comment on how it affects Disney's rendering of adult films, see Henry A. Giroux, *Disturbing Pleasures* (New York: Routledge, 1994), especially pp. 25–45.

51. Fjellman, *Vinyl Leaves*, op. cit., p.400.

52. Rustom Bharacuha, "Around Ayodhya: Aberrations, Enigmas, and Moments of Violence." *Third Text* 24 (Autumn, 1993): 51.

53. Tony Bennett, "Texts in History," op. cit., p. 80.

54. Eric Smoodin, "How to Read Walt Disney," in *Disney Discourse* op. cit., pp.4–5.

55. Mark Crispin Miller, "Free the Media." *The Nation* 262.22 (June 3, 1996): 9–15.

56. For an example of such an analysis, see Stanley Aronowitz, *Roll Over Beethoven* (Middletown, CT: Wesleyan University Press, 1993); Giroux, *Disturbing Pleasures, op. cit.*

57. Inderpal Grewal and Caren Kaplan, "Introduction: Transnational Feminist Practices and Questions of Postmodernity," in Inderpal Grewal and Caren Kaplan (eds.), *Scattered Hegemonies* (Minneapolis: University of Minnesota Press, 1994).

8

The Politics of Pedagogy, Gender, and Whiteness in *Dangerous Minds*[1]

Introduction

In the early 1990s the debate over race took a provocative turn as "whiteness" became increasingly visible as a symbol of racial identity. Displaced from its widely understood status as an unnamed, universal moral referent, "whiteness" as a category of racial identity was appropriated by diverse conservative and right-wing groups, as well as critical scholars, as part of a broader articulation of race and difference, though in different ways and for radically opposed purposes. For a disparate group of whites, mobilized in part by the moral panic generated by right-wing attacks on immigration, race-preferential policies, and the welfare state, "whiteness" became a signifier for middle-class resistance to "taxation, to the expansion of state-furnished rights of all sorts, and to integration."[2] Threatened by the call for minority rights, the rewriting of American history from the bottom up, and the shifting racial demographics of the nations' cities, whites felt increasingly angry and resentful over what was viewed as an attack on their sense of individual and collective consciousness.[3]

As "whiteness" came under scrutiny by various social groups as an oppressive, invisible center against which all else is measured, many whites began to identify with the "new racism" epitomized by right-wing conservatives such as popular talk show host, Rush Limbaugh.[4] Winning over vast audiences with the roar of the "angry white male" bitter over imagined racial injuries committed against whites, Limbaugh's popularity affirmed that race had become the most significant social force of the 1980s and 1990s. In an era of unprecedented unemployment, poverty, and diminishing opportunities for most black Americans, right-wing whites had convinced themselves of their loss of privilege. For these groups, archconservative actor and mythic white male, Michael Douglas, becomes less a symbol of "falling down" in a tragic Hollywood morality film about white supremacy and paranoia and more a moral crusader fighting a holy if lost war. Thus, the discourse of race became a vehicle for appeasing white anxiety and reinventing both the subject and meaning of what one might loosely call "racial justice." The progressive legacy of identity politics as "a crucial movement to expand citizenship to people of color and other subordinated groups" was either trivialized or dismissed as conservatives appropriated the politics of identity as a defining principle of "whiteness."[5] Cultural critic John Brenkman highlights this appropriation by claiming that "the constituency whose beliefs and fears have been most significantly molded to their racial identity in the 1980s are white."[6]

A siege mentality arose for policing cultural boundaries and re-asserting national identity. The discourse of "whiteness" as an ambivalent signifier of resentment and confusion gives expression to a mass of whites who feel victimized and bitter, while it masks deep inequalities and exclusionary practices within the current social order. Shifting the politics of race from the discourse of white supremacy, the historical legacy of slavery and segregation, as well as the ongoing burden of racial injustice endured by African-American and other minorities in the United States, politicians such as Pat Buchanan, David Duke, Jesse Helms, and Pat Robertson mobilized a new populist discourse about family, nation, traditional values, and individualism as part of a broader resistance to multicultural democracy and diverse racial culture. In the rapidly expanding medium of talk radio, conservatives bashed blacks for many of the social and economic problems facing the country.[7] Conservative columnist Mickey Kaus exemplifies this sensibility in his comment: "I may want to live in a society where there is no alienated race and no racism, where I need not feel uncomfortable walking down the street because I'm white."[8] As race became paramount in shaping American politics and everyday life from the 1980s on, racial prejudice in its overt forms was considered a taboo. While the old racism maintained some cachet among the more vulgar, right-wing conservatives (e.g., New York city's radio talk show host Bob Grant), a new racist discourse emerged in the United States. The new racism was coded in the language of "welfare reform, neighborhood schools, toughness on crime and 'illegitimate' births." Cleverly designed to mobilize white fears while relieving whites of any semblance of social responsibility and commitment, the new racism, articulated by conservatives such as Jim Sleeper and David Horowitz, served to rewrite the politics of "whiteness" as a besieged racial identity. As the racial backlash intensified in the broader culture, "whiteness" assumed a new form of political agency visible in the rise of right-wing militia groups, skinheads, and the anti-PC crusades of indignant white students and conservative, academic organizations such as the National Association of Scholars and the Southern League.[9]

Rather than being invisible, as left-wing critics such as Richard Dyer and bell hooks have claimed, "whiteness" was aggressively embraced in popular culture in order to rearticulate a sense of individual and collective identity for besieged whites.[10] Celebrated in the mass media in the 1990s, the new cartography of race has emerged as the result of an attempt to rewrite the racial legacy of the past while recovering a mythic vision of "whiteness" associated with purity and innocence. Popular films such as *Forrest Gump* (1994) and *The Patriot* (2000) attempted to rewrite public memory by cleansing the American past of racial tensions and endorsing "a preferred understanding of racial relations that work on the behalf of the public mourning of the 'victimized white male.'"[11] Widely discussed books such as *The Bell Curve* by Richard Herrnstein and Charles Murray and *The End of Racism* by Dinesh D'Souza revised and reaffirmed the basic principles of the eugenics debate of the 1920s and 1930s and provided a defense of racial hierarchies.[12]

In the popular press, the discourse of racial discrimination and social inequality gave way to lurid stories about black crime, illegal aliens taking jobs, the threat to the deficit posed by government welfare payments to single teen mothers, and the assertion that black "gangsta" rap artists such as Snoop Doggy Dogg and Ice Cube corrupt the moral values of white suburban youth.[13] While liberal academic journals such as *The New Republic* and *The Atlantic Monthly* shunned the extremist discourses of David Duke, Ralph Reed, and Jerry Falwell, they produced editorials and stories legitimating the popular perception that black culture is a culture of crime, pathology, and moral degeneracy. *The New Republic* devoted an entire issue to an analysis of *The Bell Curve*, justifying its decision in a shameful editorial statement which declared, "The notion that there might be resilient ethnic differences in intelligence is not, we believe, an inherently racist belief."[14] Of course, the refusal to acknowledge that such a position grew historically from a eugenics movement that legitimated diverse racial hatreds as well as some of the most barbarous and atrocious massacres of the twentieth century appeared irrelevant next to the editorial's self-congratulatory assertion of intellectual flexibility. *The Atlantic Monthly* echoed similar racial fears in a barrage of sensationalist cover stories and articles about how crime, disease, gangsta rap, unwed (black) mothers, and the breakdown of public order were about to wreak havoc on "everyone – even white people in Back Bay."[15]

The tawdry representations of black experience that these magazines produced gained increasing currency in the dominant media. Racial coding parading as common sense populism associated blacks with a series of negative equivalencies that denied racial injustice while affirming the repressed, unspeakable, racist unconscious of dominant white culture. Images of menacing black youth, welfare mothers, and convicts, framed by the evocative rhetoric of fear-mongering journalists, helped to bolster the image of a besieged white middle-class suburban family threatened by "an alien culture and peoples who are less civilized than the native ones. . . . a people who stand lower in the order of culture because they are somehow lower in the order of nature, defined by race, by color, and sometimes by genetic inheritance."[16]

While the popular press was signaling the emergence of a politics of identity in which white men were defining themselves as the victims of "reverse" racial prejudice, academics were digging in and producing a substantial amount of scholarship, exploring what it might mean to analyze "whiteness" as a social, cultural, and historical construction. Such work was characterized by diverse attempts to locate "whiteness" as a racial category and to analyze it as a site of privilege, power, and ideology, but also to examine critically how "whiteness" as a racial identity is experienced, reproduced, and addressed by those diverse white men and women who identify with its common sense assumptions and values.

In some quarters, the call to study "whiteness" provoked scorn and indignation. For instance, *Time* magazine held up to ridicule a professor who named a standard American literature survey course she taught, "White Male Writers."[17] *Newsweek* took a more mainstream position, constructing an image of white men in the United States as undergoing an identity crisis over their changing public image. According to the editors of *Newsweek*, white males were no longer secure in an identity ravaged by "feminists, multiculturalists, P.C. police persons, affirmative-action employers, rap artists, Native Americans, Japanese tycoons, Islamic fundamentalists and Third World dictators."[18] Not to be outdone in their equation of feminists, multiculturalists, and Native Americans with Third World dictators, *Newsweek* further lamented the clobbering white men were taking in the media, buttressing their argument with comments from a "rancorous" female employee as well a prominent psychiatrist who assured readers that "For white men in their 30s and 40s, this is not a joke at all. Their whole future is at stake, in their minds. They're scared."[19] While the demise of the power of white men seemed a bit exaggerated to the editors of *Newsweek*, they also made it quite clear that the current white panic was not entirely unfounded since whites may find themselves in the twenty-first century living in a society consisting largely of "diverse racial and ethnic minorities."[20]

Youth and the Rearticulation of Whiteness

Race increasingly matters as a defining principle of identity and culture as much for white students in the 1990s as it did for youth of color in the 1970s and 1980s. As a marker of difference, race significantly frames how white youth experience themselves and their relationships to a variety of public spaces marked by the presence of people of color. In contrast to the position popular among white educators who claim that "We [whites] do not experience ourselves as defined by our skin color,"[21] white youth have become increasingly aware of themselves as white. Two major forces affecting the racial divide have served to make "whiteness" more visible and fragile as a site of privilege and power, while at the same time limiting opportunities for youth to be both white and oppositional.[22] The first is the emergence of identity politics in the United States as it emerged in the 1960s to the present. While contradictory and diverse in its manifestations, identity politics has largely resulted in the formation, consolidation, and visibility of new group of racial identities. But such identities have emerged within a highly charged public debate on race, gender, and sexual orientation and have made it more difficult for white youth to either ignore "whiteness" as a racial category or to "safely imagine that they are invisible to black people."[23] White students may see themselves as nonracist, but they no longer view themselves as colorless. As Charles Gallagher points out, "whiteness" has become "a salient category of self-definition emerging in response to the political and cultural challenges of other racialized groups."[24]

Contrary to its advocates' claims, identity politics did not seek the transformation of society in general; rather it promoted a politics of difference that asserted itself through the separate and often essentialized banners of race, gender, sexuality, ethnicity, and nationality. Within this recoding of the politics of recognition and difference, the experiences, rights, and histories of subordinate groups have been affirmed. However, these groups have been simply unable to articulate a new social vision rooted in the principles of equality or solidarity that organized progressive "interactions between white and black people in addressing such a politics."[25]

Unfortunately, for many white youth, whose imaginations were also left fallow, unfed by a larger society's vision or quest for social justice, identity politics engendered a defensive posture. White students assumed that the only role they could play in the struggle against racism was either to renounce their "whiteness" and become black or suffer the charge that any claim to white identity was tantamount to racism. Within this paradigm, racism was configured through a politics of representation that analyzed how whites have constructed, stereotyped, and delegitimated racial others, but it had practically nothing to say about how racial politics might address the construction of "whiteness" as an oppositional racial category. Moreover, while the debate within identity politics made important theoretical gains in rewriting what it meant to be black, it did not question the complexity of "whiteness" with the same dialectical attentiveness. Although "whiteness" has become an object of critical scrutiny, it appeared to have no connotation except to "signify the center which pushes out, excluded, appropriates, and distorts the margins."[26] "Similarly, liberal ideology has provided only a one-item agenda for how blacks and whites might work together in the struggle for social and racial justice. It replaces the recognition of the importance of racial identities with calls for tolerance and appeals to a color-blind society.

Identity politics, in part, has served to undermine the possibilities for white youth to engage critically the liberal appeal to a color-blind society; it also had the unintended consequence of reinforcing the divide between blacks and whites. Furthermore, the absence of an oppositional space between separatism and a power-evasive liberalism has provided an opportunity for conservatives and right-wing activists to step into the fray and appropriate "whiteness" as part of a broader backlash against blacks and people of color. In this case, conservatives and the far right actively engaged in the process of recovering "whiteness" and redefining themselves as the victims of racial antagonism while simultaneously waging a brutal and racially coded attack against urban youth, immigrants, and the poor. Seemingly unresponsive to the needs of white youth, the white working class, and the white underclass, the discourse of "whiteness" has been easily appropriated as part of a broader reactionary cultural politics that in its most extreme manifestations fueled the rise of white militia groups, the growing skinhead movement among white youth, and a growing antipolitical correctness movement in both higher education and the mass media.

The second force at work in reconstructing "whiteness" as a racial category among youth is the profound changes that have taken place regarding the visibility of blacks in the media. While it would be foolish to equate the increased visibility of blacks in the media with an increase in power, especially around issues of ownership, diverse representations of black culture throughout the media have made issues of white identity inextricably more fragile and fluid. This is evident in the ways in which popular culture is increasingly being reconfigured through the music, dance, and language of hip hop. Similarly, the emergence of Black Entertainment Television, MTV, and cable television, in general, testify to the ubiquitous, though far from unstereotypical, presence of people of color in television dramas, sports, and music, while the popular press touts the emergence of the "new" black public intellectuals in academia. All of these changes in the media signal that whites can no longer claim the privilege of not "seeing" blacks and other people of color; white youth now have to confront cultural difference as a force that affects every aspect of their lives. Coupled with the rise of an incendiary racial politics, the racialization of the media culture, and growing economic fears about their future, a significant number of white American youth are increasingly experiencing a crisis of self-esteem. Similar to cultural critic Diana Jester's comment about British youth, white American youth "do not feel that they have an 'ethnicity', or if they do, that it's not one they feel too good about."[27]

Jester has further suggested that white youth have few resources for questioning and rearticulating "whiteness" as an identity that productively narrates their everyday experiences. This seems to be borne out in the ways in which many white college students have reacted to the racial politics of the last decade. One indication of the way in which "whiteness" is being negotiated among students is evident in the rising racist assaults on students of color on campuses across the United States in the last few years. As a resurgent racism becomes more respectable in the broader culture, racist acts and assaults have once again become a staple of college life. At the same time, large numbers of white students appear to support the ongoing assaults on affirmative action programs that have been waged by the courts and state legislatures. Moreover, white students increasingly express a general sense of angst over racial politics and an emphatic indifference to politics in general.[28]

Charles Gallagher's ethnographic study of white college students suggests that many of them view the emergence of multiculturalists, feminists, and other progressive groups as an attack on "whiteness" and a form of reverse discrimination. For example, Gallagher writes "It is commonly assumed among many white students that any class that addresses issues of race or racism must necessarily be anti-white. More specifically, students believe that the instructors of these classes will hold individual white students accountable for slavery, lynching, discrimination, and other heinous acts."[29] Many of the white students that Gallagher interviewed did not see themselves as privileged by virtue of skin color; some went so far as to claim that, given the rise of racial preferences, whites no longer had a fair chance when competing with minorities in the labor market. Gallagher asserts that white students are resentful over being blamed for racism and that "ignoring the ways in which whites 'get raced' has the making of something politically dangerous...[and that] [w]hiteness must be addressed because the politics of race, from campus clubs to issues of crime to representation in the statehouse, permeate almost every social exchange."[30] Unfortunately, Gallagher offers little in the way of suggesting how "whiteness" might be rearticulated in oppositional terms. In fact, he concludes by suggesting that as "whiteness" becomes more visible it will be further appropriated and mediated through a racist ideology, and that any notion of white solidarity will result in a reactionary politics. Hence, "whiteness" as a marker of identity is confined within a notion of domination and racism that leaves white youth no social imaginary through which they can see themselves as actors in creating an oppositional space to fight for equality and social justice.[31]

Central to any pedagogical approach to race and the politics of "whiteness" is the recognition that race as a set of attitudes, values, lived experiences, and affective identifications has become a defining feature of American life. However arbitrary and mythic, dangerous and variable, the fact is that racial categories exist and shape the lives of people differently within existing inequalities of power and wealth.[32] As a central form of difference, race will neither disappear, be wished out of existence, or become somehow irrelevant in the United States and the larger global context. Howard Winant insightfully argues:

Race is a condition of individual and collective identity, a permanent, though tremendously flexible, element of social structure. Race is a means of knowing and organizing the social world; it is subject to continual contestation and reinterpretation, but it is no more likely to disappear than any other forms of human inequality and difference.... To rethink race is not only to recognize its permanence, but also to understand the essential test that it poses for any diverse society seeking to achieve a modicum of freedom.[33]

Pedagogically this suggests providing the conditions for students to address how their "whiteness" functions in society, not only as marker of privilege and power, but also how it can be used as a condition for expanding the ideological and material realities of democratic public life. Moreover, it is imperative that all students understand how race functions systemically as it shapes various forms of representations, social relations, and institutional structures. Rather than proposing the eradication of the concept of race itself, educators and other cultural workers need to fashion pedagogical practices that take a detour through race in order to address how "whiteness" might be renegotiated as a productive force within a politics of difference linked to a radical democratic project.

Analyzing "whiteness" as a central element of racial politics becomes useful in exploring how "whiteness" as a cultural practice promotes race-based hierarchies, how white racial identity structures the struggle over cultural and political resources, and how rights and responsibilities are defined, confirmed, or contested across diverse racial claims.[34] "Whiteness" in this context becomes less a matter of creating a new form of identity politics than an attempt to rearticulate "whiteness" as part of a broader project of cultural, social, and political citizenship.

I want to begin to take up this challenge pedagogically by building upon James Snead's pertinent observation that the emergence of mass visual productions in the United States requires new ways of seeing and making visible the racial structuring of white experience.[35] The electronic media – television, movies, music, and news – have become a powerful pedagogical force, veritable teaching machines in shaping the social imaginary of students regarding how they view themselves, others, and the larger society. Central to the formative influence of the media is a representational politics of race in which the portrayal of black people abstracts them from their real histories while reinforcing all too familiar stereotypes ranging from lazy and shiftless to the menacing and dangerous.

Recent films from a variety of genres, such as *Pulp Fiction* (1995), *Just Cause* (1995), *Ace Ventura: When Nature Calls* (1996), and *Black and White* (2000) offer no apologies for employing racist language, depicting black men as drug-dealing killers, or portraying blacks as savage or subhuman. Antiracist readings of these films often position white students to define and critique racism as the product of dominant racist stereotypes that unfairly depict black identities, experiences, histories, and social relations. As important as these critiques are in any antiracist discourse or pedagogy, they are severely limited theoretically because they do not make problematic how "whiteness" as a racial identity and social construction is taught, learned, experienced, and identified within certain forms of knowledge, values, and privileges. Hollywood films rarely position audiences to question the pleasures, identifications, desires, and fears they experience as whites viewing dominant representational politics of race. More specifically, such films almost never problematize either the structuring principles that mobilize particular pleasures in audiences or how pleasure as a response to certain representations functions as part of a broader public discourse. At worst, such films position whites as racial tourists, distant observers to the racist images and narratives that fill Hollywood screens. At best, such films reinforce the liberal assumption that racism is something that gives rise to black oppression but has little or nothing to do with promoting power, racial privilege, and a sense of moral agency in the lives of whites.[36]

In what follows, I want to explore the pedagogical implications for examining representations of "whiteness" in *Dangerous Minds* (1995). Through my analysis of *Dangerous Minds*, I hope to provide some pedagogical insights for examining how "whiteness" as a cultural practice is learned through the representation of racialized identities, how it opens up the possibility of intellectual self-reflection, and how students might critically mediate the complex relations between "whiteness" and racism not by having them repudiate their "whiteness" but by grappling with its racist legacy and its potential to be rearticulated in oppositional and transformative terms. I also want to stress that I am not suggesting that *Dangerous Minds* is a film that should be trashed and dismissed. Its importance lies in its relevance as an exemplary representation of "whiteness" within the dominant media. *Dangerous Minds* is an important film to analyze pedagogically in order to address how the media is creating a representational racial politics that turns a generation of youth of color into a generation of suspects.

Dangerous Minds and the Production of Whiteness

Dangerous Minds, a Hollywood blockbuster starring Michelle Pfeiffer, was produced for a mass, general audience, and grossed millions for its producers within its first week. The film's popularity, in part, can be measured by the appearance of a short-lived pilot television series called *Dangerous Minds*, that premiered in the fall of 1996. While some may argue that *Dangerous Minds* is too popular and too unoriginal to be taken seriously as a cultural text, it is precisely because of its popularity and widespread appeal that it warrants an extended analysis. Like many Hollywood films, *Dangerous Minds* is not only offensive in terms of its racial politics but also in its fundamentally debased depiction of teaching and education. The 1995 summer hit is also symptomatic of how seemingly "innocent" entertainment gains its popularity in taking part in a larger public discourse on race and "whiteness" largely informed by a right-wing and conservative notion of politics, theory, and pedagogy.

At first glance, *Dangerous Minds* resembles a long tradition of Hollywood movies recounting the sorry state of education for dispossessed kids who bear the brunt of poverty, crime, violence, and despair in the inner cities of the United States. Unlike earlier films such as *Blackboard Jungle* (1955), *To Sir With Love* (1967) and *Stand and Deliver* (1988) which also dealt with the interface of schooling and the harsh realities of inner-city life, *Dangerous Minds* does more than simply narrate the story of an idealistic teacher who struggles to connect with her rowdy and disinterested students. *Dangerous Minds* functions as a dual chronicle. In the first instance, the film attempts to represent "whiteness" as the archetype of rationality, "tough" authority, cultural literacy, and high academic standards in the midst of the changing racial demographics of urban space and the emergence of a resurgent racism in the highly charged politics of the 1990s. In the second instance, the film offers viewers a mix of compassion and consumerism as a pedagogical solution to motivating teenagers who have long given up on schooling as either relevant or meaningful to their lives. In both instances, "whiteness" becomes a referent for not only rearticulating racially coded notions of teaching and learning, but also for redefining how citizenship can be constructed for students of color as a function of choice linked exclusively to the marketplace. At the same time, gender provides a subtext for both marking public school teaching as a feminine profession and for positioning women and other marginalized groups as prime recruits for the new army of part-time workers that are increasingly becoming a central part of the educational labor force recruited to work in the most downtrodden sections of the urban centers in the United States.

Providing an allegory for representing both the purpose of schooling and the politics of racial difference as they intersect within the contested space of the urban public schools, *Dangerous Minds* skillfully mobilizes race as an organizing principle to promote its narrative structure and ideological message. Black and Hispanic teenagers provide the major fault line for developing classroom pedagogical relations through which "whiteness" – located in the authority of the teacher – privileges itself against the racially coded images of disorder, chaos, and fear. The opposition between teacher and student, white and nonwhite, is clearly established in the first few scenes of the film. The opening sequence, shot in grainy monochrome, depicts a rundown urban housing project teeming with poverty, drug dealing, and immanent danger. Against this backdrop, disaffected, black and Hispanic children board a school bus which will take them to Parkmount High School and out of their crime- and drug-infested neighborhoods. This is one of the few shots in the film that provides a context for the children's lives, and the message is clear: the inner city has become a site of pathology, moral decay, and delinquency synonymous with the culture of working-class black life. Featuring a rap music score that includes hard core artists such as Coolio, Sista, and Aaron Hall, the soundtrack is present only as a backdrop to the film. While the driving beat of hip hop reinforces the gritty urban realism that provides a tidy summation of these kids' everyday lives, it is completely ignored as a cultural or pedagogical resource by the teachers for learning about their students' histories, experiences, or the economic, social, and political limits they face daily. Moreover, the musical score's marginality to the plot of *Dangerous Minds* serves to reinforce the right-wing assumption that rap music signifies black culture as a culture of crime and violence. Framed by a racial iconography and musical score that constructs minority students as both the objects of fear and subjects in need of discipline and control, the audience is prepared for someone to take charge. Enter LouAnne Johnson, a good-hearted ingenue thrust into the classroom of "at risk" kids like a lamb led to the slaughter.

A divorced ex-marine, LouAnne Johnson turns up at Parkmount High in order to student teach and finish her degree. She is immediately hired as an English teacher in the "Academy School," a euphemism for warehousing students who are considered unteachable. Dressed in dowdy tweeds and white lace, LouAnne enters her class triumphant and full of high hopes to meet a room filled with Hispanic and black kids who have brought the "worst" aspects of their culture into the classroom. Music blares amidst the clatter of students shouting, rapping, dancing, presenting LouAnne with a classroom in an inner-city school that appears to be disorderly and out of control. Leaving the safety of her white, middle-class culture in order to teach in a place teeming with potential danger, LouAnne Johnson is presented to the audience as an innocent border crosser. Against this image of innocence and good-will, white America is provided with the comforting belief that disorder, ignorance, and chaos are always somewhere else – in that strangely homogenized, racial space known as the urban ghetto.[37]

The students respond to LouAnne's attempt to greet them with the taunting epitaph, "white bread." Confused and unable to gain control of the class, LouAnne is accosted by a male student who makes a mockery of her authority by insulting her with a sexual innuendo.

Frustrated, she leaves the class and tells Hal, a friend who teaches next door, that she has just met the "rejects from hell." He assures her that she can reach these students if she figures out how to get their attention. These opening scenes work powerfully in associating black and Hispanic kids with the culture of criminality and danger. These scenes also make clear that "whiteness" as a racial identity, embodied in LouAnne Johnson, is both vulnerable and under siege as well as the only hope these kids have for moving beyond the context and character of their racial identities. In other words, "whiteness" as a racial identity is being constructed through the stereotypical portrayal of black and Hispanic kids as intellectually inferior, hostile, and childish while coding "whiteness" as a norm for authority, orderliness, rationality, and control.

The structuring principles at work in *Dangerous Minds* perform a distinct ideological function in their attempt to cater to white consumers of popular culture. Pedagogy performs a doubling operation as it is used in this film. As part of the overt curriculum, the film focuses on teaching in an inner-city school and constructs a dominant view of race as embodied in the lives of urban black and Hispanic children. On the other hand, the hidden curriculum of the film works pedagogically to recover and mark the ideology, culture, and values that construct "whiteness" as a dominant form of racial identity and gender as a metaphor for linking family values, privatization, and personal caring to a notion of empowerment that rests largely with gate keeping and warehousing those racialized others who are seen as beyond hope and possibility. Hollywood films about teaching have a long tradition, but rarely do such films merely use the theme of teaching as a pedagogical tool for legitimating a conservative view of "whiteness" as a besieged social formation, and subordinate racial identities as a threat to public order. The conservative and ideological implications of how "whiteness" is constructed in this film can ben seen through a series of representations presented in the film.

Dangerous Minds tells us nothing about the lives of the students themselves. The audience is given no sense of their histories or experiences outside of the school. Decontextualized and dehistoricized, the cultural identities of these students appear marginal to the construction of race as an organizing principle of the film. Racial differences in this film are situated within the spatial metaphor of center and margins, with the children of color clearly occupying the margins. At the center of the film is the embellished "true story" of LouAnne Johnson, who not only overcomes her initial failure to motivate these students but also serves as a beacon of light by convincing them that who they are and what they know needs to be ditched if they are to become more civilized and cultured (and so more "white"). Racial conflict in this context is resolved through a colonial model in which white paternalism and missionary zeal provide the inspiration for kids from deprived backgrounds to improve their character and sense of responsibility by reading poetry. The kids in this movie simply appear as a backdrop for expanding LouAnne's own self-consciousness and self-education; the film shows no interest in their coming of age and examining how racism works in the schools and larger society. Whenever these kids do face a crisis – an unwanted pregnancy, the threat of violence, or dropping out of school – LouAnne invades their homes and private lives, using the opportunity to win the kids' allegiance or draw attention to her own divorce, physical abuse, or sense of despair. If any notion of identity occupies center stage, it is not that of the kids but that of a white woman trying to figure out how to live in a public space inhabited by racialized others.

The notion of authority and agency in *Dangerous Minds* is framed within a pedagogy of "tough love" that serves to mask how racial hierarchies and structured inequality operate within the schools and connect them to the larger society. Authority in *Dangerous Minds* is asserted initially when LouAnne Johnson shows up on the second day of class wearing a leather jacket and jeans. Reinventing herself as a military officer on leave, she further qualifies her new "tough" no-nonsense look by informing her students she is an ex-marine who knows karate. Suggesting that fear and danger are the only emotions they recognize as important, she crosses a racial divide by rooting her sense of authority in a traditionally racist notion of discipline and control. Once she gets the group's attention, she moves onto more lofty ground and begins the arduous task of trying to develop a pedagogy that is both morally uplifting and pedagogically relevant. Choice becomes for LouAnne the theoretical axis that organizes her classroom approach. First, on the side of moral uplift (complete with a conservative nineties whitewashing of history), she tells her students that there are no victims in her class. Presumably, this is meant as a plea to rouse their sense of agency and responsibility, but it rings entirely hollow since LouAnne has no understanding of the social and historical limits that shape their sense of agency on a daily basis. Of course, some students immediately recognize the bad faith implicit in her sermonizing call, and urge her to test it with a dose of reality by living in their neighborhood for a week.

Moreover, LouAnne appears to confuse her own range of choices – predicated, in part, on her class and racial privileges – with those of her students, even though they lack the power and resources to negotiate their lives politically, geographically, or economically with the same ease or options. She has no sense that choice springs from power and those who have limited power have fewer choices. The subtext here reinforces the currently popular right-wing assumption that character, merit, and self-help are the basis on which people take their place in society. Of course, within a hierarchical and social structure organized by race, as well as economic power, gender, and other key determinants, "whiteness" emerges as the normative basis for success, responsibility, and legitimate authority. By suggesting that white educators can ignore how larger social considerations impact on racial groups, white privilege, experience, and culture is relieved of complicity with, if not responsibility for, racist ideology and structural inequalities.

Choice is not only trivialized in LouAnne's classroom, it also provides the basis for a pedagogy that is as indifferent to the lives of poor inner-city kids as it is demeaning. Relying on the logic of the market to motivate her kids, LouAnne rewards classroom cooperation with candy bars, a trip to an amusement park, and dinner at a fancy restaurant. Baiting students with gimmicks and bribes does more than cast a moral shadow on the pedagogical value of such an approach or the teacher as a kind of ethical exemplar; it also makes clear how little LouAnne knows about the realities of her students' lives. Indifferent to the skills they need to survive, LouAnne is unconcerned about their experiences, interests, or cultural resources. This becomes clear in three pivotal instances in the movie.

In the first instance, LouAnne attempts to motivate the students by giving them the lyrics to Bob Dylan's "Mr. Tambourine Man." Indifferent to the force of hip hop culture (though, in designing the soundtrack, marketing executives appeared to know the draw and impact of hip hop on the films' audience), her attempt to use popular culture appears as nothing less than an act of cultural ignorance and bad pedagogy. But more revealing is her attempt to relate Bob Dylan's lyrics to the most clichéd aspects of the students' culture – namely violence and drugs. Not only does she disregard the complex and often contradictory cultural resources and interests of her students, but she also frames her notion of popular culture in a text from the 1960s – almost 20 years before these kids were born. Rather than excavating the traditions, themes, and experiences that make up her students' lives in order to construct her curriculum, she simply avoids their voices altogether in shaping the content of what she teaches. Beneath this form of symbolic violence there is also the presupposition that whites can come into such schools and teach without theory, ignore the multilayered histories and narratives that students bring to schools, and perform miracles in children's lives by mere acts of kindness.

In LouAnne's romantic version of schooling and teaching, there is no sense of what it means to give urban youth survival skills. The teacher's ignorance is reflected in another scene when she visits the grandmother of two black students missing from school for several days. The boys' grandmother has pulled them out of school and LouAnne decides to reason with her in order to get the students back into her class. The grandmother meets her in the yard, and refers to her as a "white bread bitch." The grandmother is indignant over what the boys have brought home for homework and tells LouAnne that "her boys have got bills to pay and that she should find some other poor boys to save." Regardless of the fact that Bob Dylan's lyrics are irrelevant to the kids' lives, the black grandmother is represented as an obstructionist. Yet, she is actually closer to the truth in suggesting that what LouAnne has passed off as useful knowledge will not help the boys survive life in the ghetto, nor will it change the conditions that give rise to urban squalor.

LouAnne's teaching is in actuality a pedagogy of diversion – one that refuses to provide students with skills that will help them address the urgent and disturbing questions of a society and a culture that in many ways ignores their humanity and well-being. These students are not taught to question the intellectual and cultural resources they need to address the profoundly antihumane conditions they have to negotiate every day. How to survive in a society, let alone remake it, is an important pedagogical question that cannot be separated from the larger issue of what it means to live in a country that is increasingly hostile to the existence of poor white and black kids in the inner cities. But LouAnne ignores these issues and offers her students material incentives to learn, and in doing so constructs them as consuming subjects rather than social subjects eager and able to think critically in order to negotiate and transform the worlds in which they live. In another pivotal exchange, students ask LouAnne what reward they are going to get for reading a poem. She surprises her students and the wider audience by insisting that learning is its own best reward. In doing so she switches her pedagogical tack, completely unaware of the consequences or limitations of the marketplace approach she has employed most of the semester.

LouAnne's sense of privilege also becomes evident in the boundless confidence she exhibits in her authority and moral superiority. She believes that somehow her students are answerable to her both in terms of their classroom performance and in terms of their personal lives; her role is to affirm or gently "correct" how they narrate their beliefs, experiences, and values. LouAnne takes for granted that she has *de facto* an unquestioning right to "save" them or run their lives without entering into a dialogue in which her own authority and purity of intentions are called into question. Authority here functions as a way of making invisible LouAnne's own privileges as a white woman, while simultaneously allowing her to indulge in a type of moralizing commensurate with her colonizing role as a white teacher who extracts from her students love and loyalty in exchange for teaching them to be part of a system that oppresses them.

The inability of LouAnne to enter into a dialogue with her students is apparent in two important interchanges with them. In one scene, LouAnne breaks up a fight between Emilio and some other students, then demands from Emilio a full explanation:

LouAnne:	Was it worth it? You like to hit people? Why? You feel angry?
Emilio:	You're trying to figure me out. You going to try to psychologize me. I'll help you. I come from a broken home, and we're poor, okay. I see the same fucking movies you do.
LouAnne:	I'd like to help you, Emilio.
Emilio:	Thank you very much. And how you going to do that? You going to give me some good advice – just say no – you going to get me off the streets? Well forget it. How the fuck are you going to save me from my life?

Emilio is trying to educate her, but LouAnne is not listening carefully. She assumes a moralizing posture that is totally indifferent to understanding the complex forces shaping Emilio's life. Nor can this great white hope consider that her students' histories and worldviews might be usefully incorporated into her pedagogy in order to teach kids like Emilio the survival skills they need to cope with the conditions and contexts of their surroundings. In another exchange, LouAnne takes Raul, a promising student, to a fancy restaurant because his group won a poetry contest. LouAnne mistakenly presupposes that it will be as easy for Raul to cross class borders as it is for her. But Raul is uncomfortable in such a context; he tells LouAnne that, in order to dress properly and avoid humiliating himself and her, he has bought his expensive leather jacket from a fence. In this scene is the underlying suggestion that, to succeed in life, working-class kids such as Raul need the cultural capital of white middle-class people like LouAnne.

Dangerous Minds mythically rewrites the decline of public schooling and the attack on poor, black and Hispanic students as a part of a broader project for rearticulating "whiteness" as a model of authority, rationality, and civilized behavior. The politics of representation at work in this film reproduces a dominant view of identity and difference that has a long legacy in Hollywood films, specifically Westerns and African adventure movies. As Robin Kelley points out, the popularity of many Hollywood films, especially the Western and African adventure genre, is as much about constructing "whiteness" as it is about demonizing the alleged racialized Other. He notes that within this racialized Hollywood legacy, "American Indians, Africans, and Asians represent a pre-civilized or anti-civilized existence, a threat to the hegemony of Western culture and proof that 'whites' are superior, more noble, more intelligent."[38] *Dangerous Minds* is an updated defense of white identity and racial hierarchies. The colonizing thrust of this narrative is highlighted through the image of Michelle Pfeiffer as a visiting white beauty queen whose success is, in part, rendered possible by market incentives and missionary talents.

Against LouAnne Johnson's benevolence and insight is juxtaposed the personality and pedagogy of Mr. Grandy, the black principal of Parkmount High. Grandy is portrayed as an uptight, bloodless bureaucrat, a professional wannabe whose only interest appears to be in enforcing school rules (Hollywood's favorite stereotype for black principals). Grandy rigidly oversees school policy and is constantly berating Johnson for bypassing the standard curriculum, generating nontraditional forms of teaching, and taking the students on unauthorized trips. As a black man in a position of leadership, he is depicted as an obstacle to the success of his charges, and ruthlessly insensitive to their needs. When Emilio visits Grandy's office to report another student who is trying to kill him, Grandy orders him out because he failed to knock on the office door. Leaving the building, Emilio is soon shot and killed a few blocks from the school.

Racial politics in this film are such that black professionals come off as the real threat to learning and civilized behavior, and whites, of course, are simply there to lend support. In contrast to Grandy, Johnson's "whiteness" provides the racialized referent for leadership, risk taking, and compassion. This is borne out at the end of the film when the students tell her that they want her to remain their teacher because she represents their "light." In this context, *Dangerous Minds* reinforces the highly racialized, though reassuring, mainstream assumption that chaos reigns in inner-city public schools, and that white teachers alone are capable of bringing order, decency, and hope to those on the margins of society.

Public Pedagogy and the Politics of Whiteness in
Dangerous Minds

Rather than being dismissed simply as a racist text by critical educators, *Dangerous Minds* should be read symptomatically for the ways in which it articulates and reproduces "whiteness" as a dominant racial identity within the public space of the inner-city classroom. Offering an unapologetic reading of "whiteness" as a trope of order, rationality, insight, and beauty, *Dangerous Minds* is an important pedagogical text for students to use in addressing how "whiteness" and difference are portrayed in the film, and how race shapes consciously or unconsciously their everyday experiences, attitudes, and worldviews. I am not suggesting that educators force students into viewing *Dangerous Minds* as either a good or bad film, but that they should encourage students to engage the broader social conditions through which the popularity of the film has to be understood. One pedagogical task is to get students to think about how *Dangerous Minds* bears witness to the ethical and racial dilemmas that animate the larger racial, gendered, and class-ridden landscape, and how it reworks or affirms their own intellectual and affective investments as organized through dominant racial ideologies and meanings at work in this highly racialized text.

Students may offer a number of responses to a film such as *Dangerous Minds*. But given the popularity of the film, and the large number of favorable reviews it received in newspapers across the country, it is reasonable to assume that the range of readings available to white students will fall within a mix of dominant and conservative interpretations.[39] Rather than stressing that students are diverse readers of culture, it is important to recognize that the issue of ownership and control of the apparatuses of cultural production limits the readings made widely available to students and shapes the popular context from which dominant notions of racism are understood. When racist difference does enter into classroom discussion, it more than likely will focus on the disruptive behavior that black and Hispanic students exhibit in schools – behavior that will often be seen as characteristic of an entire social group, a form of cultural pathology that suggests minorities are largely to blame for the educational problems they experience. Similarly, when "whiteness" is destabilized or critically addressed by students, it more than likely will be taken up within a power-evasive discourse in which white racism is often reduced to an act of individual prejudice cleanly removed from the messy contexts of history, politics, and systemic oppression.[40] This suggests that it is unlikely that white students will recognize LouAnne's pedagogy and insistence on the value of middle-class cultural capital as a racist attempt to teach black and Hispanic students that their own narratives, histories, and experiences are uncivilized and crude. And yet, however popular such dominant readings might be, they offer educators a prime pedagogical opportunity to interrogate and rupture their codes and ideologies. For instance, the ideological link between the privileging of white cultural capital and the ongoing, degrading representation of the Other in Hollywood films about Africa, in television sitcoms, or more recently in violent black youth films may not be evident to students on a first reading of the film, but certainly can become an object of analysis as various students in the class are provided with alternative readings.

At best, *Dangerous Minds* offers white students an opportunity to engage with a popular text that embodies much of what they generally learn (or mislearn) about race without initially putting their own racial identities on trial. Moreover, the film provides educators with an opportunity to talk about how white people are raced, how white experience is constructed differently within a variety of public spaces, and how it is mediated through the diverse but related lens of class, gender, and sexual orientation. As such the film can be taken up as part of a representational politics that illuminates "whiteness" as a shifting, political category whose meaning can be addressed within rather than outside of the interrelationships of class, race, ethnicity, and gender. Films such as *Dangerous Minds* can be taken up intertextually, particularly with other cultural texts (i.e., antiracist films, books, articles, etc.) that provide a theoretical basis for challenging "whiteness" as an ideological and historical construction; it is precisely the tension generated between such texts that invites entrance into a pedagogy that commences with what Gayatri Spivak refers to as "moments of bafflement."[41] While such pedagogical tensions do not guarantee the possibility of decentering "whiteness" in order to render "visible the historical and institutional structures from within which [white teachers and students] speak,"[42] they do provide the pedagogical conditions for students and teachers alike to question and unlearn those aspects of "whiteness" that position them within the privileged space and relations of racism.

While it is impossible to predict how students will actually react to a pedagogy of bafflement that takes "whiteness" and race as an object of serious debate and analysis, it is important to recognize that white students will generally offer enormous resistance to analyzing critically the "normative-residual space [of] white cultural practice."[43] Resistance in this case should be examined for the knowledge it yields, the possibilities for interrogating its silences and refusals. Pedagogically this suggests allowing students to air their positions on "whiteness" and race regardless of how messy or politically incorrect such positions might be. But there is more at stake here than providing a pedagogical space for students to narrate themselves, to speak without fear within the contexts of their own specific histories and experiences. Rather than arguing that students be simply allowed to voice their racial politics, I am suggesting that they be offered a space marked by dialogue and critique in which such positions can be engaged, challenged, and rearticulated through an ongoing analysis of the material realities and social relations of racism.

Needless to say, the issue of making white students responsive to the politics of racial privilege is fraught with the fear and anger that accompany having to rethink one's identity. Engaging in forms of teaching that prompt white students to examine their social practices and belief systems in racial terms may work to reinforce the safe assumption that race is a stable category, a biological given, rather than a historical and cultural construction. For instance, AnnLouise Keating points out that when teaching her students to interrogate "whiteness" critically, many of them come away believing that all whites were colonialists, in spite of her attempts pedagogically to distinguish between "whiteness" as the dominant racial and political ideology and the diverse, contingent racial positions white people take up.[44]

In spite of the tensions and contradictions that any pedagogy of "whiteness" might face, it is imperative that teachers address the histories that have shaped the normative space, practices, and diverse relationships that white students have inherited through a legacy of racial privilege. Analyzing the historical legacy of "whiteness" as an oppressive racial force necessitates that students engage in a critical form of memory work while fostering less a sullen silence or paralyzing guilt and more a sense of outrage at historical oppression and a desire for racial justice in the present. Keating illuminates the problems she faced when attempting to get students to think critically about racism and its systemic nature and to interrogate or reverse their taken-for-granted assumptions about "whiteness" and racial privilege. She writes:

> These reversals trigger a variety of unwelcome reactions in self-identified "white" students, reactions ranging from guilt to anger to withdrawal and despair. Instructors must be prepared to deal with these responses. The point is not to encourage feelings of personal responsibility for the slavery, decimation of indigenous peoples, land theft, and so on that occurred in the past. It is, rather, to enable students of all colors more fully to comprehend how these oppressive systems that began in the historical past continue misshaping contemporary conditions. Guilt-tripping plays no role in this process.[45]

However, Keating is not entirely clear on how educators can avoid guilt-tripping students or to what degree they are not to be held responsible (accountable) for their present attitudes within this type of pedagogy. Making "whiteness" rather than white racism the focus of study is an important pedagogical strategy. Analyzing "whiteness" opens up theoretical and pedagogical spaces for teachers and students to articulate how their own racial identities have been shaped within a broader racist culture and what responsibilities they might assume for living in a present in which whites are accorded privileges and opportunities (though in complex and different ways) largely at the expense of other racial groups. Yet, as insightful as this strategy may prove to be, more theoretical work needs to be done to enable students to critically engage and appropriate the tools necessary for them to politicize "whiteness" as a racial category without closing down their own sense of identity and political agency.

While *Dangerous Minds* provides a pedagogical opportunity for students to see how dominant assumptions about "whiteness" can be framed and challenged, it does not address what it means to rearticulate "whiteness" in oppositional terms, related to but not reduced to forms of racial oppression. Neither the portrayal of "whiteness" as a form of racial privilege nor as a practice of domination necessarily establishes the basis for white students to rearticulate their own "whiteness" in ways that go beyond their overidentification with or desire to be "black" at the expense of their own racial identities.

All students need to feel that they have a personal stake in how the discourse of race marks their own identities (however fluid, multiple, and unstable). This is not a call to inscribe them within a discourse of race, but to eventually challenge those notions of race that prevent them from locating forms of identification that will allow them to assert a view of political agency in which they can join with diverse groups around a notion of democratic public life that affirms ethnic, cultural, and perceived racial differences through a "rearticulation of cultural, social, and political citizenship."[46] This demands that educators and others recognize the multiple and varied connections that link the legacy of diverse racisms with existing practices of race as an ongoing and shifting site of struggle and power relations. Difference in this context cannot be abstracted from the discourse of power, equality, and social justice. Linking identity, race, and difference to a broader vision of radical democracy suggests a number of important pedagogical considerations. First, students need to investigate the historical relationship between race and ethnicity. Historian David Roediger is right in warning against the conflation of race and ethnicity by critical theorists, especially in light of a history of ethnicity in which white immigrants saw themselves as white and ethnic. According to Roediger, the claim to ethnicity among white immigrants, especially those from Europe, did not prevent them from defining their racial identities through the discourse of white separatism and supremacy.[47] In this case, white ethnicity was not ignored by such immigrants; it was affirmed and linked in some cases to the dominant relations of racism.

The issue of racial identity can be linked to what Stuart Hall has called the "new ethnicity."[48] For Hall, racial identities can be understood through the notion of ethnicity, but not the old notion of ethnicity which depends in part on the suppression of cultural difference and a separatist notion of white identity. Hall's attempt to rewrite ethnicity as a progressive and critical concept does not fall into the theoretical trap described by Roediger. By decoupling ethnicity from the traditional moorings of nationalism, racism, colonialism, and the state, Hall posits the new ethnicity as a referent for acknowledging "the place of history, language, and culture in the construction of subjectivity and identity, as well as the fact that all discourse is placed, positioned, situated, and all knowledge is contextual."[49]

Extending Hall's insights about ethnicity, I want to argue that the diverse subject positions, social experiences, and cultural identities that inform "whiteness" as a political and social construct can be rearticulated in order for students to recognize that "we all speak from a particular place, out of a particular history, out of particular experience, a particular culture without being constrained by [such] positions.... We are all, in that sense, ethnically located and our ethnic identities are crucial to our subjective sense of who we are."[50] In Hall's terms, "whiteness" cannot be addressed as a form of identity fashioned through a claim to purity or some universal essence, but as one which "lives with and through, not despite difference."[51]

Hall provides a theoretical language for racializing "whiteness" without essentializing it; he also argues, correctly, that ethnicity must be defined and defended through a set of ethical and political referents that connect diverse democratic struggles while expanding the range and possibilities of democratic relations and practices. Redefined within the theoretical parameters of a new ethnicity, "whiteness" can be read as a complex marker of identity defined through a politics of difference subject to the shifting currents of history, power, and culture. That is, "whiteness" can no longer be taken up as fixed, naturally grounded in a tradition or ancestry, but as Ien Ang claims in another context, must be understood as a form of postmodern ethnicity, "experienced as a provisional and partial site of identity which must be constantly (re)invented and (re)negotiated."[52]

The notion of "whiteness" being in transit, hybrid, but at the same time grounded in particular histories and practices, extends the political potential of Hall's new ethnicity thesis in that it provides a theoretical space for engaging racial identity as a fundamental principle of citizenship and radical democracy the aim of which is the "expansion of egalitarian social relations, and practices."[53]

The new ethnicity defines racial identities as multiple, porous, complex, and shifting, and in doing so provides a theoretical opening for educators and students to move beyond framing "whiteness" as either good or bad, racially innocent or intractably racist. "Whiteness" in this context can be addressed through its complex relationship with other determining factors that usurp any claim to racial purity or singularity. At the same time, "whiteness" must be addressed within power relations that exploit its subversive potential while not erasing the historical and political role it plays in shaping other racialized identities and social differences. Unlike the old ethnicity, which posits difference in essentialist or separatist terms, Hall's notion of the new ethnicity defines identity as an ongoing act of cultural recovery, acknowledging that any particular claim to racial identity offers no guarantees regarding political outcomes. But at the same time, the new ethnicity provides a theoretical service by allowing white students to go beyond the paralysis inspired by guilt, or the racism fueled by anxiety and fear of difference. In this context, "whiteness" gains its meaning only in conjunction with other identities such as those informed by class, gender, age, nationality, and citizenship. For progressive whites, "crossing over does not mean crossing out."[54] Whites have to learn to live with their "whiteness" by rearticulating it in terms that allow them to formulate what it means to develop viable cross relations political coalitions and social movements. Whites have to learn and unlearn, engage in a critical pedagogy of self-formation that allows them to cross racial lines, not in order to become black but so they can begin to forge multiracial coalitions based on an engagement rather than a denial of "whiteness."

By positioning "whiteness" within a notion of cultural citizenship that affirms difference politically, culturally, and socially, students can take notice of how their "whiteness" functions as a racial identity while still being critical of forms of "whiteness" structured in dominance and aligned with exploitative interests and oppressive social relations. By rearticulating "whiteness" as more than a form of domination, white students can construct narratives of "whiteness" that both challenge and, hopefully, provide a basis for transforming the dominant relationship between racial identity and citizenship, one informed by an oppositional politics. Such a political practice suggests new subject positions, alliances, commitments, and forms of solidarity between white students and others engaged in a struggle over expanding the possibilities of democratic life, especially as it affirms both a politics of difference and a redistribution of power and material resources. George Yudice argues that as part of a broader project for articulating "whiteness" in oppositional terms, white youth must feel that they have a stake in racial politics that connects them to the struggles being waged by other groups. At the center of such struggles is both the battle over citizenship redefined through the discourse of rights, and the problem of resource distribution. He writes:

> This is where identity politics segues into other issues, such as tax deficits, budget cuts, lack of educational opportunities, lack of jobs, immigration policies, international trade agreements, environmental blight, lack of health care insurance, and so on. These are the areas in which middle- and working-class whites historically have had an advantage over people of color. However, today that advantage has eroded in certain respects.[55]

As part of a wider attempt to engage these issues, Yudice suggests that white youth can form alliances with other social and racial groups who recognize the need for solidarity in addressing issues of public life that undermine the quality of democracy for all groups. As white youth struggle to find a cultural and political space from which to speak and act as transformative citizens, it is imperative that educators address what it means pedagogically and politically to help students rearticulate "whiteness" as part of a democratic cultural politics. Central to such a task is the need to challenge the conventional left-wing analysis of "whiteness" as a space between guilt and denial, a space that offers limited forms of resistance and engagement. In order for teachers, students, and others to come to terms with "whiteness" existentially and intellectually, we need to take up the challenge in our classrooms and across a wide variety of public sites of confronting racism in all its complexity and ideological and material formations. But most importantly, "whiteness" must provide a diverse but critical space from which to wage a wider struggle against the myriad of forces that undermine what it means to live in a society founded on the principles of freedom, racial justice, and economic equality. Rewriting "whiteness" within a discourse of resistance and possibility represents more than a challenge to dominant and progressive notions of racial politics; it provides an important challenge for educating cultural workers, teachers, and students to live with and through difference as a defining principle of a radical democracy.

Notes

1. A much shorter version of this essay appeared in *Cineaste* 22(4) (1997): 46–9.
2. Howard Winant, "Amazing Grace." *Socialist Review* 75.9 (1992): 166.
3. For an excellent analysis of this issue, see Thomas Byrne Edsall and Mary D. Edsall, *Chain Reactions: The Impact of Race, Rights, and Taxes on American Politics* (New York: W.W. Norton, 1992).
4. On the meaning of the new racism and its diverse expressions, see Howard Winant, *Racial Conditions* (Minneapolis: University of Minnesota Press, 1994). See also Henry A. Giroux, *Border Crossing* (New York: Routledge, 1992).
5. George Yudice, "Neither Impugning Nor Disavowing Whiteness Does a Viable Politics Make: The Limits of Identity Politics," in Christopher Newfield and Ronald Strickland (eds.), *After Political Correctness* (Boulder, CO: Westview, 1995), pp. 255–81.
6. John Brenkman, "Race Publics: Civic Illiberalism, or Race After Reagan." *Transition* 5.2 (1995): 14.
7. I take up this issue in extensive detail in Henry A. Giroux, *Fugitive Cultures: Race, Violence, and Youth* (New York: Routledge, 1996).
8. Kaus cited in John Brenkman, "Race Publics," op. cit., p. 34.
9. On the rise of right-wing groups in the United States, see Sara Diamond, *Roads to Domination: Right-Wing Movements and Political Power in the United States* (New York: Guilford Press, 1995) and Sara Diamond, *Facing the*

Wrath (Monroe, ME: Common Courage Press, 1996). On racism and right-wing movements, see Michael Novick, *White Lies, White Power* (Monroe, ME: Common Courage Press, 1995). For a number of articles on the right-wing backlash, see Chip Berlet (ed.), *Eyes Right!: Challenging the Right Wing Backlash* (Boston: South End Press, 1995).

10. Both Richard Dyer and bell hooks have argued that whites see themselves as racially transparent and reinscribe whiteness as invisible. While this argument may have been true in the 1980s, it no longer makes sense as white youth, in particular, have become increasingly sensitive to their status as whites because of the racial politics and media exposure of race in the last few years. See Richard Dyer, "White." *Screen* 29.4 (1988): 44–64; bell hooks, *Black Looks: Race and Representation* (Boston: South End Press, 1992).

11. Aaron D. Gresson III, "Postmodern America and the Multicultural Crisis: Reading Forrest Gump as the 'Call Back to Whiteness.'" *Taboo* 1 (Spring, 1996): 11–33.

12. Richard J. Herrnstein and Charles Murray, *The Bell Curve: Intelligence and Class Structure in American Life* (New York: The Free Press, 1994); Dinesh D'Douza, *The End of Racism: Principles for a Multiracial Society* (New York: The Free Press, 1995).

13. The sources documenting the growing racism in the dominant media and popular culture are too extensive to cite. Some important examples, include Jimmie L. Reeves and Richard Campbell, *Cracked Coverage: Television News, The Anti-Cocaine Crusade, and the Reagan Legacy* (Durham, NC: Duke University Press, 1994); John Fiske, *Media Matters* (Minneapolis: University of Minnesota Press, 1994); Jeff Ferrell and Clinton R. Sanders (eds.), *Cultural Criminology* (Boston: Northeastern University Press, 1995); Herman Gray, *Watching Race* (Minneapolis: University of Minnesota Press, 1995); Michael Dyson, *Between God and Gangsta Rap* (New York: Oxford University Press, 1996), and Henry A. Giroux, *Fugitive Cultures: Race, Violence and Youth* (New York: Routledge, 1996). For a summary of the double standard at work in the press coverage of rap music, see Art Jones and Kim Deterline, "Fear of a Rap Planet: Rappers Face Media Double Standard." *Extra* 7.2 (March/April, 1994): 20–1.

14. Editorial, "The Issue." *The New Republic* (October 31, 1994): 9.

15. For a brilliant analysis of the racial politics of *The Atlantic Monthly*, see Charles Augnet, "For Polite Reactionaries." *Transition* 6.1 (1966): 14–34.

16. Stuart Hall, "Race, Culture, and Communications: Looking Backward and Forward at Cultural Studies." *Rethinking Marxism* 5.1 (1992): 13.

17. William A. Henry III, "Upside Down in the Groves of Academe." *Time* (April 1, 1991): 66–9.
18. David Gates, "White Male Paranoia." *Newsweek* (March 29, 1993): 48.
19. Ibid., p. 51.
20. Ibid, p. 49.
21. James Joseph Scheurich, "Toward A White Discourse on White Racism." *Educational Researcher* (November, 1993): 6.
22. Two excellent articles addressing the possibilities for rearticulating whiteness in oppositional terms are: Diana Jester, "Roast Beef and Reggae Music: The Passing of Whiteness." *New Formations* 118 (Winter 1992): 106–21; Yudice, "Neither Impugning Nor Disavowing Whiteness Does a Viable Politics Make," op. cit. I have relied heavily on both of these piece in developing my analysis of white youth.
23. hooks, *Black Looks*, op. cit., p. 168.
24. Charles A. Gallagher, "White Reconstruction in the University." *Socialist Review* 94: 1&2 (1995): 166.
25. Jester, "Roast Beef and Reggae Music," op. cit., p. 111.
26. Ibid., p. 115.
27. Ibid., p. 107.
28. A comprehensive survey of freshmen conducted in 2000 by the Higher Education Research Institute at the University of California at Los Angeles reported that "Only 28.1 percent of entering college students reported an interest in 'keeping up to date with political affairs,' the lowest level since the survey was established, in 1966, when the figure was 60.3 percent." Cited in Alex P. Kellog, "Looking Inward, Freshmen Care less About Politics and More About Money." *The Chronicle of Higher Education* (January 26, 2001): A47.
29. Gallagher, "White Reconstruction in the University," op. cit., p. 170.
30. Ibid., pp. 182, 185.
31. This theme is explored in Howard Pinderhughes, *Race in the Hood: Conflict and Violence Among Urban Youth* (Minneapolis: University of Minnesota Press, 1997).
32. I want to thank my colleague at Penn State University, Bernard Bell, for this insight (personal communication).
33. Howard Winant, *Racial Conditions* (Minneapolis: University of Minnesota Press, 1994), p. xiii.
34. I think Houston Baker is instructive on this issue in arguing that race, for all its destructive tendencies and implications, has also been used by blacks and other people of color to gain a sense of personal and historical agency. This is not a matter of a positive image of race canceling out its negative underside. On the contrary, Baker makes a compelling case for the

dialectical nature of race and its possibilities for engaging and overcoming its worse dimensions while extending in the interest of a transformative and democratic polis. See Houston Baker, "Caliban's Triple Play," in Henry Louis Gates, Jr. (ed.), *Loose Canons: Notes on the Culture Wars* (New York: Oxford University Press, 1992): 381–95.

35. James Snead, *White Screens, Black Images* (New York: Routledge, 1994), especially chapter 10, "Mass Visual Productions," pp. 131–49. For an analysis of the importance of race in the broader area of popular culture, two representative sources include: Michael Dyson, *Reflecting Black* (Minneapolis: University of Minnesota Press, 1993); Henry A. Giroux, *Fugitive Cultures*, op. cit.

36. Ruth Frankenberg, *The Social Construction of Whiteness* (Minneapolis: University of Minnesota Press, 1993): 49.

37. On the localization of crime as a racial text, see David Theo Goldberg, "Polluting the Body Politic: Racist Discourse and the Urban Location," in Malcolm Cross and Michael Keith, (eds.), *Racism, the City and the State* (New York: Routledge, 1993): 45–60.

38. Robin D. G. Kelley, "Notes on Deconstructing 'the Folk.'" *The American Historical Review* 97.5 (December, 1992): 1406.

39. For instance, see Jon Glass, "'Dangerous Minds' Inspires Teachers." *The Virginian-Pilot* (September 2, 1995): B1; Catherine Saillant, "School of Soft Knocks." *Los Angeles Times* (October 11, 1995): B1; Sue Chastain, "Dangerous Minds No Threat to this Tough Teacher." *The Times Union* (August 13, 1995): G1.

40. For example, in Ruth Frankenberg's study of white women, radical positions on race were in the minority; and in Gallagher's study of white college students, liberal and conservative positions largely predominated. See Frankenberg, *The Social Construction of Whiteness*, op. cit.; Gallagher, "White Reconstruction in the University," op. cit.

41. Gayatri Chakravorty Spivak, *Post-Colonial Critic: Interviews, Strategies, Dialogues*, Sarah Harasym (ed.) (New York: Routledge, 1990): 137.

42. Ibid, p. 67.

43. Frankenberg, *The Social Construction of Whiteness*, op. cit. p. 234.

44. AnnLouise Keating, "Interrogating 'Whiteness,' (De) Constructing 'Race.'" *College English* 57.8 (December, 1955): 907

45. Ibid., p. 915.

46. See Yudice, "Neither Impugning Nor Disavowing Whiteness Does a Viable Politics Make," op. cit, pp. 276–7.

47. David Roediger, "'White Ethnics' in the United States," in *Towards the Abolition of Whiteness* (London: Verso, 1994): 181–198.

48. Stuart Hall takes up the rewriting of ethnicity in a variety of articles, see especially "New Ethnicities," in David Morley and Kuan-Hsing Chen (eds.), *Stuart Hall: Critical Dialogues in Cultural Studies* (New York: Routledge, 1996), pp.441–9; Stuart Hall, "Cultural Identity and Diaspora," in Jonathan Rutherford (ed.), *Identity, Community, Culture, Difference* (London: Lawrence and Wishart, 1990), pp. 222–37; Stuart Hall, "Ethnicity: Identity and Difference." *Radical America* 13.4 (June, 1991): 9–20; Stuart Hall, "Old and New Identities, Old and New Ethnicities," in Anthony D. King (ed.), *Culture, Globalization and the World System* (Binghampton: State University of New York Press, 1991): 41–68.

49. Hall, "New Ethnicities," op. cit., p. 29.

50. Ibid.

51. Hall, "Cultural Identity and Diaspora," op.cit., p. 235.

52. Ien Ang, "On Not Speaking Chinese: Postmodern Ethnicity and the Politics of Diaspora." *Social Formations* 24 (Winter, 1995): 110.

53. Chantal Mouffe, "Feminism, Citizenship, and Radical Democratic Politics," in Judith Butler and Joan Scott (eds.), *Feminists Theorize the Political* (New York: Routledge, 1992), p. 380.

54. Peter Erickson, "Seeing White." *Transition* 5.3 (Fall, 1995): 185.

55. Yudice, "Neither Impugning Nor Disavowing Whiteness Does a Viable Politics Make," op. cit., p. 276.

9

Media Panics and the War Against "Kids": Larry Clark and the Politics of Diminished Hopes[1]

Representing Youth as a Problem

Representations of youth in popular culture have a long and complex history and habitually serve as signposts through which American society registers its own crisis of meaning, vision, and community. The presentation of youth as a complex, shifting, and contradictory category is rarely narrated in the dominant public sphere through the diverse voices of the young. Prohibited from speaking as moral and political agents, youth become an empty category inhabited by the desires, fantasies, and interests of the adult world. This is not to suggest that youth don't speak; they are simply restricted from speaking and intervening in those spheres where public conversation shapes social policy. Under such conditions, youth bear the brunt of adult power as a form of containment and as such are refused the resources necessary to give substance to their own individual and collective needs.

When youth do speak – the current generation, in particular – their voices generally emerge on the margins of society, in underground magazines, alternative music spheres, computer-hacker clubs and other subcultural sites. The places youth inhabit, especially since the beginning of the 1980s, increasingly point to the dangerous erosion of noncommodified public space and spheres and the undermining of the collective safety nets and nurturing systems that historically have provided some sustenance and hope for youth.[2] Quality public schools, youth clubs, religious institutions, public art programs, urban shelters, and drug- and crime-free urban neighborhoods seem to have receded and been replaced, in part, by public spaces largely marked by the absence of adult support. The basketball court, the shopping mall, the darkly lit street corner, the video arcade, the urban dance hall, the suburban home inhabited by latchkey children, the decaying housing projects, and the second-hand automobile have become the privileged sites for working-class youth. In alarming numbers, young people in the 1990s are being distanced from both the values, language, and practices necessary to shape a democratic social order and those public terrains that traditionally have been used to promote and embody civic discourse and critical reflection.

Lauded as a symbol of hope for the future while scorned as a threat to the existing social order, youth have become objects of ambivalence caught between contradictory discourses and spaces of transition. While pushed to the margins of political power within society, youth nonetheless become a central focus of adult fascination, desire, and authority. Increasingly denied opportunities for self-definition and political interaction, youth are transfigured by discourses and practices that subordinate and contain the language of individual freedom, social power, and critical agency. Symbols of a declining democracy, youth are located within a range of signifiers that largely deny their representational status as active citizens. Associated with coming-of-age rebellion, youth become a metaphor for trivializing resistance. At the same time, youth attract serious attention as both a site of commodification and a profitable market. For many aging baby boomers, youth represent an invigorated referent for a midlife consciousness aggressively in search of acquiring a more "youthful" state of mind and lifestyle.[3]

Caught up in an age of increasing despair, youth no longer appear to inspire adults to reaffirm their commitment to a public discourse that envisions a future in which human suffering is diminished while the general welfare of society is increased. The relations between youth and adults have always been marked by strained generational and ideological struggles, but the new economic and social conditions that youth face today, along with a callous indifference to their spiritual and material needs, suggest a qualitatively different attitude on the part of many adults toward American youth – one that indicates that the young have become our lowest national priority. Put bluntly, American society at present exudes both a deep-rooted hostility and chilling indifference toward youth, reinforcing the dismal conditions that young people are increasingly living under.

For many youth, especially those who experience ruthless subordination and oppression, nihilism often translates into senseless violence, racism, homophobia, drug addiction, date rape, suicide pacts, escalating homicide rates, and a refusal to participate in building communities of hope and alliances with other oppressed groups. This is not meant to portray youth merely as reproducing a larger social pathology as much as it is meant to make visible the political, economic, and cultural conditions that undermine democratic public life and takes the young and the very old as its first victims.

Of course, conditions of oppression do not simply produce victims or ongoing forms of resistance, but also social systems that become ethically frozen because they have become indifferent to forms of political courage and civic responsibility necessary to engage critically the most pressing problems of the times. The distinctive change of attitude toward working-class and black youth in America, while rooted in histories of racism and class struggle, can be seen, in part, by the dismal statistics concerning the quality of life of children in this country that reflect new economic and ideological realities. Statistics are often too abstract to capture the day-to-day suffering they attempt to register; nonetheless, they serve as reminders of what can only be judged as a national crisis regarding the deteriorating conditions in which many children currently find themselves.

Nationwide, the number of children living in poverty increased by 2.2 million between 1979 and 1989. Child poverty among European-Americans increased from 11.8 percent to 14.8 percent, among Latinos from 28 percent to 32 percent, and among blacks from 41.2 percent to 43.7 percent. . . . The United States has one of the worst infant mortality rates among industrialized nations. Out of every thousand babies born in the U.S., 9.8 die in infancy–a rate worse than sixteen other nations. Black children die at almost twice the national average–18.2 per thousand births.[4]

Not only are there fourteen million children living in poverty in the United States, but the USA ranks in the lower half of Western industrialized countries in providing services for family support. Moreover, the United States has experienced an alarming growth in cases of child abuse. It is also a country where more teenagers "die from suicide than from cancer, heart disease, HIV infection or AIDS, birth defects, pneumonia, influenza, stroke and chronic lung disease combined."[5] Similarly, behind the meager distribution of resources allotted for children of the poor looms an oppressive and exploitative structure of economic inequality in which the top 1 percent of the population "holds 46.2 percent of all stocks and 54.2 percent of all bonds."[6] In a recent study by the Organization for Economic Cooperation and Development it was revealed that the United States, out of the top 17 wealthiest industrial countries, has the biggest gap between the rich and poor.[7] It appears that for the richest and most powerful groups in American society youth represent one of their lowest priorities.

The most striking example of such callous indifference can be seen in the passing of the Welfare Reform Bill signed into law by former President Bill Clinton. Peter Edelman, former Undersecretary of Health and Human Services, resigned over Clinton's support of the bill, calling it in an article in *The Atlantic Monthly* the worst thing that Bill Clinton has done. Not only did the bill produce budget cuts that affect low income people, but Edelman predicted that 10 percent of all families would lose income; moreover, Edelman estimated that the bill would move 2.6 million people, including 1.1 million children, into poverty. The bill also results in drastic cuts in child nutrition programs–$3 billion in six years, and support for social services–$2.5 billion in over six years as well.[8] Even more disturbing is the fact that the largest growing population of homeless in this country are children and the average age of such children is nine years old. For white working-class youth, prospects are also bleak; they can look forward to dead-end jobs, unemployment without the benefit of health care, or perhaps homelessness.

Black teenagers face an unemployment rate of 57 percent and unprecedented levels of poverty while impoverishment and hunger become the rule of the day.[9] But what sets black youth off from their white counterparts is that the preferred method of containing white teenagers is through constitutional controls exercised through schooling, where working-class youth suffer the effects of school choice programs, tracking, and vocationalization. On the other hand, black youth are increasingly subjected to the draconian strategies of "tagging," surveillance, or more overt harassment and imprisonment through the criminal justice system.[10] A Justice Department Report points out that on any given day in this country "more than a third of the young African-American men aged 18–34 in some of our major cities are either in prison, on probation, or under some form of criminal justice supervision."[11] The same department reported in April of 2000 that "black youth are forty-eight times more likely than whites to be sentenced to juvenile prison for drug offenses."[12]

As the political tide has turned against the well-being, support, and happiness of working-class and black children, further weakening support for the very young in troubled families and social circumstances, a new form of representational politics has emerged in media culture fueled by degrading visual depictions of youth as criminal, sexually decadent, drug crazed, and illiterate. In short, youth are viewed as a growing threat to the public order.

Hollywood Youth and the Politics of Representation

The antiteen impulse that surfaces in Hollywood films in the late 1980s and early 1990s had begun to emerge in dramatic Hollywood style in slasher films such as *Halloween* (1978), *Friday the 13th* (1980), and *Nightmare on Elm Street* (1984). While a hateful misogyny swept through the horror genre films, a dismal and dystopian depiction of working-class youth spread across the Hollywood screens in the late 1980s, and seemed to forecast a new politics of representation through which dominant media culture attempted to rewrite and represent the identities and social status of youth by persistently placing them in communities "whose older local support institutions had been all but demolished."[13]

If a crisis of representation regarding youth has emerged in the 1990s, it is rooted less in a transformation of representational ideologies than in a host of complex national and global forces changing the face of the contemporary urban landscape: a downward spiraling economy, a resurgent racism, a diminishing allocation of funds for crucial public services, the creation of Tipper Gore's Parent's Music Resource Center, and the hostile public response from many adults to rap and urban contemporary music as it entered the mainstream. These factors, among many others, appear to register a shift in media culture's simplistic but sometimes sympathetic portrayal of youth as a problem through which to analyze the social and political dynamics at work in the larger society to its current more racist and brutalizing view. Young people are no longer seen as a symptom of a wider social dilemma – they are the problem.

A representational politics began to emerge that strongly resonated with a growing neoconservative demonization of urban white and black youth in the commercially dominated sectors of media culture. In films such as *River's Edge* (1987), *My Own Private Idaho* (1991), and *Natural Born Killers* (1995), white youth are framed and presented through the degrading textural registers of pathological violence, a deadening moral vacuum, and a paralyzing indifference to the present and future. On the other hand, Hollywood blockbusters such as *Wayne's World* (1992), *Dazed and Confused* (1993), *Dumb and Dumber* (1995), *American Pie* (1999), and *Scary Movie* (2000) project onto post-Watergate youth a long legacy of anti-intellectualism that has been a defining principle of American culture. In this script, idiocy, over-the-top raunchiness, and empty-headed, deliberate outrageous behavior become the principle characteristics of a youth culture that defines its relationship to each other through spectacle of brutality, humiliation, and a self-centered indifference. In this instance, Jim Carrey exemplifies the new teenager whose sense of agency appears to be drawn from a cross between Beavis and Butthead and David Duke. No longer a site of resistance, high school is now portrayed in films such as *Clueless* (1995), *Varsity Blues* (1999), *Jawbreaker* (1999), *Election* (1999), and *Ten Things I Hate about You* (1999) as either irrelevant or as simply providing students with the opportunity to use their sexuality or athletic prowess to satisfy their own narcissistic needs while delighting in their ability to manipulate others. High school is now modeled after the shopping mall where students can package themselves and wield their social and sexual wares to advance their reputations in the school pecking order. Needless to say, simplistic Hollywood portrayals of youth as either potential muggers or dead from the neck up legitimates real futures that offers the horrifying images of the prison, mental hospital, or the local fast food outlet. As youth are conceived in images of demonization, sexual decadence, and criminality, the only public sites that appear available to them are unskilled work, highly policed public spaces, or the brute reality of incarceration.

Hollywood representations of black youth in the last decade seem to be largely inspired by the dynamics of class hatred as well as the powerful resurgent racism in American society. In films that include *Boyz N the Hood* (1991), *Menace II Society* (1993), *Clockers* (1995), *Belly* (1998), and *Black and White* (2000), black male youth are framed through narrow representations that strongly articulate with the dominant neoconservative image of "blackness as menace and 'other'."[14] Within these films, violence resonates with the popular perception that everyday black urban culture and the culture of criminality mutually define and feed off each other. If white working-class and middle-class youth are seen as a problem to be contained, black youth are seen as a dangerous threat to be eliminated.

Media representations of white and black working-class youth in the 1990s differ from the portrayal of such youth historically in that the contemporary construction of youth appears to be aggressively attacked as a generation of suspects, particularly around issues of sexuality and violence. Demonized as both a threat to the larger social order and located within a debased notion of sexuality – defined as either a commodity or as a problem – contemporary youth appear as both excess and threat, a referent for desire and emulation and a reminder that their bodies and minds are no longer the privileged space of either critical agency or hope within the commercially driven social order. The bodies of youth now symbolize death and depravity, on the one hand, and the embodiment of the full-scale desire for commodification on the other. Media representations extending from Calvin Klein ads to Hollywood youth films largely define teenagers in terms of their sexuality, and in doing so reaffirm both their limited sense of agency and portray them as a generation of suspects, by suggesting that the brutality and violence associated with young people is the consequence of an adolescent libido that is out of control.

Within the new representational politics of youth, the body is increasingly being commodified and disciplined through a reactionary, postmodern cultural politics. The struggle over the body and sexuality as a sign becomes as important as the more traditional practices of containing and disciplining the body as a threat to the social order. In part, the new crisis of representation erases the body of youth as a site of resistance, whether expressed through a transgressive sexuality, an appropriation of popular culture, or in the formation of underground cultural formations. The bodies of youth in the age of Tom DeLay and the Christian Coalition signify one of the most unsettling threats to American society as an increasingly conservative agenda dominates the discourse about the rights of children and the nature of the social problems facing the United States. Surely there is more than irony at work in a conservative discourse that defines its notion of family values, in part, on an image of the completely pure and sexually innocent child (read white and middle-class) while it refuses to acknowledge the "immense sexualization of children within consumer capitalism."[15] The hypocrisy of such a discourse cannot be easily dismissed. As Marilyn Ivy points out, "For to think about the child as a sexual object in capitalism is already to have violated the pristine space the child must occupy to guarantee the crumbling social order, with its insistence on the sanctity of the nuclear family and standardized gender relations."[16]

In what follows, I want to analyze the representations of teenage sexuality in the bleak depiction of urban youth in Larry Clark's film, *Kids*. The representations of youth presented in this film need to be addressed as part of a broader public struggle over how "technologies of power produce and manage...the individual and social body through the inscription of sexuality" within the visual and pedagogical machinery of Hollywood culture.[17] The primary issue is not whether artists, educators, and the general public should be condemned for finding pleasure in representations of youth as depicted in films such as *Kids*. Finding pleasures in sexually charged images of children does not make people morally culpable. At the same time, the emergence of a representational politics in which the bodies of youth are no longer seen as the privileged site of critical thinking, agency, resistance, or productive desires raises important questions regarding the moral responsibility and limits of one's pleasures at a time when subordinate youth are under massive assault by conservatives. In doing so, I want to illuminate how Larry Clark's *Kids* functions pedagogically within a broader discourse about youth, focusing specifically on how such representations resonate with specific conservative attacks on related issues of sexuality, race, and gender. Central to this analysis is a critique of a transgressive art that serves to deploy teenage sexuality as decadent and predatory.

Related to this criticism is the call to challenge the current fascination by many cultural workers with forms of aesthetic and textual criticism and the ways in which such criticism ignores representations of children's culture and bodies as part of a larger debate about power, ideology, and politics. Textual criticism that celebrates the formal aesthetic principles at work in "realistic representations" of teenage sexuality often provides justification for flaunting the commodification of young bodies. Moreover, portraying teenage sexuality as decadent and predatory is neither critically transgressive nor worthy of being labeled as progressively transformative. Artists, critics, and others who respond to these representations by retreating to an ideologically "neutral" defense of aesthetics and artistic freedom often reproduce the very problems such representations legitimate. That is, by failing to engage in a broader public dialogue about the messy political realities of exploitation and social injustice that result from current attacks on poor, urban, white and black youth, such critics often legitimate rather than challenge the current conservative agenda for dispensing with those youth they view as disposable, if not dangerous, to the imperatives of the free market and global economy.

Kids and the Politics of Diminished Hopes

Seeing comes before words. The child looks and recognizes before it can speak. But there is also another sense in which seeing comes before words. It is seeing which establishes our place in the surrounding world; we explain that world within words, but words can never undo the fact that we are surrounded by it. The relation between what we see and what we know is never settled.[18]

One of the most controversial films to appear about teenage sexuality and youth in 1995 was *Kids*, a film directed by Larry Clark from a script written by 19-year old Harmony Korine. Most of the characters in the documentary-like film are nonactors and skateboarding friends of Korine. The film opens with a close-up of a teenage boy and girl loudly kissing each other. The image is crucial both aesthetically and politically. Aesthetically, the camera focuses on open mouths, tongues working overtime, a sucking noise highlights the exchange of saliva – the scene is raw, rubbing against the notion of teenage sex as "a scaled down version of adult couplings, glamorized and stylized."[19] And it seems to go on forever, positioning the audience as voyeurs watching sex explode among kids who look too young to be acting on their own passions. In voice over, Telly (Leo Fitzpatrick), the 15-year-old known to his friends as the Virgin Surgeon, says "Virgins. I love 'em." After seducing a young blond virgin in her bedroom, Telly bolts from the Manhattan brownstone and joins his friend, Casper (Justin Pierce), who has been waiting for him. Telly provides an account of his conquest in intimate detail, and so begins Clark's rendition of urban teenage youth in the 1990s.

After Telly's initial seduction, he and Casper head out to wander through the streets of Manhattan. Along the way, they knock off a 40-ounce bottle of beer, urinate in public, jump over subway turn-stiles, and steal some fruit from a Korean grocer. They end up at a friend's apartment where they do drugs, talk sex, and watch skateboarding movies. The scene becomes more violent as Telly and his friends end up at Washington Square Park where they smoke some more dope, insult two gays who walk by, and viciously beat with their skateboards a black youth who Casper gets into an argument with. After stealing some money from Telly's mother, the youths break into the local YMCA for a swim. The day's activities culminate in a night of excessive drinking and drugs at a party given by a kid whose parents are out of town. The party degenerates into a haze of narcotized and drunken bodies, hands plunged randomly into crotches. Telly scores his second virgin. In the meantime, Jennie (Chloe Sevigny) appears at the party looking for Telly to inform him that she has tested positive for the HIV virus, but she is too drugged to prevent him from infecting another young girl. Too numb to do anything, she falls asleep on a couch. In a grotesque and perverse reversal of the fairytale plot, Clarke's sleeping beauty, Jennie, is not awakened with a kiss and the promise of living happily ever after. Rather, she suffers the brutal humiliation of a rape by Casper and will awaken to the nightmare reality of her eventual death and potentially his as well. The scene ends with Casper looking directly into the camera and asking "Jesus Christ, what happened?"

Irresponsible sex becomes lethal violence as it becomes clear that Jennie contracted the HIV virus from Telly, who now emerges as the infector, "the ultimate villain of American culture in the age of AIDS."[20] If Telly's story is one of sexual conquest, Jennie's is one of tragedy and powerlessness in the face of a ruthless urban youth culture that celebrates reckless sexuality and violence while it reduces young girls to one of two sexist stereotypes. They are sexual objects to be taken up and put down at will or they are sex-crazed and on the make. When the girls come together in the film, they are sitting around talking about oral sex, titillating the guys or each other, or getting set up to be exploited, as in the case of Darcy, Telly's last sexual conquest, to become another AIDS statistic.

As for the younger generation of preteens, their future is fore-shadowed as the camera focuses on a quartet of dope-smoking 11-year-old boys who watch the older kids drink and drug themselves into a stupor at the party. The future they will inherit holds no positive role models nor encouraging signs of hope.[21] For even younger girls, there is the ominous and disturbing message that they will soon become sexual trophies for the predatory male buffoons who stalk them in the dangerous space of the city. Film critic Michael Atkinson captures this sentiment in noting that the camera "lingers on a stepside moptop 3-year-old girl as if to grimly intone, it's only a matter of time."[22] Clark's gaze, which captures the bodies of young girls as wholly gendered and sexualized, sustains "the representation of the female body as the primary site of sexuality and visual pleasure."[23] Passivity and helplessness become the privileged modes of behavior as the girls in the film follow the lead of the male characters, silently observe their expressions of brutality, and plead tearfully when they become the objects of such violence. Predatory sexuality permeates the ruthless world of misogynist teenage males filled with a sense of themselves and their desire to prey on young girls who wait passively to be pulled into a ritual of seduction and possibly death.

Decontextualized Youth and the Swindle of Agency

Floating on the surface of a dead-end cynicism, Clark's film refuses to probe where identity resides for the urban youth he represents. The teenagers in *Kids* are portrayed as if they live in a historical, political, and cultural vacuum. Lacking any depth, memories, or histories, Clark's teenagers are drawn in personal and stylized terms. For example, he provides no larger context for understanding the cultural, social, and institutional forces working on the lives of these urban teenagers. In this severely decontextualized perspective, it is almost impossible to understand the absence of adults in the film, the at-risk sexuality, the rabid homophobia, or the random violence practiced by these teenagers. Representing teen life as if it existed outside of the forces of history, politics, and the dominant culture too easily resonates with a dominant, conservative ideology that blames the "psychological instability" of poor and black urban youth for the social decay, poverty, and endless disruptions that influence their everyday lives. Not unlike the Calvin Klein jeans advertising campaign, Clark's narrative about youth plays on dominant fears about the loss of moral authority while reinforcing images of demonization and sexual license through which adults can blame youth for existing social problems, and be titillated at the same time.

Clark's realism is too easily used – under the pretext of historical and social consideration – to transform the jolting experiences of the teenagers he represents into raw, celebratory, and stylized evocations of shock and transgression. Failing to come to grips with considerations of politics, power, and ideology, Clark avoids serious questions regarding how the viewer can account for the simultaneous aggression and powerlessness portrayed by teenagers in *Kids*, and he offers no resistance to the brutality and limited options that define their lives. Lacking depth and detail, the teenagers who inhabit Clark's film are one-dimensional to the point of caricature. David Denby is right in insisting that Clark "turns the youth of his subjects into aesthetic shock. His teens have arrived at decadence without passing through maturity. They seem to have no dimensions – intellectual, spiritual, even physical – apart from carnality. They're all tongues."[24] Clark's attempt to let the film speak for itself results in a stylized aesthetic of violence that renders the reality of violence voyeuristic, spectacular, and utterly personal rather than social and political. *Kids* avoids a central pedagogical lesson in dealing with any segment of teenage culture: unsafe sexual practices, violence, and drug use are learned behaviors that "society seems to be going all out to teach."[25] Similarly, Clark seems unacquainted with the notion that any serious portrayal of teens in this culture "that wishes to force a shift in ways of seeing, feeling and perceiving begins by questioning established power."[26] In the end, pathology and ignorance become the basis for defining the identity and agency of urban youth in Clark's world of casual violence, rampart nihilism, and incorrigible depravity. While Clark has been quick to defend his film as a cautionary tale about safe sex, as well as an indictment of adults who either don't understand teenagers or are simply not around to provide guidance for them, he fails to understand – or at least represent – that it is precisely adult society with its celebration of market values, market moralities, and its attack on civil society that "undermines the nurturing system for children."[27]

Realism and the Politics of Teenage Sexuality

Clark's framing of *Kids* in pseudodocumentary style – an aesthetic rendition of representing the world directly as it is – serves to legitimate his claim that *Kids* provides a full-blown, "no holds barred" journey into the culture of contemporary urban youth. But the cinema verité approach and loosely structured narrative cannot salvage Clark's surface exploration of a typical 24 hours in the lives of some drug and sex-crazed, morally rudderless adolescents, regardless of the aura of "truth" that structures *Kids*. Clark's use of and appeal to realism as a testimony to the film's authenticity obscures his own political and ethical responsibility in depicting a brutal and bitter portrait of a specific group of young people.[28] The invocation of truth that accompanies appeals to gritty realism serve to sanction the severity of right-wing images of urban youth at work in broader popular representations.

Clark's reliance on the verisimilitude of documentary-like narrative, playing on the audiences' fears and anxieties, and the positing of sexuality and hedonism as the driving forces of agency among urban youth, reveals the ideological conservatism that undergirds *Kids*. The consequences of portraying youth through the "transparent" lens of realism is a viewpoint marked by the absence of a reflective moral perspective, and one that offers critics and viewers a dose of media sensationalism that serves as an apology for a specific view of reality by making it appear natural, matter-of-fact and outside of human control.[29] Teen sexuality in Clark's discourse becomes a metaphor for insincerity, crudeness, violence, and death. Missing from this perspective is a political understanding of the relationship between violence and sexuality as a daily experience for those who inhabit the places and spaces that promote suffering and oppression. The dangers of such a position are exemplified in a review of *Kids* by Amy Taubin, the film critic, writing for *Sight and Sound*.

Fascinated by Clark's use in *Kids* of light, shade, and color and the film's realistic portrayal of teenage sexuality, Taubin adds an ideological twist to Clark's chic aesthetic by suggesting that adolescent socialization is determined less by culture than by biology – that is, high-powered libidos out of control. For Taubin, it is precisely this high intensity libidinal energy that gives Clark's representations of teenage youth "their feverish energy, their mad humor, their extravagantly blunt language.... [making them] mean, sordid, hungry and radiant at the same time."[30] Taubin's fascination with the aesthetics of teen sexuality excludes ideological considerations even as they are invoked, betraying the conservative politics – or the perversion – underlying her analysis. This is particularly clear when she describes the horrible rape scene of Jennie at the end of the film. Taubin writes, "it seems to take forever, leaving one time to feel as helpless as the semi-conscious Jennie, and perhaps (if one is totally honest) slightly turned on."[31] Not unlike Clark, Taubin is fascinated with teenage sexuality even when it legitimatizes voyeuristic titillation in the face of a ruthless and gruesome rape. What the perspectives of Clark and Taubin have in common is that teenage sexuality is not only a negative force in teen's lives, it also pushes the limits of an aestheticism that provides fodder for the celebration of stylized perversion and teen lust. What such thinking shares with current right-wing attempts to demonize youth is the assumption that young people are primarily identified with their bodies, especially their sexual drives. Stripped of any critical capacities, youth are defined primarily by a sexuality that is viewed as unmanageable and in need of control, surveillance, legal constraint, and other forms of disciplinary power. Similarly, this reductionist rendering of sexually active youth is a short step from stereotypical portrayals of black sexuality in which sexuality becomes a metaphor for disease, promiscuity, and social decadence.

Race Talk and Contaminating Youth

There is another disturbing aspect of *Kids* that has received little attention in the popular press. Though Telly and Casper are white, they communicate in black street lingo and call each other "nigger." Their clothes, walk, and street style mimic the black cultural fashion of hip hop. Though the black characters in *Kids* are not central to the film, they are either the recipients of violence or serve as comic backdrop for sexual stereotyping. The role of blackness is not an incidental aspect of Clark's film because it articulates too strongly with the broader dominant view that black culture is responsible for the self-destructive journey that white youth are making through the urban landmines of drugs, sex, and violence. Marcus Reeves captures this sentiment explicitly:

> Taken alongside the right's urgent moves to demonize and eliminate African American cultural influences in America and abroad (especially hip-hop music, language, and fashion) Clark's unyielding and "verité" focus on the summer-day transgressions of two hip-hop dressing/street slang-wielding/40 ounce-drinking/blunt-smoking/pussy-conquering white teenage males...provides a focus on what's making white American youth so crazy: Dey hanging out and acting like dem nasty, demoralizing niggas. That the race baiting is unintentional doesn't help.[32]

While Clark's alleged racism and demonization of youth may be unintentional, it participates in what Toni Morrison calls race talk: "The explicit insertion into everyday life of racial signs and symbols that have no meaning other than pressing African Americans to the lowest level of the racial hierarchy...the rhetorical [and representational] experience renders blacks as noncitizens, already discredited outlaws."[33] The pertinent question is not whether one can accurately declare Clark a racist, but whether the effects of his cinematic representations perpetuate racist discourse and practices in the wider society. Clearly his representations about working class and black youth hint at an ideological irresponsibility rooted in an over-identification with the recklessness of the young.

Clark's own tortured childhood reveals in part his infatuation with teenage culture. Ignored by his father and forced to accompany and aid his mother who went from door to door peddling baby photography, Clark started using his own camera to shoot his friends, many of whom were petty hoodlums, speed freaks, and thugs. Eventually Clark produced a number of books of photography, including *Tulsa* (1971), *Teenage Lust* (1983), *Larry Clark* (1992), and *The Perfect Childhood* (1993). The first two books secured Clark's image as a tough guy photographer. Despite his notoriety, Clark drifted around in the 1970s and eventually spent 19 months in jail in Oklahoma on an assault and battery charge. After the jail stint, he headed for New York and became a professional photographer. By Clark's own account, he came into puberty too late and suffered a lousy adolescence for not measuring up to his peers. In part, this experience betrays his obsession with adolescence and the horror, excitement, and intensity it reflects.[34] In a revealing comment to Terrence Rafferty, he says "Since I became a photographer I always wanted to turn back the years. Always wished I had a camera when I was a boy. Fucking in the backseat. Gangbangs. . . . A little rape. In 1972 and 1973 the kid brothers in the neighborhood took me with them in their teen lust scene. It took me back."[35] Clark reveals more than nostalgia about adolescence in general; he uncritically romanticizes the very violence he portrays in *Kids*. Clark's film replicates the erotic compulsion of the voyeur, as a middle-aged man whose infatuation with teen sex is more narcissistic than socially or politically revealing, more symptomatic than productively educational.

Where *Kids* fails in this sense, the popular British film, *Trainspotting* (1996), directed by Danny Boyle, offers a more complex and politically nuanced portrayal of youth. *Trainspotting* chronicles the lives of six young people in an economically impoverished Scotland as they descend into the world of heroin, drugs, alcoholism, and despair. Favoring the surreal over social realism, Boyle tries to capture the exhilarating highs and the debilitating lows of heroin addiction. Kids lose themselves in ecstatic numbness and dissipate into Christ-like figures as the heroin pumps through their veins to the sound of Iggy Pop's "Lust for Life." Faithful to depicting the pleasures that draw young people to smack, the film begins early on with a junkie in the shooting gallery rhapsodizing about heroin: "Take the best orgasm you've every had, multiply it by a thousand, and you're still nowhere near." Whereas *Kids* dwells on the surface of free-floating hormones, drug use, and rage, or represent the reality of AIDS and youth, *Trainspotting* depicts the horrors of addiction, withdrawal, and indiscriminate violence. In one scene, Ewan McGregor's Renton plunges into a shit-filled toilet to retrieve the heroin-laced suppositories he has lost. Trying to kick his habit, Renton is haunted by distorted images of his life on the streets, violent friends, and the horrifying memory of the neglected baby who died in the shooting gallery he occupied with his heroin-addicted mates. *Trainspotting* refuses the cheap voyeurism of Larry Clark's *Kids*. Instead, it explores with humor, surreal images, and unflinching sensitivity the complex dynamic of pleasure, pain, and unchecked narcissism that accompanies heroin use.

Crackling with dead-end grittiness, *Trainspotting* posits a similarity between drugs and the stifling repression of ruthless capitalism. Conventional tensions between critique and celebration are bypassed in this film, just as the politics of the film refuses a preachy moralism. *Trainspotting* never lets the audience forget that behind the drugs, pleasure, narcissism, and violence is a society that creates the economic, social, cultural, and historical conditions for youth who engage in such behavior. Bob Dole got it wrong when he claimed in his 1996 presidential campaign that *Trainspotting* celebrates heroin use. On the contrary, Boyle's film argues that heroin usage is not going to go away by telling young people to just say no as long as civic life is modeled on crass consumerism and young people live under impoverished economic and social conditions. With society dominated by a particularly harsh and hypocritical form of capitalist accumulation as the only alternative, drugs will retain their allure within a broader cycle of extremity and hopelessness.

Recovering an Ethical Discourse for a Pedagogy of Representations

For too long, progressives have viewed the struggle over culture as less significant than what is often referred to as the "real" world of politics, that is, the world of material suffering, hunger, poverty, and physical abuse. While such a distinction suggests that representations of rape and its actual experience cannot be confused, it is also imperative to understand how both modalities interact in providing the basis for constructing moral arguments as practices, recognizing how interpretations have a consequential impact regarding how people make discriminatory judgments about what is better or worse, and in doing so provide the grounds to act by addressing grave human problems in both their symbolic and material forms.[36] Struggles over popular culture, for instance, represent a different but no less important site of politics. For it is precisely on the terrain of

culture that identities are produced, values learned, histories legitimated, and knowledge appropriated. Culture is the medium through
which children fashion their individual and collective identities and
learn, in part, how to narrate themselves in relation to others. Culture
is also the shifting ground where new and old literacies – ways of
understanding the world – are produced and legitimated in the
service of national identity, public life, and civic responsibility. As a
site of learning and struggle, culture becomes the primary referent for
understanding the multiple sites in which pedagogy works, power
operates, and authority is secured or contested. More specifically,
Hollywood films represent more than weak politics or innocent
entertainment. In fact, they are powerful pedagogical sites where
children and adults are being offered specific lessons in how to
view themselves, others, and the world they inhabit. In this sense,
such films must be seen as a serious object of social analysis by anyone
who takes education seriously. But recognizing that Hollywood films
function as teaching machines demands more than including them in
the school curricula; it also demands that educators and other cultural
workers bring questions of justice and ethics to bear on the form and
content of such films. This becomes particularly important when
raising questions about the limits of such representations, particularly
when they portray children in degrading terms, legitimate the culture
of violence, and define agency and desire outside of the discourse of
compassion and moral responsibility.

As the right wing wages war against sex education, condom
distribution in schools, sex on the Internet, and video stores that
carry pornographic films, there is a curious silence from progressive
and other radical cultural workers about the ways in which children
and sex are portrayed in films, advertising, and media culture in
general. While it is important for progressives to continue to argue
for freedom of expression in defending films or other cultural forms
that they might find offensive, they also need to take up what it
means to provide an ethical discourse from which to criticize those
images, discourses, and representations that might be destructive to
the psychological health of children or serve to undermine the
normative foundations of a viable democracy. Appeals to the First
Amendment, the right of artistic expression, and the dignity of

consent, are crucial elements in expanding cultural democracy, but they are insufficient for promoting an ethical discourse that cultivates an ethics of concern, self-responsibility, and compassion. Progressives must be more open about their commitment to political and ethical principles that recognize how structures of oppression operate through the media, and particularly through those public spheres that shape children's culture. How children derive meaning from the media suggests a broader concern for making those who control media culture in this society accountable for the pedagogies they produce. Cultural workers such as Larry Clark have a responsibility, both political and moral, to reflect upon the possible implications of their work. The obligation here is not legal, it is moral – to consider whether young people will benefit from representations of sexuality that legitimate a "callous culture of self-centered individuals for whom physical pleasure is all."[37] At stake here is the need to be attentive to media culture as a site of cultural politics where the struggle over the content and context of representations must be linked to broader struggles in the society to improve the quality of democracy itself.

Notes

1. A version of this essay appeared in *Review of Education/Pedagogy/Cultural Studies* 18.3 (1996): 307–31.
2. Cornel West, "America's Three-fold Crisis." *Tikkun* 9.2 (1994): 42.
3. Deena Weinstein, "Expendable Youth: The Rise and Fall of Youth Culture," in Jonathon S. Epstein (ed.), *Adolescents and Their Music* (New York: Garland, 1994), pp. 67–83.
4. George Lipsitz, "We Know What Time It Is: Race, Class and Youth Culture in the Nineties," in Andrew Ross and Tricia Rose (eds.), *Microphone Fiends: Youth Music and Youth Culture* (New York: Routledge, 1994), p. 18.
5. Camille Sweeney, "Portrait of the American Child." *The New York Times Magazine* (October 8, 1995): 52–3.
6. Cited in Robert Kuttner, "The Overclass is Waging Class Warfare With a Vengeance." *The Boston Globe* (July 24, 1995): 11.

7. Cited in Associated Press, "Global Study: U.S. Has Widest Gap Between Rich and Poor." *Chicago Tribune* (October 28, 1995): Section 1, p. 21.

8. See Peter Edelman, "The Worst Thing Bill Clinton Has Done." *The Atlantic Monthly* 279.3 (1997): 43–58. See also the moving analysis by Deborah R. Connolly of the problems experienced daily by a group of poor women trying their best to negotiate a social service system that is under served and overburdened. In Deborah R. Connolly, *Homeless Mothers: Face to Face with Women and Poverty* (Minneapolis: University of Minnesota Press, 2000).

9. Holly Sklar, "Young and Guilty by Stereotype." *Z Magazine* 6 (July/ August, 1993): 54.

10. "Tagging is the police practice of picking up all Black men at least once and entering their names into police records." In Denver, it has been reported that tagging was so successful that an "estimated two-thirds of all Black men between the ages of 12 and 24 were on the list. Whites made up only 7 percent of the list in a city that is 80 percent Caucasian." Cited in Christian Parenti, "Urban Militarism." *Z Magazine* (June, 1994): 49.

11. Steven R. Donziger, *The Real War on Crime: The Report of the National Criminal Justice Commission* (New York: Harper Perennial, 1996), p. 101.

12. Cited in Eyal Press, "The Color Test." *Lingua Franca* (October, 2000): 55.

13. Tricia Rose, "A Style Nobody Can Deal With: Politics, Style and the Postindustrial City in Hip Hop," in Andrew Ross and Tricia Rose, *Microphone Fiends* op.cit., p. 78.

14. Herman Gray, *Watching Race: Television and the Struggle for "Blackness"* (Minneapolis: University of Minnesota Press, 1995), p. 165. Gray's book provides an excellent analysis of the racial coding that goes on in the electronic and mass-mediated culture.

15. Marilyn Ivy, "Memory, Silence and Satan." *The Nation* 261.22 (December 25, 1995): 834–5.

16. Ibid.

17. Lee Quinby, *Anti-Apocalypse: Exercises in Genealogical Criticism* (Minneapolis: University of Minnesota Press, 1994), p. 6.

18. John Berger, *Ways of Seeing* (London: BBC, 1972), p. 7.

19. Trip Gabriel, "Think You Had a Bad Adolescence?" *The New York Times* (July 31, 1995): C1.

20. Cited in Michael Warner, "Negative Attitude." *Voice Literary Supplement* (September 6, 1995): 25.

21. In response to a interviewer who suggests that one message of the film is that boys are bad news and girls should beware, Clark responded, maybe ironically, that "the girls come off as the most honest, the strongest." One can't help but wonder how Clark defines these terms, and in comparison

to what references, both within and outside of the film. Cited in Jack Womack, "Teenage Lust." *Spin* (September, 1995): 70.

22. Michael Atkinson cited in Ed Morales, "Skateboard Jungle." *The Village Voice* (September 12, 1995): 66.

23. Teresa de Lauretis, *Technologies of Gender* (Bloomington: Indiana University Press, 1987), p. 13.

24. David Denby, "School's Out Forever." *New York* (July 31, 1995): 44.

25. Sklar, "Young and Guilty by Stereotype," op.cit., p. 11.

26. Stanley Aronowitz, *Dead Artists, Live Theories and Other Cultural Problems* (New York: Routledge, 1994), p. 42.

27. Cornel West, "America's Three-Fold Crisis." *Tikkun* 9.2 (1994): 42. For two books that deal specifically with the complex forces that poor kids negotiate while retaining a sense of dignity and agency, see Sharon Thompson, *Going All the Way: Teenage Girls' Tales of Sex, Romance & Pregnancy* (New York: Hill and Wang, 1995); Jane Pratt and Kelli Pryor, *For Real: The Uncensored Truth About America's Teenagers* (New York: Hyperion, 1995).

28. On Clark's documentary realism, see James Crump, "Quasi-Documentary: Evolution of a Photographic Style." *The New Art Examiner* (March, 1996): 22–8.

29. On the issue of how public memory is constructed, see Geoffrey Hartman, "Public Memory and Its Discontents." *Raritan* XIII.4 (Spring 1994): 28.

30. Amy Taubin, "Chilling and Very Hot." *Sight and Sound* (November, 1995): 17.

31. Ibid.

32. Marcus Reeves cited in Ed Morales, "Skateboard Jungle," op.cit., p. 64.

33. Toni Morrison, "On the Backs of Blacks." *Time* (Fall, 1993): 57.

34. Some interesting interviews and comments on Clark's life can be found in Jim Lewis, "Larry Clark's First Feature Film, 'Kids.'" *Harper's Bazar* (August, 1995): 144–5, 190–1; Gabriel, "Think You Had a Bad Adolescence?" op.cit., pp. C1, C7; Jack Womack, "Teenage Lust," op.cit., pp. 65–70; Terrence Rafferty, "Growing Pains." *The New Yorker* 51.22 (July 31, 1995): 80–2.

35. Rafferty, "Growing Pains." op.cit., p. 80.

36. For a brilliant analysis of ethics and social action, see Beverly Harrison, *Making Connections: Essays in Feminist Social Ethics* (Boston: Beacon Press, 1985).

37. David Smith Allyn, "Sex With a Heart." *Tikkun* 10.6 (November/December, 1995), p. 92.

PART III

Race and the Culture of Violence in Hollywood Films

10

Racism and the Aesthetic of Hyper-real Violence: *Pulp Fiction* and Other Visual Tragedies[1]

I have no responsibility to anything other than my shit and the characters and being as true to them as I possibly can. . . . They [the audience] don't have to watch, and that's fine. I don't have any patience with all that self-righteous shit. Just don't watch it, man.

Quentin Tarantino[2]

Cinema and the Culture of Violence

American cinema has increasingly provided a site of convergence for depicting both the inner-city "reality" of black-on-black youth violence and for promoting a renewed "acceptability and/or tolerance of straightforward racist doctrine."[3] Recent films focusing on black urban violence such as *Boyz N the Hood* (1991), *Juice* (1992), *Menace II Society* (1993), *Sugar Hill* (1994), *Fresh* (1994), *New Jersey Drive* (1995), and *Belly* (1998) have attracted national media coverage because they do not simply represent contemporary urban realities but also reinforce the popular perception that everyday black urban life and violent crime mutually define each other. Cinema appears to be providing a new language and aesthetic in which the city becomes the central site for social disorder and violence, and black youth in particular become agents of crime, pathology, and moral decay.

Real life and celluloid images blur as the representations of race and violence proliferate more broadly through the news media's extensive coverage of youth violence. Such coverage, not infrequently, highlights gore, guts, hysteria, and other tawdry Hollywood effects to punctuate its sensationalist, often racist, commentary. The relationship between the everyday and cinematic representations is often taken up as causal, as when the national media recently focused on Hispanic youth in Los Angeles, New York, and New Jersey who rioted or fought each other outside of the movie theaters in which gangsta films were being shown. In examining these real and symbolic representations of black-on-black violence, the popular press used the incident to link exposure to media violence with aggressive antisocial behavior in real life. The press did not use these events to call public attention to the "violence to the mind, body, and spirit of crumbling schools, low teacher expectations, unemployment and housing discrimination, racist dragnets and everyday looks of hate by people who find [black youth] guilty by suspicion."[4] Instead of focusing on how larger social injustices and failed policies, especially those at the root of America's system of inequality, contribute to a culture of violence that is a tragedy for all youth, the dominant media transformed the growing incidence of youth violence into a focus on black-on-black fratricide. In this particular instance, the representation of black youth was used as a vehicle to thematize the causal relationship between violence and the discourse of pathology. Such racially coded discourse serves to mobilize white fears and legitimate "drastic measures" in social policy in the name of crime reform.[5] Moreover, the discourse of race and violence provides a sense of social distance and moral privilege that places dominant white society outside of the web of violence and social responsibility.

Another example of how cinematic representations and "objective" reporting mutually reinforce a narrow, racial coding of violence can be seen in an incident that happened at a local movie theater in Oakland, California. A group of Castlemont High School students in Oakland, California were taken to see *Schindler's List* (1993) on Martin Luther King Day as part of the school's effort to deepen their sense of history and oppression, and to broaden their understanding of the struggle for human rights. The students, most of them black and Hispanic, laughed at some of the most violent scenes in the film.

The manager of the theater reacted in shock and asked them to leave. The story received national attention in the popular press, and echoed the stereotypical assumption that these students mirrored in their own personalities the nihilism and pathology that inevitably lead to increased disorder and criminality. In the age of Trent Lott and Tom DeLay, pathology has become a characteristic of the racially marginal space of the urban city, a space of gruesome violence that threatens to spread outward to the "safe" confines of middle-class America.

Hardly a paragon of objectivity, the media betrays through its portrayal of this episode a certain tragic irony in representing black youth as the source rather than the victim of violence. In fact, recent statistics reveal that "young black males constituted 17.7 percent of all homicide victims, even though they made up only 1.3 percent of the US population. [Moreover] black men over age 24 were victims of homicide at a rate of 65.7 per 100,00, compared with 7.8 per 100,00 for white men."[6] The media portrait nonetheless reflects the conservative mood of the country: treating violent youth as dangerous urban aliens is a guaranteed crowd pleaser; focusing on the devastating effects of (white) racism, rising poverty and unemployment for a generation of black youth is less popular.[7]

What is so crucial about the above examples is that the largely white dominant media, while critical of the particular response of black and Hispanic children to the inhumane consequences of Nazi violence, refused to analyze in any significant way the larger culture of violence that permeates the United States. Such an investigation might explain both the insensitive response of the schoolchildren to the violence portrayed in *Schindler's List* but it would also demand that white society examine its own responsibility and complicity in producing an ever-spreading culture of violence, whose hip nihilism makes it difficult for anyone to draw a meaningful line between the normal and the pathological. Moreover, as the context and the conditions for the production of violent representations are justified in the name of entertainment and high box office profits, youth increasingly experience themselves as both the subject and the objects of everyday violence and brutality. The cheap editorializing by the popular press and dominant media offer skewed portrayals of youth that cover over the fact that "young people aged 12 to 17 are the most common victims of crime in America, with a 1 in 13 chance of being raped, robbed, or assaulted."[8] While the relationship between representational violence and its impact on children and youth is not clear, the culture of violence spawned by television, videos, and film is too pervasive to be ignored or dismissed.

I want to argue that media culture is the central terrain on which the new racism has emerged. What counts as a source of education for many youth appears to reside in the spawning of electronic media, including radio talk shows, television, and film. This is evident in the resurgent racism that has become popular among many talk show hosts such as Bob Grant, who refers to African-Americans as "primates." It is also apparent in films such as *Just Cause* (1995) in which traditional stereotypes of young black males as rapists are recycled in order to fuel conservative enthusiasm for legalizing the death penalty. Television culture increasingly reduces black youths to the figure of the urban gangsta and rap music as the musical signifier for legitimating a drug culture, violence, and sexism. Violence has become increasingly a source of pleasure in a media-saturated culture. Either displayed as a site of voyeuristic titillation and gory spectacle, or defined primarily as an ideology of the aesthetic, violence functions as a defining principle in all the major mediums of information and entertainment. Given the ways in which violence becomes part of a new aesthetic, it is all the more imperative for educators and cultural workers to find ways of scrutinizing its mechanisms. They must explore its political and pedagogical implications for producing and legitimizing particular ideologies and representations of youth. How do educators prepare youth and others to think through representations of violence in order to understand them critically as "vehicles through which society's racial contradictions, injustices, and failed policies are mediated?"[9] Educators need pedagogical strategies that move between dominant and oppositional appropriations of violence. These will enable them to develop alternative understandings of how violence is produced, framed aesthetically, circulated, and ruptured. Violence may then be connected with broader considerations of critique, public discourse, and social engagement.[10]

RACE AND THE CULTURE OF VIOLENCE

The moment of violence in films is never arbitrary nor innocent. Yet, there is no singular reading or simple yardstick that can be used to either condone or condemn how violence is represented, taken up by diverse audiences, or used to maximize pleasure so as to give the aesthetics and content of violence a liberatory or oppressive edge. Cinematic violence can be used to probe the depths of everyday life in ways that expand one's understanding of tyranny and domination; such violence can also be used to maximize the sleazy side of pleasure, reinforce demeaning stereotypes, or provoke cheap voyeurism. Cinematic violence operates on many registers, and any theoretical and pedagogical attempt to deal with complex representations of violence must be discriminatory in taking up such distinctions. As widespread as the culture of violence might be, it is especially imperative that educators, parents, and citizens challenge the representations of violence that have become a defining principle of the visual media. Such a challenge needs to be enunciated critically as part of a broader public policy to both protect youth, especially young children, and enable them to distinguish between two kinds of violence—violence of the spectacle and a representational violence that allows them to identify with the suffering of others, display empathy, and bring their own ethical commitments to bear.

In what follows, I want to offer first an arbitrary and schematic definition of different representations of violence in order to provide a theoretical groundwork for making important discriminations about how violence is constructed in films, how it mobilizes specific forms of identification, and how it might be addressed pedagogically. Second, I will examine how the ultraviolence emerging in popular films heralded as part of a new avant garde constructs forms of cultural racism. (This ultraviolence is an aestheticized violence that appeals to a generation of youth raised on the fast-paced programming of MTV and the ethical indifference of the 1980s). In addition, I will take up how racially coded violence works to exclude dominant white society from any responsibility or complicity with the larger culture of violence while simultaneously shifting the burden of crime and social decay to people of color, working-class whites, and other subordinate groups. In developing this perspective, I will explore the important intersections of what can be called entertainment, politics, and pedagogy in the electronic media by addressing the widely acclaimed films by Quentin Tarantino, *Reservoir Dogs* (1992) and *Pulp Fiction* (1994). Finally, I will conclude by suggesting how educators and other cultural workers can think through pedagogical and political strategies to understand and critically engage racism as inextricably linked to the rising culture of violence in the United States.

Ritualistic, Symbolic, and Hyper-real Violence

Statistics regarding the representation of violence in media culture border on the outrageous. George Gerbner, a professor and dean emeritus at the Annenberg School for Communication at the University of Pennsylvania, has been monitoring violence on television for the last 20 years. According to Gerbner's studies, the major broadcast networks average about five acts of violence an hour in their prime-time programming. This is an alarming figure given that the visual media has become an overwhelming fact of cultural life. "The [television] set is on an average of 7 hours a day in the average American home. . . . Most viewers watch by the clock and not by the program."[11] For example, it has been reported that for the last 15 years on Saturday morning, when children do most of their viewing, the networks averaged about 25 acts of violence an hour. Moreover, "researchers estimate that the average child will watch 100,000 acts of simulated violence before graduating from elementary school. And studies have shown that poor children see even more."[12] In addition, "by the age of 18, the average American child has witnessed 18,000 simulated murders on television."[13] Increasingly, motion picture violence has followed the path of television, especially since much of the profits generated from theater movies will be made through videocassette sales. Serious films have given way to the blockbuster, and the trade-off has been an increase in the number of violent films shown in movie theaters across the United States.

If educators are going to move beyond simply condemning representational violence in a wholesale fashion, it becomes necessary to draw distinctions, however crudely, between violence that is an empty spectacle and violence that can illuminate important messages about the basis of humanity and inhumanity. Thus, the imperative for teachers and others goes beyond simply quantifying violence in the visual media. For example, the violence portrayed in films as different as *Schindler's List* (1993) and *Die Hard With a Vengeance* (1995) register disparate interests and assumptions. In the former, violence is used to inscribe in public memory the tragic event of the Holocaust, an historical event that should be neither forgotten nor repeated. However, the violence in spectacle films such as *Die Hard With a Vengeance* (1995) is kitsch, serving up cheap entertainment. This particular form of violence celebrates the sensational and the gruesome; it contains no redeeming value except to parade its endless stream of blood and gore at the expense of dramatic structure, emotional depth, and social relevance.

Hence, in analyzing visual violence, I will loosely distinguish three forms: ritualistic, symbolic, and hyper-real. First, there is what I will call ritualistic violence, ritualistic in the sense that violence is at the center of the genres that produce it–horror, action-adventure, Hollywood drama – utterly banal, predictable, and often stereotypically masculine. This type of violence is pure spectacle in form and superficial in content. Audiences connect with such depictions viscerally; yet it is not edifying in the best pedagogical sense, offering few insights into the complex range of human behavior and struggles. Ritualistic violence is racy, sensationalist, and testosterone-laden. It does not recast ordinary events or critically attempt to shift sensibilities. On the contrary, it glows in the heat of the spectacle, shock, and contrivance, yet it is entirely formulaic. This is the Bruce Willis and Arnold Schwarzenegger school of violence, fueling blockbusters such as *Die Hard With a Vengeance* (1995) and *True Lies* (1994). Other examples can be found in films such as *Speed* (1994), *Blown Away* (1994), and *The Fugitive* (1994).

Within these films there is an "echo of the pornographic in maximizing the pleasure of violence."[14] Representations of ritualistic violence derive their force through countless repetitions of graphic cruelty, serving to numb the senses with an endless stream of infantilized, histrionic flair. For example, the hero of *Robocop II* (1990) massacres 81 people, while Bruce Willis yields a body count of 264 killings in *Die Hard 2* (1990).[15] Excessive violence, in this case, is valorized to the degree that it reproduces the genre with new psychological and visual twists, yet never asking more from the audience than the programmed response. Referencing only itself as heightened spectacle, violence in the Hollywood blockbuster film offers viewers voyeuristic identification rather than providing an opportunity for the audience to think through and scrutinize the mechanisms and implications of violence.

One of the pedagogical consequences of ritualistic violence is that it contributes to the commonsensical assumption that Hollywood film is strictly about entertainment and need not be judged for its political and pedagogical implications. Hence, as a formalist principle, it is complicitous with other forms of media culture that offer no challenge to the current conservative attempt to construct public memory as part of a broader effort to demonize the legacy of the 1960s with their association of youth and resistance. Passing for simply entertainment, ritualistic violence in film draws attention away from representational politics, which often codes black youth as criminals, welfare recipients as morally depraved, and the city as a site of degeneracy. But ritualistic violence in films does more than entertain: it erases history as it rewrites it and in doing so appeals to an earlier age when the model of youth was suburban, white, and raised by down-to-earth parents of the Ozzie and Harriet lookalike variety.

Ritualistic violence in many ways serves as a prop to evoke and legitimate a largely conservative view of public memory, and often plays to both the fear of crime and the desire for another time in history when minorities knew their place and women were not on the picket lines fighting for their rights. Amidst the glut of violent, blockbuster films, Hollywood movies like *Forrest Gump* (1994), *Nell* (1994), and *I.Q.* (1994) appear as welcomed, clean family fun, a cinematic antidote that harks back to a nostalgic past. But such films do more than serve as a relief from the overdose of cinematic violence; they are also indicative of how public memory gets rewritten Hollywood-style. Such "harmless" films serve largely both to entertain and legitimate a past cleansed of conflict. Within this cinematic script, cultural differences become un-American, and a wilfully anti-intellectual individualism provides the model for citizenship. But Hollywood films do more than induce historical amnesia; they are also sites of struggle and resistance both in terms of what they try to say and how they are taken up by diverse audiences. It is precisely through the defining principles of a critical self-consciousness regarding their own location within the larger culture and their concern with social criticism that Hollywood film has engaged and taken up what can be called symbolic violence.

The second type of violence, symbolic violence, has a long cinematic tradition and can be recognized in more recent films such as Oliver Stone's *Platoon* (1987), Clint Eastwood's *Unforgiven* (1992), Neil Jordan's *The Crying Game* (1992), and Steven Spielberg's *Schindler's List* (1993). Symbolic violence attempts to connect the visceral and the reflective. It couples the mobilization of emotion and the haunting images of the unwelcome with an attempt to "give meaning and import to our mortal twitchings. . . . it shakes everything up, reforming the fictive environment around itself."[16] Symbolic violence does not become an end in itself; it serves to reference a broader logic and set of insights. Instead of providing the viewer with stylistic gore that offers the immediacy of visual pleasure and escape, symbolic violence probes the complex contradictions that shape human agency, the limits of rationality, and the existential issues that tie us to other human beings and a broader social world. Symbolic violence refuses the techniques of fast-paced rhythmic frames, or a dizzying pattern of repetitious images. Instead, it attempts to "find ways of scrutinizing the mechanisms and implications of violence through different processes of framing, juxtaposing, repeating and quoting images"[17] within a context that invites critical and meaningful commentary.

For example, in *Platoon* Oliver Stone uses violence as a vehicle for rewriting the Hollywood war movie and in doing so attempts to demystify national chauvinism as a legitimation for waging war in Vietnam. *Platoon* also foregrounds violence as an explosive index of class and racial tensions that give rise to contradictory loyalties, acts of aggression, and the painful psychological experiences many troops endured in the jungles of Vietnam. In this case, violence has a determining role, that is, it has consequences portrayed in the film that connect morality and human agency.

A similar example of symbolic violence can be seen in Clint Eastwood's film, *Unforgiven*, which virtually rewrites the traditional John Wayne version of the American West. Against the romantic narratives of helpless heroines, shootouts at sundown, and cowboy heroism, Eastwood creates a film in which violence serves as both a spectacle and an ethical referent for exploding the myth of a West in which women are only ornaments, justice is pristine and unadulterated, and white male heroes bask in the splendor of the fast draw. *Unforgiven* rewrites the traditional and revisionist Western and in doing so raises ethical questions concerning how violence has been mythologized and decontextualized so as to reinvent a nostalgic and utterly false version of the American past, a past that once again seemed to shape public memory and national identity with the election of Ronald Reagan in 1980.[18] Through a cinematic rupturing of the culture of violence, *Unforgiven* engages in a critical form of memory work that ruptures a conservative rendering of history.

The third type of cinematic violence I want to address is hyper-real violence. This form of violence has emerged relatively recently and can be seen in a number of contemporary films that include *Reservoir Dogs*, a nicely textured film that boldly chronicles the gang violence and torture of a police officer after a botched jewelry heist; *Natural Born Killers* (1994), which tells the story of Mickey and Mallory, two young serial killers who become media sensations; *Killing Zoe* (1993), which tells the story of a failed bank robbery as a pretext for exploring the loss of intimacy, romance, and the psychological depths of psychotic violence; and *Pulp Fiction*, the most recent and celebrated of films depicting the new violence. *Pulp Fiction* is constructed loosely around three stories that pays homage to the pulp crime genre of the 1930s in the United States. On the international scene, hyper-real violence can be seen in films such as Johnny Woo's Hong Kong production, *The Killer* (1989), and in the 1992 Belgian movie *Man Bites Dog* by Remy Belvaux and Andre Bonzel.

What is new in these films is the emergence of a form of ultra-violence marked by technological overstimulation, gritty dialogue, dramatic storytelling, parody, and an appeal to gutsy realism. Whereas ritualist violence is shorn of any critical social engagement, hyper-real violence exploits the seamy side of controversial issues. It appeals to primal emotions and has a generational quality that captures the actual violence that youth encounter in the streets and neighborhoods of an increasingly racially divided America.

Hyper-real violence – with its technological wizardry and its formalist appeals, irony, guilt-free humor, wise guy dialogue, and genuflection to the cultural pap of the 1970s – represents a marker of the age. In some ways it both demonstrates and redefines Hannah Arendt's insightful comment about the banality of violence.[19] For Arendt, violence is banal because its ubiquity makes it more difficult for human beings in the twentieth century not to be implicated or addressed by it. It was precisely the ubiquity and the mundane nature of violence that Arendt believed made it a serious danger to civil society. The hyper-real violence of the new gangsta genre parading as film noir appears to mock Arendt's insight by isolating terrifying events from wider social contexts. Films in this genre are filled with an endless stream of characters who thrive in a moral limbo and define themselves by embracing senseless acts of violence as a defining principle of life legitimated by a hard dose of cruelty and cynicism. For the mostly young directors of the new hyper-real violent films, it is precisely the familiarity and commonality of everyday violence that renders it a prime target to commodify, sensationalize, and subordinate to the ideology of the aesthetic of realism. Audiences can gaze at celluloid blood and gore and comfortably refuse any complicity or involvement for engaging the relationship between symbolic and real violence.

But hyper-real violence in the new cinema represents more than moral indifference coupled with cultural slumming. The form and content of the new hyper-real films go beyond emptying representations of violence of any ethical content, they also legitimate rather than contest, by virtue of their documentary appeal to what is, the spreading acts of symbolic and real violence rooted in and shaped by a larger racist culture.[20] Representations of violence can no longer be separated from representations of race; they mutually inform each other in terms of what is both included and left out of such representations. Nowhere is this more evident than in the wave of new avant garde films informed by hyper-real violence. But before I discuss *Reservoir Dogs* and *Pulp Fiction* as exemplary films in this

205

regard, I want to map out briefly some representative signposts indicating the extent to which race, white panic, and dominant media images of violence circulate in the wider culture of representations so as to lend credibility to the racism being produced in the new wave of hyper-real violent films.

White Panic and the Racial Coding of Violence

Incidents of material violence in the United States have become so commonplace that they seem to constitute the defining principle of everyday life. Acts of violence ranging from the banal to the sensational increasingly dominate the contents of newspaper accounts, television news programs, and popular magazines. What I want to explore, however, are the ways in which the never-ending images of violence seem to cancel out the actual experience and suffering caused by violence as the American public is bombarded with daily images of violence ranging from coverage of the O.J. Simpson trial to reports of serial killers who maim and murder victims with bombs sent in packages through the mail. Featured in the newspaper, the evening news, or talk radio, the reality of everyday violence is supplemented by a culture of violence produced as entertainment for broadcast and cable television programs, movie theater films, and video games. Within this expanding culture of violence, the relationship between fact and fiction becomes more difficult to comprehend as real life crimes become the basis for television and movie entertainment and newscasting becomes increasingly formulaic, sensational, and less neutral and objective.

While violence appears to cross over designated borders of class, race, and social space, the representation of violence in the popular media is largely depicted in racial terms.[21] As the fact reporting and entertainment spheres merge in media culture, representations of violence are largely portrayed through forms of racial coding that suggests that violence is a black problem, a problem outside of white suburban America. In fact, white Americans fancy themselves the new besieged group of the late 20th/early 21st century – voiceless and powerless before the thought police of the political correctness movement. No longer safe from the threat of urban violence they increasingly view themselves as prisoners in their own homes and neighborhoods.

Beneath the growing culture of violence, both real and simulated, there lies a deep-seated racism that has produced what I want to call a white moral panic. The elements of this panic are rooted, in part, in a growing fear among the white middle class over the declining quality of social, political, and economic life that has resulted from an increase in poverty, drugs, hate, guns, unemployment, social disfranchisement, and hopelessness. Expressions of the white panic can be seen in the passing of Proposition 187, which assigns increasing crime, welfare abuse, moral decay, and social disorder to the flood of Mexican immigrants streaming across the borders of the United States. White panic can also be read in the depictions of crime that appears in national newspapers and magazines. For example, *Time* magazine, following the arrest of O.J. Simpson, presented his jail mug shot on its cover with a much darkened face, feeding into the national obsession of the black male as a dreaded criminal – a racist gesture for which the magazine subsequently had to issue an apology. Even more aggressively, *The New York Times Magazine* ran a cover story on June 27, 1993 titled "A Predator's Struggle to Tame Himself" accompanied with a picture of a tall, black male prisoner on the cover. In August of 1994, *The Times Magazine* ran another cover story on youth gangs, and put a picture of an Afro-American woman on the cover. Again in December of 1994, it ran yet another story titled, "The Black Man is in Terrible Trouble. Whose Problem is That?" The story was accompanied by a cover picture of the back of a black man's shaved head, displayed with a gold ring prominently hanging from his ear. The following week *The New York Times Magazine* ran a lead story on welfare and referenced it with the image of a black woman on the cover. What is reprehensible about the endless repetition of these images is that they not only reproduce racist stereotypes about blacks by portraying them as criminals and welfare cheats, but they remove whites from any responsibility or complicity for the violence and poverty that has become so endemic to American life. Racist representations feed and valorize the assumption that unemployment, poverty, disenfranchisement, and violence are a black problem. One of the more recent expressions of resurgent racism in the media can be seen in the massive popular news, television, and magazine coverage given to *The Bell Curve* by Richard Herrnstein and Charles Murray, a book that legitimates the position that racism "is a respectable intellectual position, and has a legitimate place in the national debate on race."[22] Herrnstein and Murray, among others, provide a discourse in which the white majority righteously situates itself in the role of moral witness and judge of the fate of black people in this country.

The racial coding of violence is especially powerful and pervasive in its association of crime with black youth. As Holly Sklar points out, "In shorthand stereotype, black and Latino boys mean dangerous, girls mean welfare, they all mean drugs. They are all suspect."[23] One need only consider widespread popular media coverage linking black rap music with gang violence, drugs, and urban terror, or former Senator Bob Dole's attack on rap artists for contributing to violence in the social order. This is the same Bob Dole who is a major supporter of the National Rifle Association and led the charge in the senate to repeal the ban on assault weapons. Motion pictures depicting "realistic" portrayals of black ghetto life add fuel to the fire by becoming a register in the popular mind for legitimating race and violence as mutually informing categories.[24] The consequences of such racist stereotyping produce more than prejudice and fear in the white collective sensibility. Racist representations of violence also feed the increasing public outcry for tougher crime bills designed to build more prisons and legislate get-tough policies with minorities of color and class. All of this is accompanied by the proliferation of pseudoscientific studies that envision the creation of a custodial state to contain "some substantial minority of the nation's population, while the rest of America tries to go about its business."[25]

In the mass-mediated cultural spheres that shape individual and social consciousness, social and political causes of violence are often elided. The media highlights the simplistic calls of conservative politicians for more prisons, orphanages for the children of poor black and white mothers, and censorship of the arts and public broadcasting. Fueled by a ruthless indifference to human suffering coupled with a penchant for simplistic answers, the conservative

208

approach to violence and other social issues ignores pedagogically appropriate alternatives such as education, community building, and public debate. Whether in the portrayal of popular black music or in Hollywood movies, a predisposition toward violence becomes the defining attribute and justification for indicting an entire racial group. Of course, violence is not absent from representations of white youth and adults, but it is rarely depicted so as to suggest that aggression and violence represent an inherent quality of what it means to be white, or that violence is a central construction in the formation of the history of dominant white society in the United States.

On the contrary, violence in films about white youth is framed almost exclusively through the language of individual pathology, political extremism, or class-specific nihilism. For example, the white youth portrayed in *Natural Born Killers* become acceptable to white audiences because the possibility for identification never emerges. They are pathological killers, children of grossly dysfunc-tional families, clearly outside of the parameters of normalcy that prevail in white society in general.[26] Another critically acclaimed avant-garde youth film, *True Romance* (1993), couples a certain post-modern penchant for popular culture, amoralism, and a slick aestheti-cism with violence. In this film, 1970s retro trash and pop cultural icons inform contemporary white youth culture, including an Elvis character with a gold jacket who dispenses advice in bathrooms, a heroin addict who enjoys kung fu movies, and a leading character who works in a comic book store. Youth in this film become a metaphor for the end of civilization. Exhaustion and despair define their connection with a society in which the only stimulation left appears to be in the spectacle of sensation and the thrill machine of gratuitous violence.

Youth are isolated and estranged in these films and can offer no indictment of American society, not only because they embrace a disturbing nihilism, but also because they appear marginal, shiftless, and far removed from Dan Quayle's notion of American family values. Youth are on the margins, and the hip violence in which they engage has the comfortable aura of low life craziness about it. You won't find these kids in a Disney film. The representation of white youth violence emerges through an endless series of repugnant characters whose saving grace, for those who might have to endure the shock of recognition, resides in their being on the extreme psychological and economic edges of society. Often when the media focuses on white youth who commit violent acts, anguished questions of agency, moral accountability, and social responsibility do not apply. Agency for violent white youth is contaminated by a personal pathology that never questions the social and historical conditions at work in its own construction. On the other hand, in the racially coded representations of violence in black films, violence does not register as the result of individual pathology. Here the violence of representation serves to indict blacks as an entire racial group while legitimating the popular stereotype that their communities are the central sites of crime, lawlessness, and immorality.

For example, in films about violent white youth such as *Laws of Gravity* (1992), *Kalifornia* (1993), *Natural Born Killers* (1994), and *Kids* (1995) the language of hopelessness and desperation cancels out any investigation into how agency is constructed as opposed to simply guaranteed in the larger political and social sense. But in black youth films such as *Menace II Society* (1993), *Jason's Lyrics* (1994), and *New Jersey Drive* (1995) there is a haunting sense that blacks are solely responsible for the narrow range of possibilities that inform their lives and result in living out their everyday existence with little hope amidst a culture of nihilism and deprivation.[27] In the end, black powerlessness becomes synonymous with criminality. By refusing to explore the complex constraints black youth have to face in everyday life, these films avoid altogether the role that historical, social, and economic determinants play in setting limits to human agency within poor urban neighborhoods. Consequently, such films offer no language for illuminating social forces outside of the discourse of racism, Social Darwinism, pathology, and cynicism. In short, dominant representations of black and white youth violence feed right-wing conservative values in the Newt Gingrich era while offering little recognition of the densely populated landscape of violence at the heart of white, dominant society.

The racist coding of representations of Black youth tells us less about such youth than it does about how white society configures public memory, national identity, and the experiences of marginal groups in American society. At the same time, the resurgence of racist culture poses a challenge to educators for redefining the politics of transformative teaching through a broader notion of what it means critically to engage various sites of learning through which youth learn about knowledge, values, and social identities. Racism in film and public life points to a widening crisis of vision, meaning, and community in the United States. It is within this broader crisis that the emergence of hyper-real violence takes on a significance that exceeds the current fascination with films that employ a combination of nihilistic violence and formalistic inventiveness, a biting sense of irony, and scornful cynicism.

Functioning as teaching machines, the new hyper-real avant garde films become both an expression of the erosion of civil society and a challenge for educators and others to rethink how such representations of violence "can be wrested away from a reality in which madness reigns."[28] In what follows, I want to address the work of writer and film director, Quentin Tarantino, focusing in particular on *Reservoir Dogs* (1992) and his most recent and controversial film, *Pulp Fiction* (1994). Both of these films are exemplary for analyzing the new genre of hyper-real violent films characteristic of the 1990s, and how the film functions as part of a broader public discourse.

Violence as Art in *Reservoir Dogs*

In 1992, Quentin Tarantino wrote and directed *Reservoir Dogs*, a low budget gangster film made in the cinematic tradition of earlier films directed by Robert Altman, Martin Scorsese, and Stanley Kubrick. But unlike his famous predecessors, Tarantino redefines the staple elements of the pulp genre – murder, drugs, sex, violence, and betrayal – by introducing self-consciously witty dialogue, formal inventiveness, and slick, yet casual, violence so as to elevate what had been judged traditionally as a B movie genre into an avant garde art form.

Organized around a botched jewelry store robbery by a group of young white men, the film follows the group to a warehouse where they hide out after the bloodbath that followed the heist. The warehouse becomes the set piece for the film as it unfolds around the fate of a wounded undercover cop posing as one of the robbers, a police officer kidnapped after the robbery, and the disputes that emerge among the tense and restless gangsters. Focusing less on the anatomy of the crime, *Reservoir Dogs* explores in decelerated time how white male identities under siege construct their lives through an endless stream of dialogue played out amidst smutty jokes, racist and sexist language, hard-edged sentiment, and gratuitous, casual violence. Tarantino rewrites the aesthetic of violence in this film in postmodern terms. Rather than relying on fast-paced images of brutality, Tarantino decelerates the violence and gives it a heightened aesthetic twist as it unfolds between a homage to realism and rupturing scenes of numbing sadism. From the onset, the plot develops in a graphic scene in which Mr. Orange (Tim Roth), who has been wounded in the robbery, lies on the barren warehouse floor slowly bleeding to death. As the film develops, the pool of blood that surrounds his body gets progressively wider until Mr. Orange appears like a small boat set adrift in a river of his own blood. In the most riveting scene in the film, one that has become a hallmark of Tarantino's style, the captive police officer is tortured by Mr. Blonde (Michael Madsen). Cranking up the volume on the radio, Mr. Blonde dances across the floor to the tune of "Stuck in the Middle With You," he then flicks open a straight razor and cuts off the police officer's right ear. He then pours gasoline over his victim's body but before he can set the cop on fire, Mr. Orange (Tim Roth) becomes conscious long enough to fatally shoot Mr. Blonde. Combining elements of stylized violence, brutal sadism, cruel irony, and pop cultural retro-kitsch, Tarantino revels in stylistic excess in order to push the aesthetic of violence to its visual and emotional limits.

The graphic violence in *Reservoir Dogs* refuses to stand alone as the centerpiece of the film. It is mediated and authenticated by a tough guy vernacular that rivals the film's bankrupt sensationalism, offering the audience the scandal of horror and the seduction of realism without any understanding of the link between violence and larger social forces. The violence embedded in language, a central structural principle of the film, becomes clear in its opening scene. A group of working-class men dressed in black suits sit around a restaurant table discussing in great detail the meaning of Madonna's song, "Like a Virgin." One of the characters, Mr. Brown, played by Tarantino, provides the following tough guy monologue:

> Let me tell you what "Like a Virgin"'s about. It's about this cooz who's a regular fuckin' machine. I'm talkin' mornin' day night afternoon dick dick dick dick dick dick dick. Then one day she meets this John Holmes motherfucker and it's like, Whoa baby. I mean this cat is like Charles Bronson in *The Great Escape*: he's diggin' tunnels. All right, she's gettin some serious dick action and she's feelin somethin' she hasn't felt since forever. Pain. Pain. It hurts, it hurts her . . . just like it did the first time. You see the pain is remindin' the fuck machine what it was once like to be a virgin. Hence, "Like a Virgin."

Working-class machismo emerges in *Reservoir Dogs* as Tarantino's assembly of characters talk and trade insults as if they are off the streets of Bensonhirst, splintering their language with terms like "cooz", "niggers," and "jungle bunnies." Sexist and racist language adds to the realistic temper of their personalities but carries with it a naturalism that makes it complicit with the very relations it so casually portrays. This is a white boys' film, unapologetic in its use of racism and sexism as rhetorical strategies for privileging an overabundance of testosterone. Their language and protracted conversations revolve around small talk, bravado laced with profanities, and streetwise insults. Abusive language parading as a gutsy realism appears hermetic and self-contained, removed from any self-conscious consideration of how it objectifies and belittles blacks and women. This is in-your-face language, guilt-free, and humorously presented so as to mock even the slightest ethical and political sensibility.[29]

Reservoir Dogs serves as a significant model for a number of films that have attempted to cash in on its overly self-conscious treatment of language, aesthetics, humor, and violence. Moreover, it seems to be a film perfectly suited for the racial, ethnic, and sexual backlash that conservatives have been mobilizing in full force throughout the 1980s and 1990s. The attack on politically correct behavior offered Tarantino and other youthful directors such as Roger Avery the opportunity to exploit the cultural mean-spiritedness of the times by taking visual and linguistic liberties that might not have been tolerated a decade before. All of a sudden it has become fashionable to blame the poor for their plight, to criticize blacks for swelling the welfare rolls or to pathologize their alleged violent tendencies, to blame unemployed youth for their inability to find jobs, and to point a cynical finger at wimpy liberals and others who dare resurrect the language of compassion and social justice.

Quentin Tarantino, capitalizing on his growing reputation with the critical acclaim of *Reservoir Dogs* (1992), wrote and produced *Pulp Fiction* (1994), a film that made him an instant star in the pantheon of Hollywood auteur directors. *Pulp Fiction* garnered a number of prestigious awards, including the Palme d'Or at the 1995 Cannes Film Festival and an Oscar for best screenplay. Highly praised by liberal and conservative film critics alike, *Pulp Fiction* received an extraordinary amount of media attention and public recognition. Given the prominence of media and public enthusiasm for this film and the cultural politics it suggests, I want to explore not only the themes at work in this text, but who this film addresses, and how it takes up the relationship between representations of cinematic violence and what it means to construct white and black identities in America.

Cinema as Pulp Fiction

Pulp Fiction consists of three interconnected stories. The film begins with a pair of petty crooks, Pumpkin and Honey Bunny, played by Tim Roth and Amanda Plummer, who decide over coffee to change their luck by robbing the very diner in which they are eating. Just as they jump up on the table and announce their intent to the patrons of the diner, the scene shifts to the first main story which involves two hit men, Vincent (John Travolta) and his black partner, Jules (Samuel Jackson), who are on their way to do a hit for their boss, Marsellus, the local drug baron (Ving Rhames). On their way to do the job, Travolta and Jackson discuss whether their boss overreacted when he had a man tossed out of a window because he massaged the feet of his wife. With perfect seriousness, the dialogue explores the moral limits of foot massaging and whether it deserves an act of revenge worthy of adultery. The conversation then shifts to Travolta's concern about being asked by his boss to entertain his wife, Mia (Uma Thurman), for the evening while he goes out of town.

What Jules and Vincent don't talk about is the task at hand which is to fetch a briefcase stolen from their boss by some young college boys. The hit men succeed in getting the briefcase, and in doing so casually kill all but one of the young men in the room. The violence is quick and unexpected, totally out of character with the conversations that preceded it. But the accelerated shock of the killing doesn't end there. As Vincent and Jules leave the apartment they take a young frightened Afro-American male with them as a hostage. While driving in the car, Vincent accidently shoots the kid, blowing his head off and splattering bone and blood all over the car with requisite pieces of bone fragments and brain lodged in Jules's jerri-curls.

That evening Vincent escorts his boss's wife out for dinner and dancing. Mia, with an endless appetite for coke, snorts the stuff as Vincent appears at the door to begin the evening. After dinner, Vincent brings her back to her apartment and while he runs off to the bathroom, Mia finds some heroin in his jacket packet and, believing it is coke, tunnels it up her nose. Vincent comes back and finds that she has overdosed, lying unconscious on the floor with blood and saliva streaming out of her nose and mouth. He panics, puts Mia in his car, and rushes over to his drug dealer's apartment. The scene climaxes in a moment so appalling that the viewer will either be riveted to the screen or driven out of the theater. Gruesome spectacle joins with black comedy as Vincent revives Mia with a jolt of adrenalin administered through a foot long needle plunged directly into her heart. Mia appears to come back from the dead and the wife of the dealer who is watching the event comments, "trippy."

The third story concerns Butch (Bruce Willis), a boxer, who has been ordered by Marsellus, the drug baron, to throw a fight. Butch double-crosses him and quickly leaves the boxing arena in order to avoid being knocked off by Jules and Vincent. The following day, Butch finds out that his lover has left his father's watch in his old apartment and Butch is forced to drive back to retrieve it. On the way, he accidently hits Marsellus who spots him as he is walking across the street. Openly brawling, both men stumble into a pawn shop and are taken captive by the owner and his corrupt cop partner. They end up as prisoners in an S&M dungeon. While Marsellus is being raped, Butch manages to set himself free. Hearing Marsellus's screams as he is about to make his escape, Butch plucks a Samurai sword from the pawn shop's wares and goes back both to save Marsellus and square his debt to him. Marsellus is rescued and one of the assailants is killed by Butch. The remaining rapist is then turned into a eunuch with a shotgun blast carefully executed by Marsellus. Marsellus gives Butch a reprieve and tells him to get out of town, while making it clear that he is never to mention the rape to anyone or the deal will be off and he will be a dead man. (One wonders what would have happened to Willis's acting career if he had been raped in this particular scene.)

Picking up the second story line, Tarantino circles back to Vincent and Jules who have to find a way to get rid of a car filled with blood and a decapitated body. Jules drives to the house of his friend Jimmie, played by Tarantino, and parks the car in his garage. Jules then calls his boss, who enlists the services of a gentleman hood named Wolf (Harvey Keitel). Mr. Wolf appears in a tux at Jimmie's house and the clean-up operation gets under way. In the meantime, Jimmie is enraged that Jules has shown up at his house. Fearing that his wife, an Afro-American woman, will return home to find the body in the garage, Jimmie asks Jules in wise-guy tones if he saw a sign for "Dead Nigger Storage" on his front lawn. To say the least, Tarantino paints himself into an interesting scene playing a yuppie creep turned gangsta spewing racist epithets and complaining that his favorite linens will be ruined in the clean-up process. Reducing the death of the boy to an inconvenience, Tarantino whines about cleaning up the garage, replacing his linens, and warding off his wife's anger. Comic irony undercuts the racist nature of Tarantino's character, which is doubly dispensed through racist language and through the assumption that since Jimmie's wife is black he can assume a familiarity with black culture that makes him an insider, a white man comfortably situating himself outside of the legacy and pitfalls of racist behavior. The film's final scene takes place back in the diner where Jules and Vincent find themselves in the midst of a holdup. Jules overtakes Honey Bunny and Pumpkin; rather than kill them he goes through what appears to be a new age conversion and allows them to escape. The film ends with Jules and Vincent casually walking out of the diner.

Pulp Fiction takes its name from the popular crime stories of Dashiell Hammett, Raymond Chandler, and others that were published in the first half of the twentieth century. "Pulp" signifies an indebtedness to the pulpwood paper on which these novels were printed, but it also serves as a more gruesome slang referent for beating somebody "to a pulp." *Pulp Fiction* appropriates a number of elements from the pulp tradition. All of the characters are from the seamy side of society, and as a collection of society's sorriest outcasts they have no dreams, hopes, or possibilities other than to cash in big on the crimes they commit. Justice and morality appear removed from their sensibilities, while violence without remorse remains one of the few legitimate options for giving meaning to their identity.

Cynicism reigns supreme in Tarantino's characters, but this is not the dead-pan realism and cynicism that leaves audiences either bored or in the throes of despair. On the contrary, blurring the line between hard-boiled realism and playful if brutal irony, Tarantino seizes upon the postmodern practice of scrambling chronologies as stories leak into each other lacking any clear-cut beginning or end. For example, in one particular scene, Vincent (John Travolta) and Mia (Uma Thurman) visit a glowing retro restaurant/club called Jackrabbit Slim's. The head waiter imitates Ed Sullivan while the help dress up like dead fifties idols such as Marilyn Monroe, Mamie Van Doren, Jerry Lewis, and Dean Martin. The menu substitutes film history for a range of culinary choices, offering junk food such as Douglas Sirk steaks and Martin & Lewis shakes. Every move in the restaurant appears stylized for dramatic, postmodern effect, and the dialogue is brisk but empty, straining to be hip and cool. *Pulp Fiction* appropriates retro-culture and cultural trash and redeems both through irony that functions as an inside joke for those film viewers in the know.

Spectacle and action never become self-referential in Tarantino's films; they always work hand in hand with swiftly executed dialogue and monologues. The acts of stylish violence that pump the adrenalin up to race car speed are always preceded by endless streams of talk. Talk gives Tarantino's characters a connection with the geographies of violence through which they endlessly travel. Experimenting with formalist devices, Tarantino mixes aesthetics and language and succeeds in elevating the crime genre to a species of avant garde filmmaking. He delights in mixing what he calls "horrible tension and creepy feelings with really funny stuff."[30]

At his best, Tarantino mediates gratuitous violence with a hard-edged realism, authenticating street dialogue, and a slick, cynical humor in order to create a novel aesthetic radicalism, one that pushes "to an extreme the pleasures of pulp . . . sensation and cheapness, and moods of shallow, voluptuous despair."[31] Tough guy sincerity and a working-class code of honor are replaced in Tarantino's films with the rhetoric of insult, hyperbole and a kind of irony for irony's sake, within an amoral universe that consciously shuns political or social engagement or the possibility of social transformation. In fact, at the heart of Tarantino's success lies his ability to focus on highly charged issues such as drug dealing, murder, corruption, rape, sex, and sadism and recast them in an aesthetic formalism that undercuts their social and moral significance. For example, Tarantino often mixes styles and combines realism and artifice so as to render the victims of such crimes either scornful or utterly foolish. Put bluntly, victims are not the object of either compassion or sympathy in Tarantino's films.

Borrowed from the media's one-dimensional portrayal of youth as Generation X, Tarantino's films delight in mundane narcissism and nihilistic self-indulgence parading as a hip postmodern posture. Cynically disposed towards any notion of political and moral accountability, this Gen-X view of society relegates the concept of the social to the bygone era of the failed 1960s. Despair surfaces as a form of sublime nihilism, and any viable notion of collective action gives way to often pathological actions governed by the immediacy of the moment and mediated by personal gain and whimsy. Indeed, part of my purpose in these pages is to explore how Tarantino articulates through his films an amoralism that legitimates the neoconservative ideology of the 1990s, one that is consistent with what Ruth Conniff has called a culture of cruelty; that is, a growing contempt in American society for those who are impoverished, disenfranchised, or powerless.[32] *Pulp Fiction* appropriates crime and violence as an everyday presence and turns it into popular cinema; but in doing so Tarantino produces a racially coded, reactionary cultural politics and pedagogy that transforms neoconservative callousness and contempt for the underclass into a hip representation of avant garde high art.

Violence, Race, and the Politics of Realism

> I have no more of a problem with violence that I do with people who like bedroom comedy versus slapstick comedy. It's an aesthetic thing.[33]

Extreme violence in Tarantino's films represents a central element in his cinematic style. Tarantino first generated a great deal of controversy through a sadistic torture scene in *Reservoir Dogs*, gruesomely played out by Michael Madsen who cuts off a hostage policeman's ear and then holds it in his hand while talking to it. *Pulp Fiction* continues the tradition of hyper-real violence – for example, when Jules, while spewing out judgment day prophecy, just for effect shoots a defenseless college kid. This act of sudden violence is not aimed at some wooden, Hollywood gangsta. On the contrary, the victim is a scared kid and his murder is senseless and disturbing. Of course, the effects are no less shocking when Vincent accidently blows off the head of a black kid who appears to be barely 17 or 18 years old. These are disturbing representations of violence, endorsed by a director who appears to have "turned murder into performance art."[34]

Tarantino makes no attempts cinematically to rupture or contest the patterns of violence that his films produce or claim to represent. On the contrary, he empties violence of any critical social consequences, offering viewers only the immediacy of shock, humor, and irony without insight as elements of mediation. None of these elements gets beyond the seduction of voyeuristic gazing so as to enlist audiences' critical engagement. The facile consumption of shocking images and hallucinatory delight that is provoked undercut the possibility of educating audiences to "comment on the image instead of allowing it to pass." There is virtually no space in which the audience can unsettle the " 'moment of violence' [to allow it to] resonate meaningfully and demand our critical involvement."[35]

Tarantino employs cruelty, humor, and postmodern parody to parade visually his extensive knowledge of film history and to rewrite the dynamic of repetition and difference. For example, the male rape scene in *Pulp Fiction* does homage to the classic film, *Deliverance* (1972), but in the end Tarantino's use of parody is about repetition, transgression, and softening the face of violence by reducing it to the property of film history.[36] In this case, aesthetics is about reordering the audience's sense of trauma through a formalism that denies any vestige of politics. This is violence with an escape hatch, one that suggests that violence is a "force over which we have no control." The film is based on an aesthetics that promotes the false assumption that "violence can be distanced from reality through its apparent autonomy of signs."[37] This is what Tarantino suggests when he claims that "Violence in real life is one of the worst aspects of America. But in movies – It's fucking fun! One of the funniest, coolest things for me to watch. I get a kick out of it – all right?"[38] Tarantino's comments reveal more than a hip aesthetics that neutralizes violence by reducing it to an arid formalism and slapstick humor; it is also about a cinematic amoralism which separates the representation of violence from real life. His films offer no language for rendering sadistic violence dangerous in its ability to numb us to the senseless brutality that has become a part of everyday life, especially for youth. Tarantino justifies his graphic representations of violence through an aesthetic appeal to realism. This is a realism that is not merely documentary, it is marked by a repertoire of stylistic excesses that rely on sensationalism and elicit visceral responses. Characters take on a frenzied and despairing quality that is as self-indulgent as it is corrupt.

Tarantino argues that his violent depiction and deceleration of pain is about "stopping movie time and playing the violence out in real time. Letting nothing get in the way of it and letting it happen the way real violence does."[39] But "real" violence comes from somewhere; it is neither innocent nor does it emerge outside of existing historical contexts and social relationships. More fundamentally, representations of violence, regardless of how realistic they are, do not rupture or challenge automatically the dominant ideologies that often justify or celebrate violence in real life. Whereas symbolic violence offers an ethical language with which to engage acts of inhumanity, an uncritical appeal to realism does not allow audiences to think imaginatively about ways to disrupt what have become conventional patterns of violence that function as part of a broader discursive arena in which race and violence are being represented by right wingers. Tarantino's celebration of realism offers no normative grounds on which to challenge violence or to resist the brutal and oppressive face of power. On the contrary, the aesthetic of realism serves pedagogically to justify abstracting the representation of violence from the ethical responsibility of both filmmakers and audiences to protest brutality for brutality's sake as an established social practice.

Tarantino's view of violence represents more than reactionary politics; it also breeds a dead-end cynicism. His films are peopled with characters who have flimsy histories, go nowhere, and live out their lives without any sense of morality or justice. In Tarantino's celluloid world, the pursuit of happiness or social justice is a bad dream; whereas self-promotion and violent action remain some of the few options for exercising human agency. Tarantino acknowledges that his own 20-something sense of the world was informed less by the social and political events of the 1960s and 1970s than by French thrillers and Hollywood gangster movies: "The attitude I grew up with was that everything you've heard is lies."[40] In the end, violence for Tarantino submits to the demands of a publicly celebrated, stylized formalism; but the price exacted exceeds instant notoriety. Tarantino ends up with ultraviolent films which serve as a gateway to sadistic humor at everyone's expense, a chance to depict brutality while assuring the audience that its own complicity and involvement, whether in symbolic terms or in real life, can be successfully suspended in the name of clever entertainment.

As I have argued, Tarantino's fame, in part, is due to his willingness to substitute an aesthetic radicalism for a political and moral one. For all of his technical cinematic virtuosity, he cannot escape the surfacing of his own politics and values in the film's narrative structure, in characterization, and in dialogue. What betrays Tarantino's attempts to render the underbelly of society on its own terms is the overt racism that informs his films, evident on a number of registers. First, there is the racist language that streams forth from his characters in *Reservoir Dogs* and *Pulp Fiction*. Racist slurs and verbal assaults abound in these films, especially in *Pulp Fiction*. There is a disturbing quality to this language, especially in a film that represents a cinematic tradition that Amy Taubin calls a "new acceptable white male art form."[41] Tarantino's use of racist language to authenticate characters aimed largely at white audiences appears to have a jokey quality about it, a kind of porno subtext that suggests that as whites "we're saying something really nasty and really evil, and let's share this secret thrill."[42] This form of verbal racist violence did not escape Allen and Albert Hughes, the black film directors behind *Menace II Society*, who protest Tarantino's repeated use of the word "nigger" in *Pulp Fiction*.

Tarantino has defended himself against the use of racist language in his films. His response is worth quoting at length:

> My feeling is the word nigger is probably the most volatile word in the English language. The minute any word has that much power, as far as I'm concerned, everyone on the planet should scream it. No word deserves that much power. I'm not afraid of it. That's the only way I know how to explain it.[43]

However, what Tarantino fails to acknowledge is the history that informs the term and how the power of the word "nigger" is tied to the power of white dominant groups who traditionally control how meanings are produced, circulated, and rewarded. The point being that the slur is powerful for a set of complex reasons that cannot be left unexplained. Moreover, the use of the term by different groups of whites and blacks has different connotations. The rapper, Ice Cube, makes this clear in his comment "Look, when we call each other nigger it means no harm, in fact in Compton [CA] it is a friendly word. But if a white person uses it, it's something different, it's a racist word."[44] Similarly, as Robin Kelley points out in *Race Rebels* the word "nigger" has multiple meanings in black history and in the current context of black popular culture.[45] Unaware of the complex nuances associated with the different contextual uses of the word "nigger," Tarantino parades the term unself-consciously before audiences for whom the signifying power of the term is far from open-ended. For many whites, the word "nigger" is deeply inscribed in their memories and consciousness less as a term of cultural resistance than as an expression of their support for racist discourse and values. The racist implications of the use of the word nigger by white men in films such as *Pulp Fiction* is captured by bell hooks:

> Yet the film (via these . . . white men) can also legitimate racist folks by providing a public space where suppressed racist slurs and verbal assaults can be voiced and heard. No one seemed to worry that the film would offer white folks license to verbalize racist aggression.[46]

Tarantino's interviews and films suggest that the use of racist language, especially the endless reference to "nigger" in *Pulp Fiction*, locates him as a postmodern version of the white beatnik hipsters of the fifties, with a cool "black" style that allows him to engage in racist transgressions. But while Tarantino may be pushing ideas about racism over the top, he ends up reinforcing nothing less than a not-so-hip racism that allows white boys to laugh when they shout "nigger." Tarantino conveniently, or should we say self-indulgently, allows white youth to believe that by reinventing racism they are somehow escaping how it marks them. Gary Indiana captures this sentiment perfectly in his own critical discussion of *Pulp Fiction*.

> Tarantino flirts with the belief that energetic posturing will make his skin turn black, a delusion shared by white entertainers like Sandra Bernhard and Camille Paglia. In its most exacerbated form, this sentimental tic of the white hipster locates all "authenticity" in the black experience, against which all other experience becomes the material of grotesque irony. To be really, really cool becomes the spiritual equivalent of blackness, and even superior to it: there are plenty of square black people but not one square cool person. For the Tarantino of *Pulp Fiction*, blackness is a plastic holy grail, a mythic substance with real effects and its own medieval code.[47]

Tarantino's racism reinforces itself through the celebration of a masculinity that asserts its identity through the representation of mindless violence and a portrayal of women who are so one-dimensional that they appear to have been invented in a Beavis and Butthead script. But in an age when it is clever to be racist and sexist, the combination of slick fun and stylish carnage provides an excuse for Tarantino to erase women from his film, *Reservoir Dogs*, except through references to their body parts. And when they do appear in his work, they either act violently, as in Uma Thurman's drug snorting in *Pulp Fiction*, or are violently abused by their pimps, as is the case of Patricia Arquette in *True Romance*. In the end, Tarantino's use of hyper-real violence is propped up by a "cool" masculinity that simply recycles a patriarchal hatred of women while barely hiding its own homophobic instincts.[48]

Tarantino's mixture of gay bashing, misogyny, and crude racist language in films that are largely white and male does little to boost his alleged moral sensitivity to the everyday implications of racist and sexist language. Tarantino's racism does not merely reveal itself in the use of racist slurs, it also pervades the one-dimensional representation of blacks in *Reservoir Dogs* and *Pulp Fiction*. Once at the Sundance Film Festival Tarantino was told by a fellow filmmaker that "you've given white boys the kind of movies black kids get."[49] Taking this as a compliment, Tarantino nonetheless betrays a profoundly white and suburban sensibility by depicting the two black characters in *Pulp Fiction* as a drug dealer and a gangster hit man. In addition, Tarantino provides a number of subtle provocations in developing these characters. Marsellus, the drug-dealer, is married to a white woman. Refusing to rupture the racist obsession with black male sexuality and gangsta drug-dealing behavior, Tarantino seems to play into the need to punish his outlaw black character by submitting him to a humiliating and scandalous rape by two hayseed lunatics. This horrendous rape scene was largely ignored in the popular press, except to reference Tarantino's gay bashing rather than racism. Further, Jules, the main black character in *Pulp Fiction* is largely defined as an urban sociopath who has a penchant for quoting scripture to those he's about to ice. In a rather scandalous political move, Tarantino appropriates the prophetic language of the black church for criminal and

224

dehumanizing ends, stripping from its tradition a legacy of dignity, compassion, and nonviolence. In the end, when Jules barely misses a rendezvous with death, he decides he has been saved and consequently gives up crime for the pleasures of a more righteous and extended life. Of course, this sudden turn of events has nothing to do with feeling remorse for his victims. The tradition of prophetic language, which has served as a language of resistance and hope in black culture, is reduced in *Pulp Fiction* into a discourse of degeneracy and a signifier for moral bankruptcy.

Given the various film awards that *Pulp Fiction* has won, one wonders why such a racist and violent film has received extensive coverage in the popular press and the highest accolades of the film community. In many ways, Tarantino's film anticipates the Newt Gingrich era with its appeal to nostalgia, hard-edged humor, greed, and an excessive individualism. Well timed to take advantage of the resurgence of racism which has emerged as a result of the United States' massive shift to the right, Tarantino's film resonates cinematically with a racism that appears to be a defining principle of economic and social policy in the 1990s.

Toward a Cultural Policy of Violence in Films

What I have tried to do with Tarantino's recent work is suggest that film occupies an important public space in American culture. As commonplace as this might sound, it should not detract from the importance of recognizing that cinema is a teaching machine. That is, cinematic representations of violence do not merely reflect reality, as many Hollywood producers claim. On the contrary, cinema carries with it a language of ethics and a pedagogy. Producers and directors constantly make normative distinctions about issues regarding whether plot and character will be formulaic and stereotypical or inventive and complex; the degree to which artistic formalism or the use of glossy, color-saturated aesthetics will supersede social and political vision; and whether violence and adult situations will provide merely spectacle and diminish the integrity of the plot. This is far from an inclusive list, but it illustrates that films perform a pedagogical function in providing "a certain kind of language for conveying and understanding violence."[50]

At the same time, cinema functions in a broader pedagogical sense in that it is consistently making a claim to particular memories, histories, ways of life, identities, and values that always presuppose some notion of difference, community, and the future. Given that films both reflect and shape public culture, they cannot be defined exclusively through a notion of artistic freedom and autonomy that removes them from any form of critical accountability. This is not to suggest that the public sphere of cinema should be subject to ruthless censorship, but at the same time it cannot it be regarded as a simple form of entertainment.

Cinematic violence, whether it be ritualistic or hyper-real, is not innocent; such violence offers viewers brutal and grotesque images that articulate with broader public discourses regarding how children and adults relate, care, and respond to others. At stake here is not whether cinematic violence directly causes crime or is the determining force in the wider culture of violence. The causes of violence lie in historically rooted, complex economic and social issues that are at the heart of American society. To blame Hollywood for the violence in American society would be a subterfuge for addressing the complex causes of violence at work in the larger social order. In a world demeaned by pointless violence, the question that must be raised concerns what responsibilities filmmakers, other cultural workers, and their respective publics have in developing a cultural policy that addresses the limits and responsibilities of the use of violence in cinema. Such a policy must address how the mass media and the film community can be held responsible for educating children and others about how to discriminate among different forms of violence, how to prevent it in real life when necessary, and how to engage its root social causes in the larger social and cultural landscape. Violence is not merely a function of power; it is also deeply related to how forms of self and social agency are produced within a variety of public spheres. Cinema exercises enormous pedagogical authority and influence. The reach, limits, and possibilities of its influence, especially on young children, can only be addressed through a coordinated effort on the part of progressives who inhabit a range of cultural spheres including schools, religious institutions, business corporations, popular culture, local communities, and the home. In addition, these important cultural sites need to articulate their efforts to develop a cultural policy that address the ethical responsibilities of a cinematic public sphere, including fundamental questions about the democratization of culture. Such concerns provide a common ground for various organizations and publics to raise questions regarding the ownership, power, and control over media culture exercised by large multinational conglomerates. They reveal who has access to the means of cultural representation and who does not, and what the possibilities for democracy are when gross financial inequalities and structures of power gain control over the apparatuses that produce popular and media culture.[51]

There appears to be a an enormous deadlock in developing a critical debate over cinematic and media representations of violence. This is evident in the public furor that emerged when Bob Dole, the former Senate majority leader, appearing at a fund-raising event in Los Angeles, condemned certain Hollywood filmmakers for debasing United States culture with images of graphic violence and "the mainstreaming of deviancy." Dole specifically condemned films such as *Natural Born Killers* and *True Romance* as "nightmares of depravity" drenched in grotesque violence and sex. Speaking for a Republican party that has increasingly moved to the extreme right, Dole issued a warning to Hollywood: "A line has been crossed – not just of taste, but of human dignity and decency. . . . It is crossed every time sexual violence is given a catchy tune. When teen suicide is set to an appealing beat. When Hollywood's dream factories turn out nightmares of depravity."[52] Dole's remarks were less an insightful indictment of the culture of violence than a shrewd attempt to win the hearts and minds of Christian conservatives and those in the general public who are fed up with the culture of violence but feel helpless in the face of its looming pervasiveness. While it is commendable that Dole has taken a stand regarding the relationship between Hollywood representations of violence and its impact in society, he fails to address a number of issues necessary to engage critically the culture of violence in this country. First, political opportunism aside, Dole's remarks do not constitute a thoughtful and sincere analysis of the culture of violence. On the surface, Dole's remarks about the orgy of violence and misogyny flooding American popular culture resonate with a deeply felt anxiety about the alleged innocence of commercial entertainment. But Dole is no spokesperson for criticizing or analyzing the violence in this country. Not only had he not viewed the films he criticized, he argued that Arnold Schwarzenegger's killfest film, *True Lies*, represented the kind of film that Hollywood should be producing for family entertainment. Dole also refused to criticize the exploitive, bloody films made by Bruce Willis and Sylvester Stallone, both prominent Republicans. Second, Dole's refusal to address the culture of violence in broader terms, coupled with his role in actually reproducing such a culture, reveal a grave theoretical omission and unfortunate disingenuousness in his criticisms. At a time when "an estimated 100,000 children carry guns to school in the United States [and] gunfire kills on average 15 children a day," Dole drew no connection between the gun culture and the violence in our nation's streets, schools, and homes. But this may be understandable since Dole has received $23,426 in "direct contributions and independent expenditures from the NRA since 1982" and has publicly committed himself to "repealing the ill-conceived gun ban passed as part of President Clinton's crime bill."[53] As Ellen Goodman points out, "anybody who is against violence in the movies and in favor of assault weapons in real life leaves himself open to all sorts of charges, the least of which is hypocrisy."[54]

It is hard to believe that following the Oklahoma City bombing Dole refused to include in his critique of the culture of violence the rise of right-wing militia groups, the hate talk emanating from right-wing talk show hosts such as G. Gordon Liddy, or the gun culture supported by the National Rifle Association, which published a fund-raising letter in which federal law-enforcement agents were referred to as "Jackbooted Thugs." The latter prompted former President, George Bush, to resign from the NRA while Dole remained silent on the issue. What is the significance of Bob Dole's attack on Hollywood films he had not viewed, or his refusal to address corporate interests aligned with the Republican party that have a big economic stake in the culture of violence?

It may be that Dole's attack signals less a concern with how the culture of violence is represented in this country than who is going to control those aspects of the cultural sphere that are influential and at the same time unpredictable, given their allegiance to the often conflicting dictates of the market and artistic expression. Maybe this explains why Dole can criticize the vulgarity of popular culture while at the same time advocating the defunding of PBS, the National Endowment for the Arts, and other government support for the arts. Conservatives want to homogenize culture rather than diversify it. To diversify culture would demand supporting those institutions or public spheres in which critical knowledge, debate, and dialogue become meaningful and work. Such interactions are necessary for people to make choices about how power works through culture and what it means to identify with, challenge, and rewrite the representations that circulate in popular and mass-mediated cultures. It suggests that any debate about the best way to reduce symbolic violence in the culture must be part of a larger discourse about educating people to change the social and economic conditions that produce and sustain such violence. This further suggests addressing how questions of pedagogy and commitment can work to provide a challenge to institutional structures of power that trade in symbolic imagery while refusing to address the limits of the media's potential for error and harm. Social justice is not part of the message that underwrites Dole's concern with media culture and its relationship with the alleged public good. On the contrary, Dole represents an ideological position that advocates abolishing the Department of Education, privatizing public schools, and limiting funding for poor students who want access to higher education. Dole's moral indignation is not merely fueled by political opportunism but also by the imperatives of a political project that engages the cultural public sphere in order to control rather than democratize it.

Unfortunately, Hollywood executives, directors, and celebrities responded to Dole's remarks by primarily focusing on his hypocrisy rather than providing a forum for critically analyzing Hollywood's complicity with, and responsibility for, addressing the growing culture of violence in the United States. Oliver Stone, the director of *Natural Born Killers*, labeled Dole's attack "a '90s form of McCarthyism," while actor James Wood compared Dole's actions to the morality crusades that inspired censors of a previous era to attempt to ban *Catcher in the Rye* or *Ulysses*. Such remarks are defensive in the extreme, and exhibit little self-consciousness regarding what Hollywood's role or responsibility might be in shaping popular culture and providing a pedagogical climate in which knowledge, values, desires, and identities are marketed on a daily basis to children and young adults, among others. The relationship between greed and the marketing of violence might inspire Hollywood executives and celebrities to be more attentive to the ravages committed in the name of the free market, or address their own ethical responsibility as cultural workers who actively circulate ideas and values for popular consumption. Claiming that the film, music, and television industries simply reflect what the public wants represents more than disingenuousness, it also suggests political and ethical cowardice. Neither Dole's one-sided criticism nor Hollywood's defensive posture provides a helpful model for dealing with the culture of violence.

It is hard to imagine how Dole's moralizing and Hollywood's defensiveness addresses constructively the daily violence that takes place in urban America. While I was writing this chapter in Boston over the hot summer weekend of July 14–15, 1995 the *Boston Globe* reported that eight young people were victims of unrelated gun shootings in the city: two youths were killed and six others were seriously wounded.[55] All of these youths lived in the poorest sections of Boston. Beneath these senseless acts of violence is a culture of enormous poverty, human indifference, unemployment, economic hardships, and needless human suffering. It seems that Hollywood executives find in these stories material for reflecting reality while disavowing any responsibility for its causes or their own complicity in reproducing it. At the same time, national leadership sinks to an all time low as social services are cut and the notion of the critical citizen is subordinated to the virtues of creating a society filled with consuming subjects.

In the coming new information age, it is imperative that various cultural workers and educators raise important questions about what kind of teacher we want cinema to be, with special concern for how the representation of violence works to pose a threat "not only to our national health but to our potential for ever becoming a true participatory democracy."[56] To simply blame filmmakers and television executives for causing violence in the United States shifts critical attention away from the poisonous roots of the violence at the heart of social and economic life in America. Blaming the media also absolves educators, community activists, politicians, and other cultural workers from assuming roles as critical citizens who need to address the complex relationships between the violence we absorb through the media and the reality of violence we experience in everyday life. Violence is not simply emanating from the movie theaters of America. Rooted in everyday institutional structures and social relations, violence has become a toxic glue that bonds Americans together while simultaneously preventing them from expanding and building a multiracial and multicultural democracy. Once the brutality of specific forms of representational violence are understood as a threat to democracy itself, it might become possible to address the violence politically and pedagogically as we would other issues concerning our national identity, public well-being, and social consciousness.

Notes

1. A version of this essay appeared in *Social Identities* 1.2 (1995): 333–54.
2. Cited in Arty Nelson, "Master of Reality." *Bikini* (January, 1996): 51.
3. Edward S. Herman, "The New Racist Onslaught." *Z magazine* 7.12 (December, 1994): 24.
4. Holly Sklar, "Young and Guilty by Stereotype." *Z Magazine* 6 (July/August, 1993): 53.
5. This issue is taken up in Christian Parenti, "Urban Militarism." *Z Magazine* 7 (June, 1994): 47–52.
6. Laurie Asseo, "Statistics on Black Crime Victims Released." *The Boston Globe* (December 9, 1994): 3.
7. The media bashing of youth is taken up in great detail in Mike Males, "Bashing Youth: Media Myths About Teenagers." *Extra* (March/April 1994): 8–14.
8. "Violence Targets America's Youth." *Centre Daily Times* (July 18, 1994): 4.
9. Ed Guerrero, "Framing Blackness: The African-American Image in the Cinema of the Nineties." *Cineaste* 20.2 (1993): 30.

10. Robert Stam and Ell Shohat, "Contested Histories: Eurocentrism, Multi-culturalism, and Media." in David Theo Goldberg (ed.), *Multiculturalism: A Critical Reader* (Cambridge, MA: Blackwell, 1994): 319.

11. George Gerbner, "Miracles of Communication Technology: Powerful Audiences, Diverse Choices, and Other Fairy Tales." in Janet Waski et. al. (eds.), *Illuminating the Blind Spots* (New York: Ablex, 1993), p. 371. See also George Gerbner, Larry Gross, Michael Morgan, and Nancy Sign-orielli, "Growing Up with Television: The Cultivation Perspective." in Jennings Bryant and Dolf Zillmann (eds.), *Media Effects: Advances in Theory and Research* (Hillsdale, NJ: Lawrence Erlbaum Associates, 1993): 17–41.

12. Elizabeth Kolbert, "Television Gets Closer Look as a Factor in Real Violence." *The New York Times* (December 4, 1994): D20.

13. Anne Nelson, "Colours of Violence." *Index on Censorship* 23.162 (May/June, 1994): 86.

14. Rustom Bharacuha, "Around Aydohya: Aberrations, Enigmas, and Moments of Violence." *Third Text* 24 (Autumn, 1993): 48.

15. These figures come from a survey done by film critic, Vincent Carnby, cited in Carl Nightingale, *On the Edge* (New York: Basic Books, 1993): 170–1.

16. Bharacuha, "Around Aydohya," op.cit., p. 51.

17. Vivian Sobchack cited in David McKinney, "Violence: The Strong and the Weak." *Film Quarterly* 46.4 (Summer, 1993): 16–22.

18. This issue is explored in Susan Jefford, *Hard Bodies: Hollywood Masculinity in the Reagan Era* (New Brunswick, NJ: Rutgers University Press, 1994).

19. Hannah Arendt, *Eichmann in Jerusalem: A Report on the Banality of Evil* (New York: Viking, 1963).

20. For a brilliant analysis of this culture, see David Theo Goldberg, *Racist Culture* (New York: Basil Blackwell, 1994). It is truly amazing the degree to which Goldberg's work is ignored by both the popular press and many academics who write about race, given that his writing far exceeds in both quality and insight most of what is being written about racism and Western culture.

21. See Gail Dines and Jean M. Humez (eds.), *Gender, Race, and Class in Media* (Thousand Oaks, CA: Sage, 1994); Charles Acland, *Youth, Murder, Spec-tacle: The Cultural Politics of 'Youth in Crisis'*" (Boulder, CO: Westview Press, 1995); John Fiske, *Media Matters* (Minneapolis: University of Minnesota Press, 1994).

22. Jim Naureckas, "Racism Resurgent: How Media Let *The Bell Curve's* Pseudo-Science Define the Agenda on Race." *Extra!* 8.1 (January/February, 1995): 12.

23. Holly Sklar, "Young and Guilty by Stereotype." *Z Magazine* 7.8 (July/August, 1993): 52.

24. On this issue, see Michael Dyson, *Reflecting Black: African-American Cultural Criticism* (Minneapolis: University of Minnesota Press, 1993); bell hooks, *Black Looks: Race and Representation* (Boston: South End Press, 1992).

25. Richard J. Herrnstein and Charles Murray, *The Bell Curve: Intelligence and Class Structure in American Life* (New York: Free Press, 1994): 526.

26. For a similar critique of the violence in Hollywood films such as *Natural Born Killers*, see "Knocking 'Em Dead At the Box Office: *Natural Born Killers*." *Border/Lines* 34/35 (1994): 10–14.

27. It is worth noting that those positive and complex aspects of African-American life that constitutes youth culture are rarely portrayed in Hollywood films. For example, representations that focus on how gangstar rap "serves up white America's most cherished gun-slinging mythologies (heroic American dreams) in the form of its worst and blackest nightmares, while it empowers Black imaginations to negate the existential terror of ghetto life (and death) by sheer force of the will" are rarely acknowledged critically in the portrayal of black youth culture in the dominant media. See Nick De Genova, "Gangster Rap and Nihilism in Black America: Some Questions of Life and Death." *Social Text* 13.2 (1995): 107.

28. Ernst Bloch et al., "Adorno's Letter to Walter Benjamin-November 10, 1938," in *Aesthetics and Politics* (London: New Left Books, 1977): 127.

29. For a brilliant commentary on "bigotry delivered as a joke by white men...", see Derrick Z. Jackson, "Laughing off Racism." *The Boston Globe* (May 24, 1995): 19.

30. Tarantino interviewed in Manhola Dargis, "A Bloody Pulp." *Vibe* (October, 1995): 66.

31. David Denby, "A Thugfest." *New York* (October 3, 1994): 98.

32. Ruth Conniff, "The Culture of Cruelty." *The Progressive* 56.9 (1992): 16–20.

33. Tarantino cited in Godfrey Cheshire, "Hollywood's New Hit Men." *Interview* (September, 1994): 130.

34. Peter Travers, "Tarantino's Twist." *Rolling Stone* 692 (October 6, 1994): 80.

35. Bharacuha, "Around Aydohya," op. cit., p. 50.

36. On the relationship of parody to art forms, see Linda Hutcheon, *A Theory of Parody* (New York: Routledge, 1991).

37. Bharacuha, "Around Aydohya" (1993), p. 50.

38. Tarantino quoted in Tony Crawley, "Quentin Tarantino." *Film Review* (November, 1994): 32.

39. Tarantino cited in Peter McAlevey, "All's Well that Ends Gruesomely." *The New York Times Magazine* (December 6, 1992): 80.

40. Cited in Peter Biskind, "An Auteur is Born." *Premiere* (November, 1994): 100.

41. Amy Taubin, "Eight Critics Talk About Violence and the Movies." *The Village Voice Film Special* (December 1, 1992): 10.

42. David Kehr, "Eight Critics Talk About Violence and the Movies." *The Village Voice Film Special* (December 1, 1992): 8.

43. Cited in Dargis, "A Bloody Pulp," op. cit., p. 66.

44. Ice Cube cited in Robin D. G. Kelley, *Race Rebels* (New York: The Free Press, 1994): 209–10.

45. See Robin Kelley, ibid., especially pages 209–14.

46. bell hooks, *Yearning: Race, Gender and Cultural Politics* (Boston: South End Press, 1990): 177. It certainly escaped Harvard University law professor, Alan A. Stone, who in his review of *Pulp Fiction* argues that:

> Although Tarantino wants to shock us with violence, his film is politically correct. There is no nudity and no violence directed against women; in fact a man, the crime boss, gets raped and the only essentially evil people in the film are two sadistic honkies straight out of *Deliverance* who do the raping. The film *celebrates* interracial friendship and cultural diversity [my emphasis]; there are strong women and strong Black men, and the director swims against the current of class stereotype. (Alan A. Stone, "Pulp Fiction." *The Boston Review* XX.2 (April/May, 1995): 24–5.

This is an amazing analysis especially since it is a black youth who gets his head blown off in the back of a car, the one black woman who appears in the film is faceless, and the films is laced with racist language. But the silence about racism in this critique is equally matched by a refusal to acknowledge the demeaning portrayal of women. For example, "Honey Bunny" and the drug dealer's wife are respectively portrayed as either drug snorting and reckless or as violent and hysterical sociopaths.

47. Gary Indiana. "Geek Chic." *Artforum* 38.7 (March, 1995): 64–5.

48. For an interesting analysis on Tarantino's view on women, See Robin Wood, "Slick Shtick." *Artforum* 38.7 (March, 1995): 63–6, 110; and bell hooks, "Cool Tool," *Artforum* 38:7 (March 1995): 63–6, 110.

49. Cited in Lisa Kennedy, "Natural Born Film Maker." *The Village Voice* (October 25, 1994): 32.

50. Bharacuha, "Around Aydohya," op. cit., p. 56.

51. Herbert I. Schiller, *Culture Inc.* (New York: Oxford University Press, 1989).
52. Dole's speech cited in Adam Petman, "Hollywood Angered by Dole's Attack on Its 'Evil' Offerings." *The Boston Globe* (June 2, 1995): 1, 20; John M. Broder, "Dole Blasts 'Deviancy' in Hollywood Films, Music." *The Boston Globe* (June 2, 1995): 1.
53. Cited in "Faces of Violence." *Rolling Stone* 710 (June 15, 1995): 60.
54. Ellen Goodman, "A New Cast, Same Script." *The Boston Globe* (June 8, 1995): 18. On the sheer hypocrisy of Dole's remarks, see Derrick Jackson, "Sen. Dole's Amazon of Hypocrisy." *The Boston Globe* (June 9, 1995): 23.
55. Susan E. Neff, "Two Killed, Six Others Hurt in Rash of Boston Shootings." *The Boston Globe* (July 15, 1995): 21.
56. Michael Roth, "Violence and the De-Meaning of America." *Tikkun* 9.1 (1994): 87.

11

Multiculturalism and the Cultural Politics of Race in *187*

In opposition to the prevailing assumption that multiculturalism is primarily an educational problem, embedded in the politics of schooling and its long-standing policies of exclusion, I want to insist that multiculturalism at its root is about the broader relationship between politics and power; it is about a historical past and a living present in which racist exclusions appear "calculated, brutally rational, and profitable"[1] and permeate all aspects of everyday life. Embedded within a systemic history of black restriction, subjugation, and white privilege, the politics of multiculturalism is still, as Supreme Court Justice Ruth Bader Ginsburg puts it, "evident in our workplaces, markets and neighborhoods."[2] David Shipler argues powerfully that race and class are the two most powerful determinants shaping American society. Based on interviews with hundreds of people over a five-year period, Shipler's book, *A Country of Strangers*, bears witness to a racism that "is a bit subtler in expression, more cleverly coded in public, but essentially unchanged as one of the 'deep abiding currents' in everyday life, in both the simplest and the most complex interactions of whites and blacks."[3]

Although there can be little doubt that racial progress has been achieved in many areas in the last 50 years,[4] it is also true that such progress has not been sustained. This is particularly evident in the dramatic increase in black prisoners and the growth of the prison-industrial complex, crumbling city infrastructures, segregated

236

housing, soaring black and Latino unemployment, exorbitant school dropout rates among black and Latino youth, coupled with the more general realities of failing schools, and deepening inequalities of incomes and wealth between blacks and whites.[5] Pushing against the grain of civil rights reform and racial justice are reactionary and moderate positions ranging from the extremism of right-wing skinheads and Jesse Helms-like conservatives to the moderate "color-blind" positions of liberals like Randall Kennedy.[6]

Crucial to the re-emergence of this "new" racism is a cultural politics that plays a determining role in how race shapes our popular unconscious. This is evident in the widespread articles, reviews, and commentaries in the dominant media that give inordinate amounts of time and space to mainstream conservative authors, filmmakers, and critics who rail against affirmative action, black welfare mothers, and the alleged threats that black youth and rap artists pose to middle-class existence. Rather than dismiss such rampant conservatism as either indifferent to the realities of racism, or deconstruct its racialized codes to see where such language falls in on itself, educators can engage these commentaries more constructively by analyzing how they function as public discourses, how their privileged meanings work intertextually to resonate with ideologies produced in other sites, and how they serve largely to construct and legitimate racially exclusive practices, policies, and social relations. Race frames the fate of many minorities of color in this society and it does so not only through the passing of retrograde social policy or in the concrete forms of harassment that people of color are subjected to daily in schools, in their cars, in the stores they frequent, and so on, but also in the space of the symbolic where images and representations are reproduced en masse that legitimate and recycle a steady stream of racist views, practices, and ideologies. For instance, an award-winning film such as Steven Soderbergh's *Traffic* is praised by critics for its realistic treatment of America's war on drugs, but nothing is said of its racist and wooden portrayals of Mexicans or its appeal to conservative family values – suggesting that what is really at stake in the drug war is saving the children of the white, upper-class rich. *Traffic* absurdly argues that the children of the rich appear to be the real victims in the drug war, and in doing so conveniently ignores the enormous number of young black men who are given long jail sentences as a result of failed drug policies. Tragedy is only real when it strikes the children of the rich, and it is made more substantial when Soderbergh pushes the race card by framing the ultimate downfall of Caroline, the daughter of conservative judge, Robert Wakefield, in a scene in which she ends up shooting heroin and being raped by her black pimp. It is difficult to believe that, after the Willie Horton media event of the last decade, respectable directors could still be shamelessly using such blatant forms of racist representation to mobilize popular support for their films. Films such as *Traffic* make clear the necessity for progressive educators, parents, and others to engage a multicultural politics that offers students and teachers opportunities to critically examine how racialized meanings carried in varied cultural texts such as Hollywood films gain the force of common sense, and how such texts can be examined in light of the broader assemblage of cultural pedagogies that are produced, legitimated, and circulated in a vast range of public spheres and institutionalized sites.

In order to deepen the cultural politics of multiculturalism, educators can address questions of culture, power, identity, and representation as part of a broader discourse about public pedagogy and social policy. In this pedagogical approach, power becomes central to the study of cultural texts and practices, and socially relevant problems can be explored through theoretical engagements with wider institutional contexts and public spaces in which multicultural discourses gain their political and economic force. If teaching students to interrogate, challenge, and transform those cultural practices that sustain racism is a central objective of multicultural education, such a pedagogy must be addressed in ways that link cultural texts to the major social problems that animate public life. Texts in this instance would be analyzed as part of a "social vocabulary of culture" that points to how power names, shapes, defines, and constrains relationships between the self and the other; constructs and disseminates what counts as knowledge; and produces representations that provide the context for identity formation.[7] Within this type of pedagogical approach, multiculturalism must find ways to acknowledge the political character of culture through strategies of understanding and engagement that link an antiracist and radically democratic rhetoric with strategies

238

to transform racist institutionalized structures within and outside of the university.

At its best, critical multiculturalism should forge a connection between reading texts and reading public discourses in order to link the struggle for inclusion with relations of power in the broader society. It is precisely within the realm of a cultural politics that teachers and students develop pedagogical practices that close the gap between intellectual debate and public life, not simply as a matter of relevance, but as a process through which students can learn the skills and knowledge to develop informed opinions, make critical choices, and function as citizen activists. Robin D. G. Kelley provides one direction such a project might take. He insightfully argues:

> [Multiculturalism cannot ignore] how segregation strips communities of resources and reproduces inequality. The decline of decent-paying jobs and city services, erosion of public space, deterioration of housing stock and property values, and stark inequalities in education and health care are manifestations of investment strategies under de facto segregation. . . . [Progressives must address] dismantling racism, bringing oppressed populations into power and moving beyond a black/white binary that renders invisible the struggles of Latino, Asian-Americans, Native Americans and other survivors of racist exclusion and exploitation.[8]

Implicit in Kelley's call for action is the recognition that any viable pedagogy and politics of representation needs to address the realities of historical processes, the actuality of economic power, and the range of public spaces and institutions that constitute the embattled terrain of racial difference and struggle. This suggests developing a critical vocabulary for viewing texts not only in relation to other modes of discourse, but also, as Randall Johnson notes, "in relationship to contemporaneous social institutions and non-discursive practices."[9] Within this approach, cultural texts cannot be isolated from the social and political conditions of their production. Nor can the final explanation of such texts be found within the texts themselves. On the contrary, such texts become meaningful when viewed both in relation to other discursive practices and in terms of "the objective social field from which [they] derive."[10] Pedagogically, this suggests addressing how cultural texts in the classroom construct themselves in response to broader institutional arrangements, contexts of power, and the social relations that they both legitimate and help to sustain.

In what follows, I demonstrate the theoretical relevance for developing a multicultural pedagogical practice in which issues of representation, everyday life, and the brutal ideologies of racism intersect and mutually inform each other. In part, I want to address how film can be used to define particular social groups through cultural representations that function as powerful public pedagogies that construct and help to legitimate racist stereotypes and social relations. In doing so I want to focus on a recent Hollywood blockbuster, *187*, illustrating how pedagogy might be taken up as a public project designed to integrate representations of cultural and racial difference with material relations of power that animate racially exclusive practices and policies. Against the decline of the public sphere, it is important to recognize that Hollywood films do more than provide pleasure, escape, and entertainment; they also produce public transcripts that for better or worse animate images, representations, discourses, and ideologies that signal the need to reclaim public spaces in which dialogue, critical reflection, and social engagement are crucial for people to engage important social issues. Hollywood reminds us that the university is not the only sphere in which issues of race, multiculturalism, and historical memory are produced and engaged in dramatic ways. Moreover, if the privileged space of the university is to be challenged and called upon to engage its social function as a democratic public sphere, it may have to find ways of engaging Hollywood films as public transcripts, rather than as simply art forms or specialized texts. Instead of ignoring the public and political dimensions of film, academics need to reconsider how Hollywood films function as public pedagogies that offer a particular sensory experience and mythic mix of sight and sound as part of its efforts to shape public consciousness and legitimate a narrowly conceived range of social relations and institutional formations. Hollywood reminds us that knowledge is always linked to desire, power, and pleasure, and that far from being innocent, such knowledge plays a crucial role in connecting individuals and groups to larger social structures and relations of power.

Unfortunately, Hollywood is one of many sites that often appear too far removed from the privileged security of the university to be included in the discourse of critical multiculturalism.

Racial Coding in the Hollywood Text

During the last five years, a number of Hollywood films such as *Dangerous Minds* (1995), *The Substitute I* (1996), and *High School High* (1996) have cashed in on the prevailing racially coded popular "wisdom" that public schools are out of control, largely inhabited by illiterate, unmotivated, and violent urban youth who are economically and racially marginalized. This increasingly familiar script suggests a correlation between urban public space and rampant drug use, daily assaults, broken teachers, and schools that do nothing more than contain deviants who are a threat to themselves and everybody else. The film *187* (1997) is a recent addition to this genre, but takes the pathologizing of poor, urban students of color to extremes so far beyond existing cinematic conventions that it stands out as a public testimony to broader social and cultural formations within American society that makes the very existence of this blatantly racist film possible.

Directed by Kevin Reynolds and written by Scott Yagemann, a former school teacher, *187* narrates the story of Trevor Garfield (Samuel L. Jackson), a science teacher who rides to work on a bike in order to teach at a high school in the Bedford-Stuyvesant section of Brooklyn. Garfield is portrayed as an idealistic teacher who, against all odds, is trying to make his classes interesting and do his best to battle daily against the ignorance, chaos, and indifference that characterizes the urban public school in the Hollywood imagination. Yet the film quickly turns away from a call for educational reform and a defense of those teachers who face a Sisyphean task in trying to improve the lives of urban youth, and rapidly degenerates into a rationale for abandoning urban public schools and the black and brown students who inhabit their hallways and classrooms.

In the film's opening scenes, students move through metal detectors under the watchful eyes of security guards – props that have become all too familiar in urban high school settings. Clearly, the students in *187* are far removed from the squeaky clean, high-tech classrooms of white suburbia: the school looks more like a prison, and the students, with their rap music blaring in the background, look more like inmates being herded into their cells. The threat of violence is palpable in this school and Garfield confronts it as soon as he enters his classroom and picks up his textbook, which has the figure *187* scrawled all over it. Recognizing that the number is the police code for homicide, Garfield goes to the principal to report what he believes is a threat on his life. The principal tells Garfield he is overreacting, dismissing him with, "You know what your problem is? On the one hand, you think someone is going to kill you, and on the other hand, you actually think kids are paying attention in your class." Garfield hasn't yet left the office before the principal reveals that he has told a student in Garfield's class that he has flunked the course. Not only has the principal violated Garfield's teacher–student relationship, but the student who he has flunked is on probation and as a result of the failing grade will now be sent back to prison. The threat of violence and administrative ineptitude set the stage for a hazardous series of confrontations between Garfield and the public school system. Garfield leaves the principal's office terrified and walks back to his classroom. Each black male student he now sees appears menacing and poised to attack; shot in slow motion, the scene is genuinely disturbing. And before Garfield reaches his classroom, he is viciously and repeatedly stabbed with a nine inch nail in the hallway by the black male student he has flunked.

Fifteen months later Garfield has relocated and finds a job as a substitute teacher at John Quincy Adams High School in Los Angeles. The students in this school are mostly Latino. They wear oversized pants and torn shirts, carry boom boxes blaring rap music, and appear as menacing as the African-American students Garfield taught in Brooklyn. As the camera pans their bodies and expressions, it becomes clear that what unites these inner-city students of color is a culture that is dangerous, crime-ridden, and violent. Assigned to teach his class in a bungalow, Garfield's first day is a nightmare as students taunt him, throw paper wads at him, and call him "bitch." Garfield has moved from New York to California only to find himself in a public high school setting that has the look and feel of hell. Heat rising from the pavement, pulsating rap music, graffiti, and oversized shadows of gang members playing basketball filter through the classroom window to paint an ominous picture of what Garfield can hope to experience.

But Garfield has to face more than dangerous students. His new principal prides himself on never having been a teacher, refers to the students as "clients," and makes it clear that his primary concern is to avoid potential lawsuits. Hollywood's message in this case is clear: public schools are filled with administrators who would rather cater to a liberal discourse about the civil rights of students – who clearly don't deserve any – than protect the welfare of teachers who face the threat of daily violence.

Garfield's fellow teachers are no better. The first teacher he meets, Dave Childress (John Heard), is an alcoholic burnout who stashes a .357 Magnum in his desk drawer, thoroughly hates his students, and, we later learn, has had sexual relations with a very young, emotionally shaken, Latina student. Hanging on for the paycheck, Childress serves as a reminder of what such schools do to teachers. Robbed of his passion, he regards every kid as a social menace or macho punk, waiting to kill or be killed. Garfield eventually strike up a friendship and romance with Ellen Henry (Kelly Rowan), a perky, blond, computer science teacher, but it soon turns sour as the bleak and dangerous environment in which they find themselves eventually pushes Garfield over the edge. Ellen tries to draw close to Garfield, but he is too battered and isolated, telling Ellen at one point that when he was assaulted in New York, it robbed him of his "passion, my spark, my unguarded self – I miss them."

Garfield's descent into madness begins when his bungalow is completely trashed by the gang members in his class. He becomes edgy, living in a shadow of fear heightened by his past. Ellen then tells Garfield that Benny, a particularly vicious gang member in his class, has threatened to hurt her, and that she doesn't know what to do. Benny soon disappears from school, and is later found to be a victim of homicide, but Ellen's troubles are not over as Benny's sidekick, Cesar, and his friends kill her dog. As a result, Cesar becomes the object of vigilante justice. Roaming drunk near an L A freeway, he is stalked, shot with a spiked arrow and, while unconscious, has his finger cut off. The tension mounts as Ellen finds Benny's rosary beads in Garfield's apartment and confronts him with the evidence that he might be the killer. Garfield is immune to her reproach, arguing that someone has to take responsibility since the system will not protect "us" from "them." Ellen tells Garfield she doesn't know him anymore, and Garfield replies, "I am a teacher just like you." As the word circulates that Garfield may be the vigilante killer and assailant, the principal moves fast to protect the school from a lawsuit by firing him. Garfield, now completely broken, goes home and is soon visited by Cesar and his gang, who, inspired by the film, *The Deer Hunter*, force Garfield into a game of Russian roulette. With little to lose, Garfield accuses Cesar of not being a real man, and ups the stakes of the game by taking Cesar's turn. Garfield pulls the trigger and kills himself. Forced into questioning his own manhood, Cesar decides to take his turn, puts the gun to his head, and fatally shoots himself as well. In the final scene of the film, when a student is reading a graduation speech about how teachers rarely get any respect, the shot switches to Ellen who is in her classroom. Ellen takes her framed teaching certificate off the wall, throws it into the wastebasket, and walks out of the school.

Accessing a Pedagogy of the Cultural Object

Pedagogically, films like *187* can be interrogated by analyzing both the commonsense assumptions that inform them as well as absences and exclusions that limit the range of meanings and information available to audiences. Analyzing such films as public discourses also provides pedagogical opportunities to engage complex institutional frameworks that create the conditions for the construction, legitimation, and meaning of such cultural texts. As public discourses, these cultural texts can be addressed in terms of how they are constituted as objects that gain their relevance through their relationship to other social institutions, resources, and practices. In this instance, *187* would be taken up as a discursive practice whose effects might be addressed in relation to issues of race in related contexts where struggles for meaning and representation are connected to struggles for power, social agency, and material resources. Some of these issues are illustrated below.

The film *187* provides ample representations of students of color as the pathological other, and public schools as not only dysfunctional but also as an imminent threat to the dominant society. Represented as a criminalized underclass, black and brown students in *187* are viewed as dangerous, and public schools as holding centers that contain such students through the heavy-handed use of high-tech monitoring systems and military-style authority. Reinforcing such stereotypes is a decontextualized and depoliticized cinematic narrative that erases the conditions that produce such denigrating images of inner-city public schools – poverty, family turmoil, highly segregated neighborhoods, unemployment, crumbling school buildings, lack of material resources, or inequities within local and national tax structures. In this instance, *187* represents more than a text that portrays a particularly offensive image of urban schools and minority students, it also participates as a public pedagogy in enabling, legitimizing, and reinforcing discursive practices whose effect is to condemn the children of the urban poor to public schools increasingly subject to electronic surveillance, private police forces, padlocks, and alarms suggestive of prisons or war zones.[11]

Clearly, if the dominant codes at work in such a film are to be questioned, it is imperative for students to address how the absences in the film tie it to prevailing discourses about public education, multiculturalism, and the ongoing assault on minorities of class and color in and outside public schooling. Marking such absences is crucial to understanding such a film – the refusal to point to the need for smaller class sizes, inspiring teachers, visionary administrators, and ample learning resources – but such absences become meaningful when understood within a broader struggle over issues of racial identity, power, representation, and everyday life.

Films like *187* carry the logic of racial stereotyping to a new level and represent one of the most egregious examples of how popular cultural texts can be used to demonize black and Latino youth while reproducing a consensus of common sense that legitimates racist policies of either containment or abandonment in the inner cities.

But such instances of racial coding cannot reside merely within the boundaries of the text to be fully understood as part of the broader landscape of racial injustice. Depictions of urban youth as dangerous, pathological, and violent must be located in terms of where different possibilities of uses and effects of such representations may ultimately reside in contexts of everyday life that are at the forefront of multicultural struggles. For example, the depictions of youth in *187* resonate powerfully with the growth of a highly visible criminal justice system whose get-tough policies fall disproportionately on poor black and brown youth. What is the pedagogical potential of a film such as *187* in addressing the political, racial, and economic conditions that promote a specious (yet celebrated) "war on drugs," a war whose policies threaten to wipe out a whole generation of young black men who are increasingly incarcerated in prisons and jails? The figures are disturbing, as the number of black men incarcerated is growing at the rate of about 7 percent a year, and annual prison costs are now higher than $30 million.[12] As statistics show:

> Between 1983 and 1998 the number of prisoners in the U.S. increased from 650,000 to more than 1.7 million. About 60 percent of that number are African-Americans and Latinos. More than one-third of all young black men in their 20s are currently in jail, on probation or parole, or awaiting trial. We are now adding 1,200 new inmates to US jails and prisons each week, and adding about 260 new prison beds each day.[13]

This state of affairs is compounded by the disturbing fact that as a result of serving time nearly half of the next generation of black males will forfeit their right to vote in several states. How might a cultural text such as *187* be used to address the relationship between the increase in prison growth and the plight caused by industrial downsizing and rising unemployment among young black men across America's inner cities in the 1990s? What might it mean for students to address their own responses to the moral panics concerning crime and race that have swept across the middle-classes in the last decade, made manifest in strong electoral support for harsh crime laws and massive increases in prison growth.

At the very least, educators can address *187* not merely in terms of what such a text might mean but how it functions within a set of complex social relations that create the conditions of which it is a part and from which it stems. Larry Grossberg insightfully argues that such a pedagogy would

> involve the broader exploration of the way in which discursive practices construct and participate in the machinery by which the way people live their lives are themselves produced and controlled. Rather than looking for the "said" or trying to derive the saying from the said, rather than asking what texts mean or what people do with texts, [a critical pedagogy] would be concerned with what discursive practices do in the world.[14]

Engaging the potential discursive effects of films like *187* might mean discussing the implication of this Hollywood film's appropriating the name of the controversial California proposition to deny mostly nonwhite students access to public schools. Or it might mean discussing how the film contributes to a public discourse that rationalizes both the demonization of minority youth and the defunding of public and higher education at a time when, in states such as California, "approximately 22,555 African Americans attend a four-year public university...while 44,792 (almost twice as many) African Americans are in prison [and] this figure does not include all the African Americans who are in county jails or the California Youth Authority or those on probation or parole."[15]

Hollywood films like *187* must be addressed and understood within a broader set of policy debates about education and crime that often serve to legitimate policies that disempower poor and racially marginalized youth. For example, state spending for corrections has increased 95 percent over the last decade, while spending on higher education has decreased 6 percent. Similarly, in the last 10 years, the rate of increase in the number of correctional officers is four times that of the increase in higher education faculty. Again, it is not surprising that the chosen setting for *187* is primarily California, a state that now, the Justice Policy Institute notes, "spends more on corrections (9.4% of the General Fund) than on higher education."[16]

While it would be absurd to suggest to students that films like *187* are responsible for recent government spending allocations, they do take part in a public pedagogy and representational politics that cannot be separated from a growing racial panic over, and fear of, minorities, the urban poor, and immigrants.

As public discourses, films like *187*, *The Substitute I* and *II*, *Dangerous Minds*, and *Belly* fail to rupture the racial stereotypes that support harsh, discriminatory crime policies and growing incidents of police brutality. Recent examples include the New York Police Department's highly publicized torture of Abner Louima, or its shooting of Amadou Diallo by four patrolmen who riddled his body and an apartment building vestibule with 41 bullets in spite of the fact that Diallo was unarmed. Such films also have little to say about police assaults on poor black neighborhoods, such as those conducted by former police Chief Daryl Gates in south-central Los Angeles. Exploiting the race-based moral panics that fuel popular antagonism toward affirmative action, immigrants, bilingual education, the inner city, and the unmarried "welfare queen," films such as *187* capitalize on modes of exclusion through what Jimmie Reeves and Richard Campbell call the "discourse of discrimination" and the "spectacle of stigmatization." Within this discourse, the urban black or brown youth is depicted as "the pathological Other – a delinquent beyond rehabilitation."[17]

What is unique about *187* is that it explores cinematically what the logical conclusion might be in dealing with urban youth for whom reform is no longer on the national agenda, and for whom containment or the militarization of school space seem both inadequate and too compromising. As social problems are increasingly criminalized, and the model of the penal system begins to define not only the public space of schooling but all aspects of public space inhabited especially by those who are considered marginal by virtue of their race, class, and gender, inner-city schools appear to be relegated to the status of institutions that largely serve as direct feeders into the criminal justice system. But as the public is reduced to a territory that is largely portrayed as a site of moral decay, danger, and violence, the logic of domestic militarization appears to reach an even more dangerous level, at least as expressed in *187*.

For example, *187* flirts with the ultimate white supremacist logic, suggesting that it is perfectly reasonable to exterminate and eliminate those others deemed beyond the pale of social reform. In this instance, black and brown inner-city youth who are deemed inhuman and despicable are now seen as legitimate targets of assassination and murder. Capitalizing on the popular media conception that public education is not safe for white, middle-class children, *187* reinforces the idea that racial violence is rampant in the public schools, that minority students have turned classroom discipline into a joke, that administrators are paralyzed by insensitive bureaucracies, and that the only thing that teachers and students share is the desire to survive the day. Yet cultural texts such as *187* cannot be easily dismissed because of their overt racist messages and ideology. As public texts and pedagogies, it is crucial for teachers and students to situate films such as *187* within existing sets of social and cultural relations in order to understand the ideological, cultural, social, and economic forces that make such films possible. Crucial to explore in this type of analysis are the conditions that enable such racist texts to be produced, distributed, and circulated within existing circuits of power. Moreover, it seems crucial that educators and students engage how it is possible for such texts to gain legitimacy in the popular media. Why is it that the racism which fuels the aggressive attack on public schools presented by such films goes almost unchallenged in the media? What should be the role of critical intellectuals in taking up such texts, given the ideological and cultural work that they perform in reproducing and reinforcing existing racist assumptions and conservative attacks on public education? Clearly, such texts are important to engage not just as strategies for understanding and raising critical questions about related discourses, narratives, and social issues, but also because they offer pedagogical opportunities for students to critically interrogate what it might mean to move beyond the narrow institutional space of the classroom to address important social issues in related public spheres marked by racial injustices and unequal relations of power.

The popularity of such films as *187* in the heyday of academic multiculturalism points to the need, in light of such representations, for educators to develop pedagogical approaches which not only deepen their understanding of multiculturalism but also engage it as part of a broader struggle to develop a multiracial democracy. This suggests that critical educators get beyond reducing the pedagogy of multiculturalism to the exclusive analyses of academic texts or falling prey to limiting such analysis to the narrow discourse of identity politics. Any viable pedagogy of multiculturalism must include how questions of representation and identity are related to wider struggles for power, meaning, and resources in a variety of public spheres. For instance, as part of a pedagogy of multiculturalism educators might attempt not only to provide the conditions for students to think critically, but also encourage them to address what it would mean to challenge and transform the "economics of school funding and school policy [that] sustain segregation in American public education [through] inhuman fiscal policies that have ensured the continuous impoverishment of schools attended wholly by black or Hispanic schoolchildren."[18] Similarly, educators might make the pedagogy of multiculturalism more politically viable by requiring students to address as part of a multicultural pedagogy what it would mean to reform a criminal justice system that disproportionately incarcerates and punishes minorities of class and color.

Issues of representation and identity, in this case, offer the opportunity for multicultural educators and students to explore cultural texts as they articulate with and make visible the ways in which multiculturalism is connected to a range of important institutional, economic, cultural, and political considerations. Such concerns suggests that critical educators develop pedagogical practices that promote a social vocabulary of cultural difference that links strategies of understanding to strategies of engagement, while recognizing both the limits and strengths of the university as a site for civic education and social engagement. Clearly, for pedagogy to do this kind of critical work it would have not only to define politics through the productive prism of language, meaning, and the representational politics of a visual culture, but also connect matters of discourse and representation to broader systemic forces involving political power, institutional control, and economic ownership.

I recognize that more is at stake here than simply providing a new theoretical framework for deepening and expanding the meaning of multiculturalism as part of a larger struggle for a substantive and more fully realized democracy. There is also the issue of taking up the responsibility and role of educators as public intellectuals willing to speak truth to power, address important social issues, and display the courage to enter into public issues in order to limit human suffering. Needless to say, academics cannot become public intellectuals by the mere force of will, given the professional and institutional constraints under which they operate. But at the same time, if multiculturalism is not going to abandon the world of public politics and take seriously the link between theory and practice, progressive educators will have to rethink collectively what it means to link the struggle for change within the university to struggles for change in the broader society.

In part, bridging the politics of representation to the social gravity and force of everyday issues rooted in concrete material relations of power requires a rethinking on the part of intellectuals about the nature and use of theory in the classroom. Theory in the best sense would not be reduced to a form of theoreticism, an indulgence in which the production of theoretical discourse becomes an end in itself, an expression of language removed from the possibility of challenging strategies of domination. Rather than treating theory as a closed circuit, critical intellectuals, cultural workers, and others must appropriate it as a resource, performing the bridging work between intellectual debates and public issues; at best, theory provides knowledge and tools to connect concrete struggles with broader public debates, opening up possibilities for new approaches to social reform, or addressing the pressing social problems. In order to mobilize its power as a political force, theory cannot be used by academics to simply name multiculturalism as a discipline, text, or set of values, but must also acknowledge and contest its presence and manifestation in public life.

Within many liberal and critical approaches to multiculturalism, the politics of meaning becomes relevant only to the degree that it is separated from a broader politics of engagement. Reading texts such as *187* becomes a hermetic process, one removed from larger social and political contexts, and engaging questions of power exclusively within a politics of representation. Such readings largely function to celebrate a textuality that has been diminished to a bloodless formalism and the nonthreatening, if not accommodating, affirmation of indeterminacy as a transgressive aesthetic. Lost here is any semblance of a radical political project that "grounds itself in the study of concrete cultural practices and . . . understands that struggles over meaning are inevitably struggles over resources."[19] By failing to connect the study of texts, identity politics, and the politics of difference to the interests of a project that expands the goals of the civil rights movement, human rights campaigns against international tyranny, radical democratic feminist visions, and the opposition to antiwelfare and immigration policies, many academic multiculturalists conceive politics as largely representational or abstractly theoretical.[20]

As citizenship becomes increasingly privatized and students are increasingly educated to renounce their obligations to substantive citizenship and political agency, it becomes all the more imperative for educators to rethink how the educational force of the culture works to both secure and resist particular identities and values. This is especially important as the force of the dominant culture is defined through its submission to the values of the economy with its emphasis on privatization and the gospel of self-help, all of which works to both undermine notions of the public good and collective responsibility and place the blame for injustice and oppression entirely on the shoulders of those who are the victims of social misfortune. In part, films such as *187* offer critical educators and others an opportunity to foreground the importance of critical work aimed at recovering the ways in which culture is related to power and how and where it functions both symbolically and institutionally as an educational, political, and economic force that refuses to live with difference.

As more and more young people face a world of increasing poverty, unemployment, and diminished social opportunities, those of us in diverse sites, including public and higher education, will have to re-evaluate the relationship between culture and power as a starting point for bearing witness to the ethical and political dilemmas that connect the university to other spheres within the broader social landscape. In doing so, progressive educators need to become more attentive to how multicultural politics gets worked out in urban spaces and public spheres that are currently experiencing the full force of the right-wing attack on culture and racial difference. It is no longer possible for academics to make a claim for a radical politics of multiculturalism by defining it merely as a set of intellectual options and curriculum imperatives. Films such as *187* make it clear that critical educators and others must examine actual struggles taking place in the name of cultural difference within institutional sites and cultural formations that bear the brunt of dominant machineries of power designed to exclude, contain, or disadvantage the oppressed. The institutional and cultural spheres bearing the brunt of the racialization of the social order are increasingly located in the public schools, in the criminal justice system, in retrograde anti-immigrant policy legislation, and in the state's ongoing attempts to force welfare recipients into workfare programs.[21] Films such as *187* remind us that as progressive educators we need to vitalize our efforts within the university by connecting the intellectual work we do there with a greater attentiveness to broader pressing public problems and social responsibilities, particularly as they are produced and presented in the public space of diverse media such as Hollywood films. A radical approach to pedagogy of representation is partly required to address how material relations of power work to sustain structures of inequality and exploitation in the current racialization of the social order. It must ask specific questions about the forms racial domination and subordination take within the broader public culture and how their organization, operation, and effects both implicate and affect the meaning and purpose of higher education. At stake here is the need for critical educators to give meaning to the belief that academic work matters in its relationship to broader public practices and policies; and that such work holds the possibility for understanding not just how power operates in particular contexts, but also how such knowledge "will better enable people to change the context and hence the relations of power"[22] that inform both the media that engage them every day and the larger society in which they live. Combining theoretical rigor with social relevance may be risky politically and pedagogically, but the promise of a multicultural democracy far outweighs the security and benefits that accompany a retreat into academic irrelevance and color-blind professionalism.

I want to conclude by arguing that the promise of a multicultural democracy hinges on more than defining educators and other cultural workers as engaged public intellectuals, linking learning to social change, or engaging the media as a form of public pedagogy. Educators, artists, and other progressives must also take up the challenge of developing pedagogies that teach kids how to use media as a mode of self-expression and social activism. We need to find new ways in which pedagogy can translate into an activist strategy that expands the opportunity for knowledge and skills that helps young people extend their participation into, and control over, those cultural, economic, and social spheres that shape daily life (mass media, schools, media, workplace, policy-making institutions, the arts). Evidence of such work can be found in films such as Marc Levin's *Slam* (1998), which narrates the complexities, struggles, and hopes of Raymond Joshua (Saul Williams), a gifted rapper in Washington, D.C., who falls prey to a racist criminal justice system and ends up in jail serving time on a petty drug charge. While in prison he meets Lauren Bell (Sonja Sohn), a writing teacher who recognizes his talents as a poet and provides the emotional support and pedagogical encouragement to nurture his talents and help him to redefine his sense of agency and collective struggle through his poetry.

Unlike *187*, despair in this film does not paralyze the body and mind; on the contrary, it becomes the emotional and intellectual fodder to connect the body back to the mind in ways that rearticulate how maps of meaning and affect can come together to create a space in which the body feels and thinks in the service of hope, possibility, sensuality, and struggle. Power in this film bypasses a rationality that has no connection to the body, affect, and emotion. *Slam* offers a model for black youth to reclaim their lives within a destructive culture of violence and drugs. Levin is no romantic, but he lets the voices of Raymond Joshua and Lauren Bell capture the complexities of their lives, their courage, and strength by giving them the space and courage to narrate critically their own experiences. These narratives become the basis for dialogue, debate, rap-style poetry, and critical mediation and engagement with dangers lurking within the prison system. This is a remarkable cultural document, full of complexities, tensions, and subtleties; moreover, it is acutely aware of its own politics and the dangers African-American men face in a country that appears intent on incarcerating most of them. At the same time, it refuses to romanticize resistance and the power of critical pedagogy and Levin holds firm in the belief that progressive pedagogical and political interventions might give rise to possibilities and real achievements for kids too often viewed as throwaways.

Levin's film moves beyond either the demonization of young black youth or the simplistic call for positive images of such youth; instead, it captures the complexities of how such youth are produced within certain social, economic, and political circumstances while simultaneously working to transform such conditions. This is film with an up-front project that takes seriously the challenge of developing a language of critique and possibility, one that confronts both racist representations of youth, and a representational politics in which youth are blamed for society's failures. *Slam* provides an example of a representational politics in which a pedagogy of the popular make it possible for educators, students, and others to understand the ways in which black youth attempt "to open social and cultural spaces in which to express themselves,"[23] as well as engage and transform the conditions through which they push against the constraints of poverty and racism. In this discourse, cultural production becomes central not only to the very definition of learning and political agency, but also to the promise of what might be gained in a society in which bigotry, rather than difference and social responsibility, becomes the enemy of a multicultural democracy.

Notes

1. David Theo Goldberg, *Racist Culture* (Cambridge, MA: Blackwell, 1993): 105.
2. Ginsburg cited in Editorial, "Race On Screen and Off." *The Nation* (December 29, 1997): 6.
3. Shipler summarized in Jack H. Geiger, "The Real World of Race." *The Nation* (December 1, 1998): 27. See also, David Shipler, "Reflections on Race." *Tikkun* 13.1 (1998): 59, 78; David Shipler, *A Country of Strangers: Blacks and Whites in America* (New York: Vintage, 1998).

4. Ellen Willis argues that the two major upheavals to America's racial hierarchy have been the destruction of the Southern caste system and the subversion of whiteness as an unquestioned norm. She also argues rightly that to dismiss these achievements as having done little to change racist power relations insults people who have engaged in these struggles. See Ellen Willis, "The Up and Up: On the Limits of Optimism." *Transition* 7.2 (1998): 44–61.

5. For a compilation of figures suggesting the ongoing presence of racism in American society, see Ronald Walters, "The Criticality of Racism." *Black Scholar* 26.1 (Winter, 1996): 2–8; "A Report from the Children's Defense Fund, Yearbook 1998," *The State of America's Children* (Boston: Beacon Press, 1998).

6. For a devastating critique of Randall Kennedy's move to the right, see Derrick Bell, "The Strange Career of Randall Kennedy." *New Politics* 7. 1 (Summer, 1998): 55–69.

7. Katya Gibel Azoulay, "Experience, Empathy and Strategic Essentialism." *Cultural Studies* 11.1 (1997): 91.

8. Robin D. G. Kelley, "Integration: What's Left." *The Nation* (December 14, 1998): 18.

9. Cited in Randall Johnson, "Editor's Introduction: Pierre Bourdieu on Art, Literature and Culture," in Pierre Bourdieu, *The Field of Cultural Production* (New York: Columbia University Press, 1993), p. 19.

10. Ibid., p. 17.

11. This issue is taken up in John Devine, *Maximum Security: The Culture of Violence in Inner-City Schools* (Chicago: University of Chicago Press, 1996). Unfortunately, Devine's remedy for the militarization of school space is to blame students for not being civil enough. Hence, Devine undermines an interesting analysis of the culture of violence in schools by framing his solutions within a paradigm that is utterly privatized and trapped within the discourse of the genteel brigade led by ultra self-righteous moralizers such William Bennett.

12. These figures are cited in Fox Butterfield, "Crime Keeps on Falling, But Prisons Keep on Filling," *The New York Times* (September 28, 1997): 1. Jimmie Reeves and Richard Campbell provide a more extensive picture of prison growth in the United States. Jimmie L. Reeves and Richard Campbell, *Cracked Coverage: Television News, the Anti-cocaine Crusade, and the Reagan Legacy* (Durham: Duke University Press, 1994): 41.

13. Manning Marable, "Beyond Color-Blindness." *The Nation* (December 14, 1998): 31.

14. Lawrence Grossberg, "The Victory of Culture, Part I." University of North Carolina at Chapel Hill, unpublished manuscript (February, 1998): 27.

15. Figures cited in The Justice Policy Institute/Center on Juvenile and Criminal Justice Policy Report, *From Classrooms to Cell Blocks: How Prison Building Affects Higher Education and African American Enrollment in California* (San Francisco, CA: Justice Policy Institute, October 1996): 2.

16. Ibid.

17. These quotes come from Jimmie L. Reeves and Richard Campbell, *Cracked Coverage*, op.cit., pp. 40–1.

18. Michael Berube, "Disuniting America Again." *The Journal of the Midwest Modern Language Association* 26.1 (Spring, 1993): 41.

19. George Lipsitz, "Listening to Learn and Learning to Listen: Popular Culture, Cultural Theory, and American Studies." *American Quarterly* 42.4 (December, 1990): 621.

20. In opposition to this type of textualism Larry Grossberg argues that Edward Said's *Orientalism* is a classic example of a text that focuses on questions of difference, identity, and subjectivity while engaging the related issues of materialism and power. See Lawrence Grossberg, "Identity and Cultural Studies. Is That All There Is?" in Stuart Hall and Paul Du Gay (eds.), *Questions of Cultural Identity* (Thousand Oaks, CA: Sage, 1996): 87–107.

21. Marable, "Beyond Color-Blindness," op.cit. p. 31.

22. Lawrence Grossberg, "Cultural Studies: What's in a Name?" in *Bringing It All Back Home: Essays on Cultural Studies* (Durham, NC: Duke University Press, 1997): 252–3.

23. Herman Gray, *Watching Race: Television and the Struggle for "Blackness"* (Minneapolis: University of Minnesota Press, 1995), p. 160.

12

Brutalized Bodies and Emasculated Politics: *Fight Club*, Consumerism and Masculine Violence[1]

Introduction

If it has now become easier to imagine the end of the earth and of nature rather than the end of capitalism, as Fredric Jameson argued in *The Seeds of Time*, it is due in large part to the redoubled efforts of a global, neoliberal capitalism.[2] The breathless rhetoric of the global victory of free-market rationality spewed forth by the mass media, right-wing intellectuals, and governments alike, has found its material expression in an all-out attack on democratic values and on the very notion of the public. Within the discourse of neoliberalism – which construes profit making as the essence of democracy and provides a rationale for a handful of private interests to control as much of social life as possible in order to maximize their personal profit – issues regarding persistent poverty, inadequate health care, racial apartheid in the inner cities, and the growing inequalities between the rich and the poor have been either removed from the inventory of public discourse and social policy or factored into talk-show spectacles. The latter highlight private woes bearing little relationship either to public life or to potential remedies that demand collective action.

As the laws of the market take precedence over the laws of the state as guardians of the public good, the government increasingly offers little help in mediating the interface between the advance of capital and its rapacious commercial interests. Neither does it aid noncommodified interests and nonmarket spheres that create the political, economic, and social conditions vital for critical citizenship and democratic public life. Within the discourse of neoliberalism that has taken hold of the public imagination, there is no vocabulary in which to speak about political or social transformation. There is no collective vision, no social agency to challenge ruthless downsizing, the ongoing liquidation of job security, or the elimination of benefits for people now hired on part-time. In the midst of this concerted attack by big business on the public, market-driven consumerism continues to mobilize desires in the interest of producing market identities and market relationships. These ultimately appear as, Theodor Adorno once put it, nothing less than "a prohibition on thinking itself."[3]

It is in this context of the ongoing assault on the public by a free market economy and corporate culture that turns everything it touches into an object of consumption that David Fincher's film *Fight Club* needs to be considered. Ostensibly, *Fight Club* offers a critique of late capitalist society and the misfortunes generated by its obsessive concern with profits, consumption, and the commercial values that underline its market-driven ethos. But *Fight Club* is less interested in attacking the broader material relations of power and strategies of domination and exploitation associated with neoliberal capitalism than it is in rebelling against a consumerist culture that dissolves the bonds of male sociality and puts into place an enervating notion of male identity and agency. Contrary to the onslaught of reviews accompanying the film's premiere that celebrated it as a daring social critique[4] – the filmic equivalent of magazines like the *Baffler* or *Adbusters*, or even of political protests in Seattle, Washington D.C., Windsor, ON, Geneva, and Prague against international agents of capitalism like the World Bank, the World Trade Organization, and the International Monetary Fund. But the truth is that *Fight Club* has nothing to say about the structural violence of unemployment, job insecurity, cuts in public spending, and the destruction of institutions capable of defending social provisions and the public good. On the contrary, *Fight Club* defines the violence of capitalism almost exclusively in terms of an attack on traditional (if not to say regressive) notions of masculinity, and in doing so reinscribes white

259

heterosexuality within a dominant logic of stylized brutality and male bonding that appears predicated on the need to denigrate and wage war against all that is feminine. In this instance, the crisis of capitalism is reduced to the crisis of masculinity, and the nature of the crisis lies less in the economic, political, and social conditions of capitalism itself than in the rise of a culture of consumption in which men are allegedly domesticated, rendered passive, soft, and emasculated.

Fight Club, along with films such as *Pulp Fiction*, *Rogue Trader*, *American Psycho*, and *Boiler Room* inaugurates a new subgenre of cult film that combines a fascination with the spectacle of violence, enlivened through tired narratives about the crisis of masculinity, along with a superficial gesture toward social critique designed to offer the tease of a serious independent/art film.[5] While appearing to address important social issues, these films end up reproducing the very problems they attempt to address. Rather than turning a critical light on crucial social problems, such films often trivialize them within a stylized aesthetics that revels in irony, cynicism, and excessive violence. Violence in these films is reduced to acts of senseless brutality, pathology, and an indifference to human suffering. Reproducing such hackneyed representations of violence ("senseless," "random"), they conclude where engaged political commentary should begin. Yet, I am less interested in moralizing about the politics of Fincher's film than I am in reading it as a form of public pedagogy that offers an opportunity to engage and understand its politics of representation as part of broader commentary on the intersection of consumerism, masculinity, violence, politics, and gender relations. Moreover, *Fight Club* signifies the role that Hollywood films play as teaching machines. A far cry from simple entertainment, such films function as public pedagogies by articulating knowledge to effects, purposely attempting to influence how and what knowledge and identities can be produced within a limited range of social relations. At the same time, I recognize that such texts "are radically indeterminate with respect to their meaning, [and] any reading of a text must be determined by factors not prescribed by the text itself."[6]

As public pedagogies, texts such as *Fight Club* attempt to bridge the gap between private and public discourses, while simultaneously putting into play particular ideologies and values that resonate with broader public conversations regarding how a society views itself and the world of power, events, and politics. Reading a film such as *Fight Club*, in more specific terms, suggests engaging how it offers up particular notions of agency in which white working-class and middle-class men are allowed to see themselves as oppressed and lacking because their masculinity has been compromised by and subordinated to those social and economic spheres and needs that constitute the realm of the feminine.

In taking up these issues, I first analyze the narrative structure of the film, addressing its simultaneous critique of consumerism and its celebration of masculinity. In doing so, I address critically the representational politics that structure *Fight Club* – especially its deeply conventional views of violence, gender relations, and masculinity– and how such representations work in conjunction with a deeply entrenched culture of cynicism. Finally, I argue that such cynicism, far from being innocent, works in tandem with broader public discourses to undermine the faith of individuals and groups to engage in the possibility of a politics designed to struggle against the rising tide of antidemocratic forces and movements that threaten the already weakened fabric of democracy. Obviously, I am not arguing that Hollywood films such as *Fight Club* are a cause of these problems but are symptomatic of a wider symbolic and institutional culture of cynicism and senseless violence that exerts a powerful pedagogical influence on shaping the public imagination. In treating *Fight Club* as a pedagogical and political text my aim is to reveal its socially constructed premises, demystify its contradictions, and challenge its reactionary views. In part, I want both to ask questions about *Fight Club* that have not been generally asked in the popular press and engage how dominant public pedagogies prevent us from asking such questions in the first place. In addition, I take up the role that *Fight Club* and other cultural texts might provide as public pedagogies that can be read against themselves, that is, how such texts can be deconstructed and reworked theoretically within a wider set of associations and meanings that can be both challenged and rearticulated in order to strengthen rather than weaken a public politics, while furthering the promise of democratic transformation.

RACE AND THE CULTURE OF VIOLENCE

Fight Club and the Crisis of Everyday Life

> In [commercial cinema's] seeming transformation of violence into entertainment, choreography, and macho ebullience, one could say that the reality of violence has been infantilized. One cannot take it too seriously, And yet, one is compelled to ask if any idiom of violence can be regarded as "innocent," distanced from reality through its apparent autonomy of signs.[7]

White heterosexual men in America have not fared well in the nineties. Not only have they been attacked by feminists, gays, lesbians, and various subaltern groups for a variety of ideological and material offenses, they have also had to endure a rewriting of the very meaning of masculinity.[8] As Homi Bhabha has recently stated, the manifest destiny of masculinity, with its hard-boiled tough image of manliness, has been disturbed, and its blocked reflexivity has been harshly unsettled.[9] Moreover, the shift from a manufacturing base to an information-based economy, from the production of goods to the production of knowledge, has offered men, at least according to Susan Faludi, fewer and fewer meaningful occupations.[10] Consequently, the male body has been transformed from an agent of production to a receptacle for consumption. A rampant culture of consumption, coupled with a loss of manufacturing and middle-management jobs, presents white males with an identity crisis of unparalleled proportions. The male hero of the modern-day workforce is no longer defined in the image of the tightly hewn worker using his body and labor to create the necessities for everyday life. The new workforce hero is now modeled on the image of the young computer whiz yuppie who defines his life and goals around the hot start-up e-commerce companies, day trading, and other "get rich before I'm 21" schemes, as well as the conspicuous consumption of expensive products. Moreover, as white, heterosexual, working-class and middle-class men face a life of increasing uncertainty and insecurity, they no longer have easy access to those communities in which they can inhabit a form of masculinity that defines itself in opposition to femininity. In simple terms, the new millennium offers white heterosexual men nothing less than a life in which ennui and domestication define their everyday existence.

David Fincher's 1999 film, *Fight Club*, based on a novel by Chuck Palahniuk, attempts to critically engage the boredom, shallowness, and emptiness of a stifling consumer culture, redefine what it might mean for men to resist compromising their masculinity for the sofa or cappuccino maker that "speaks them," and explore the possibilities for creating a sense of community in which men can reclaim their virility and power. The film opens with an inside shot of Jack's brain, tracking a surge of adrenalin that quickly finds an opening in Jack's mouth and then exits up the barrel of a gun. Jack (played by Edward Norton) then proceeds to lead the audience into the nature of his predicament and in doing so narrates his journey out of corporate America and his evolving relationship with Tyler Durden (Brad Pitt), who functions as Jack's alter-ego and significant other. The first section of the film functions primarily as a critique of contemporary consumerism and how corporate culture positions men in jobs and lifestyles that are both an affront to their manhood and male sociality, leaving them to seek refuge in communities of self-help/support – portrayed as the dreaded cult of victimhood–which only accentuates the contemporary crisis of masculinity. As the film unfolds, Jack is portrayed as a neoliberal Everyman–an emasculated, repressed corporate drone whose life is simply an extension of a reified and commodified culture.

As a recall coordinator, Jack travels around the country investigating accidents for a major auto company in order to decide whether it's cheaper for the corporation to assign recalls or payment to a likely number of lawsuits. Alienated from his job, utterly lacking any sense of drive or future, Jack's principle relief comes from an insatiable urge for flipping through and shopping from consumer catalogues. A slave to the "IKEA nesting instinct," Jack self-consciously offers up rhetorical questions such as "What kind of dining set defines me as a person?" But Jack's IKEA-designed apartment appears to offer him no respite from the emptiness in his life, and his consumerist urges only seem to reinforce his lack of enthusiasm for packaging himself as a corporate puppet and presenting himself as a Tom Peters up-and-coming "brand name."[11] Tormented by the emptiness of his daily life and suffering from near terminable insomnia, Jack visits his doctor claiming he is in real pain. His 30-something doctor refuses to give him drugs and tells him that if he really wants to see pain to visit a local testicular cancer survivor group. Jack not only attends the self-help meeting, but discovers that the group offers him a sense of comfort and community and in an ironic twist he becomes a support group junkie. At his first meeting of the Remaining Men Together survival group Jack meets Bob (Meat Loaf Aday), a former weightlifter who has enormous breasts (described as "bitch tits") as a result of hormonal treatments. The group allows Jack to participate in a form of male bonding that offers him an opportunity to release his pent-up emotions and provides a cure for his insomnia. Bob becomes a not too subtle symbol in the film, personifying how masculinity is both degraded (he has breasts like a woman) and used in a culture that relies upon the "feminine" qualities of support and empathy rather than "masculine" attributes of strength and virility to bring men together. When Bob hugs Jack and tells him "You can cry now," *Fight Club* does more than mock new age therapy for men; it is also satirizing and condemning the "weepy" process of femininization that such therapies sanction and put into place.

Jack eventually meets Marla (Helena Bonham-Carter), a disheveled, chain-smoking, slinky street urchin who is also slumming in the same group therapy sessions as Jack. Jack views Marla as a tourist – addicted only to the spectacle of the meetings. Marla reminds him of his own phoniness and so upsets him that his insomnia returns, and his asylum is shattered. Jack can't find emotional release with another phony in the same session. In the voiceover, Jack claims that "if he had a tumor he would name it Marla." Once again, repressed white masculinity is thrown into a crisis by the eruption of an ultraconservative version of post-1960s femininity that signifies both the antithesis of domestic security, comfort, and sexual passivity – offering only neurosis and blame in their place. We now begin to understand Jack's comment in the beginning of the film, after the gun is pulled from his mouth, that "Marla is at the root of it."

On the heels of this loss, Jack meets Tyler Durden (Brad Pitt) on an airplane. Tyler is the antithesis of Jack—a bruising, cocky, brash soap salesman, part-time waiter, and movie projectionist with a whiff of anarchism shoring up his speech, dress, and body language. If Jack is a model of packaged conformity and yuppie depthlessness, Tyler is a no-holds-barred charismatic rebel who as a part-time movie projectionist offers his own attack on family values by splicing frames of pornography into kiddie films, or when working as a banquet waiter in a luxurious hotel urinates into the soup to be served to high-paying yuppie customers. Tyler also creatively affirms his disgust for women by making high-priced soaps from liposuctioned human fat and proudly telling Jack that he is "selling rich ladies their own fat asses back to them at $20.00 a bar." Jack is immediately taken with Tyler, who taunts him with the appellation "IKEA boy," and offers himself as his personal guide through the pitfalls of consumer culture. Mesmerized by Tyler's high octane talk and sense of subversion, Jack exchanges phone numbers with him.

When Jack returns home, he finds that his apartment has been mysteriously blown to bits. He calls Tyler who meets him at a local bar and tells him that things could be worse: "a woman could cut off your penis while you are sleeping and toss it out the window of a moving car." Tyler then launches into a five minute cliché-ridden tirade against the pitfalls of bourgeois life, mixing critique with elements of his own philosophical ramblings about the fall of masculinity. He tells Jack that issues such as crime and poverty don't trouble him. According to Tyler, the real problems men like him confront are "celebrity magazines, television with five hundred channels, some guy's name on my underwear, Rogaine, Viagra, Olestra." And as for the IKEA consumer hype of an idyllic domesticated existence, Tyler indignantly tells Jack "Things you own end up owning you. . . . Fuck Martha Stewart. . . . Fuck off with your sofa units. . . . stop being perfect. Let's evolve." And evolve they do. As they leave the bar, Tyler offers Jack the opportunity to move in with him in what turns out to be a dilapidated, abandoned house near a toxic dump.

Then the magic happens. Before they go back to Tyler's place, Tyler asks Jack to hit him, which Jack does and then Tyler returns the favor. Pain leads to exhilaration and they sit exhausted, bloodied, and blissful after their brute encounter. Soon Tyler and Jack start fighting repeatedly in a bar parking lot, eventually drawing a crowd of men who want to participate in brutally pummeling each other. Hence,

Fight Club, a new religion and secret society open only to males, is born. Groups of men soon afterwards start meeting in the cellar of a local nightclub in order to beat each other's heads into a bloody mess so as to reclaim their instincts as hunters within a society that has turned them into repressed losers and empty consumers. While Tyler enumerates several rules for the members of Fight Club ("The first rule of Fight Club is that you don't talk about Fight Club"), the one that actually captures the driving sentiment of his philosophy is the exhortation that "Self-improvement is masturbation. . . . self-destruction is the answer." For Tyler, physical violence becomes the necessary foundation for masculinity and collective terrorism the basis for politics itself. In other words, the only way Tyler's followers can become agents in a society that has deadened them is to get in touch with the primal instincts for competition and violence, and the only way their masculine identity can be reclaimed is through the literal destruction of their present selves – beating each other senseless – and their only recourse to community is to collectively engage in acts of militia-inspired terrorism aimed at corporate strongholds.

Eventually Jack has second thoughts about his homoerotic attraction to Tyler as a self-styled antihero when Tyler's narcissism and bravado mutates into an unbridled megalomania that appears more psychotic than anarchistic. Before long Tyler is spending more and more time with Marla, who appears to Jack's chagrin to be screwing him on an almost hourly basis. And Tyler ups the stakes of Fight Club by turning it into Operation Mayhem, a nationwide organization of terrorists thugs whose aim is to wage war against the rich and powerful. The acts of "resistance" carried out by Operation Mayhem, range from what has been described as "culture jamming" (transforming advertising billboards into political slogans, replacing airline safety cards with ones whose images depict the real outcome of a plane crash) to various forms of petty vandalism (demagnetizing an entire storeworth of video rentals, encouraging pigeons to shit all over a BMW dealership) to outright anarchic violence against what Tyler sees as the central symbols of domesticated masculinity: computers, the chief agents behind the end of industrialization; yuppie coffee bars, taken as symptomatic of the fetishization and feminization of a drink once associated with labor; and credit-card companies, whose products lie at the very center of contemporary consumer culture.[12] Eventually, the line between giving pain and risking death as part of the redeeming power of "masculine recovery" and the performance of barbaric fantasies worthy of the most ruthless right-wing militia movements becomes blurred. Before long one of Operation Mayhem's terrorist forays is botched and one of their members is killed by the police. The victim is Bob, the oversized testicular cancer survivor who has recently reaffirmed his own manliness by joining Fight Club. Jack is shocked by the killing, which in turn enables him to recognize that Tyler has become a demagogue and that Fight Club has evolved into a fascist paramilitary group more dangerous than the social order it has set out to destroy.

In a psychic meltdown that is long overdue, Jack realizes that he and Tyler are the same person, signaling a shift in the drama from the realm of the sociological to the psychological. Jack discovers that Tyler has planned a series of bombings around the unmentioned city and goes to the police to turn himself in. But the cops are members of Operation Mayhem and attempt to cut off his testicles because of his betrayal. Once more Jack rescues his manhood by escaping and eventually confronting Tyler in a building that has been targeted for demolition by Operation Mayhem. Jack fares badly in his fight with Tyler and ends up at the top of the building with a gun in his mouth. Jack finally realizes that he has the power to take control of the gun and has to shoot himself in order to kill Tyler. He puts the gun in his mouth and pulls the trigger. Tyler dies on the spot and Jack mysteriously survives. Marla is brought to the scene by some Operation Mayhem members. Jack orders them to leave and he and Marla hold hands and watch as office buildings explode all around them. In an apparent repudiation of all that he/Tyler has been about, Jack turns to Marla and tells her not to worry, "You met me at a weird time in my life," suggesting that life will get better for the both of them in the future.

Consumerism, Cynicism, and Hollywood Resistance

Consumerism . . . is less of an ideological falsification of well-being than a mark that no benefit exterior to the system can be imagined.[13]

As I have attempted to demonstrate, central to *Fight Club* is the interrelated critique of late capitalism and the politics of masculinity. The central protagonists, Jack and Tyler, represent two opposing registers that link consumerism and masculinity. Jack is representative of a generation of men condemned to corporate peonage whose emotional lives and investments are mediated through the allure of commodities and goods. No longer a producer of goods, Jack exemplifies a form of domesticated masculinity – passive, alienated, and without ambition. On the other hand, Tyler exemplifies an embodied masculinity that refuses the seductions of consumerism, while fetishizing forms of production – from soaps to explosives – the ultimate negative expression of which is chaos and destruction. Tyler represents the magnetism of the isolated, dauntless antihero whose public appeal is based on the attractions of the cult personality rather than on the strengths of an articulated democratic notion of political reform. Politics for Tyler is about doing, not thinking. As the embodiment of aggressive masculinity and hyperindividualism, Tyler cannot imagine a politics that connects to democratic movements, and is less a symbol of vision and leadership for the next millennium than a holdover of early-twentieth century fascist ideologies that envisioned themselves as an alternative to the decadence and decay of the established order of things. Tyler, played by the Hollywood superstar Brad Pitt (a contradiction that cannot be overlooked), seems appropriate as the founding father of Operation Mayhem – a vanguardist political movement, hierarchically organized through rigid social relations and led by a charismatic cult leader – as the only enabling force to contest the very capitalism of which it is an outgrowth. If Jack represents the crisis of capitalism repackaged as the crisis of a domesticated masculinity, Tyler represents the redemption of masculinity repackaged as the promise of violence in the interests of social and political anarchy.

While *Fight Club* registers a form of resistance to the rampant commodification and alienation of contemporary neoliberal society, it ultimately has little to say about those diverse and related aspects of consumer culture and contemporary capitalism structured in iniquitous power relations, material wealth, or hierarchical social formations. *Fight Club* largely ignores issues surrounding the breakup of labor unions, the slashing of the U.S. workforce, extensive plant closings, downsizing, outsourcing, the elimination of the welfare state, the attack on people of color, and the growing disparities between the rich and the poor. All of these issues get factored out of *Fight Club*'s analysis of consumerism and corporate alienation. Hence, it comes as no surprise that class as a critical category is non-existent in this film. When working-class people do appear, they are represented primarily as brownshirts, part of the nonthinking herd looking for an opportunity to release their tensions and repressed masculine rage through forms of terrorist violence and self-abuse. Or they appear as people who willingly take up jobs that are dehumanizing, unskilled, and alienating. There is one particularly revealing scene in *Fight Club* that brings this message home while simultaneously signaling a crucial element of the film's politics. At one point in the story, Tyler takes Jack into a convenience store. He pulls out a gun and forces the young Korean clerk to get on his knees. Putting the gun to the clerk's head, Tyler tells him he is going to die. As a kind of parting gesture, he then asks Raymond, the clerk, what he really wanted to be in life. A vetinarian, Raymond replies, but he had to drop out of school for lack of money. Tyler tells him that if he isn't on his way to becoming a vetinarian in six weeks he is going to come back and kill him. He then lets Raymond go and tells Jack that tomorrow morning will be the most important day in Raymond's life because he will have to address what it means to do something about his future. Choice for Tyler appears to be an exclusively individual act, a simple matter of personal will that functions outside of existing relations of power, resources, and social formations. As Homi Bhabha points out, this notion of agency "suggests that 'free choice' is inherent in the individual [and] . . . is based on an unquestioned 'egalitarianism' and a utopian notion of individualism that bears no relation to the history of the marginalized, the minoritized, the oppressed."[14]

This privatized version of agency and politics is central to understanding Tyler's character as emblematic of the very market forces he denounces. For Tyler, success is simply a matter of getting off one's back and forging ahead; individual initiative and the sheer force of will magically cancels out institutional constraints, and critiques of the gravity of dominant relations of oppression are dismissed as either an act of bad faith or the unacceptable whine of victimization. Tyler hates consumerism but he values a "Just Do It" ideology appropriated from the marketing strategists of the Nike corporation and the ideology of the Reagan era. It is not surprising that in linking freedom to the dynamics of individual choice, *Fight Club* offers up a notion of politics in which oppression breeds contempt rather than compassion, and social change is fueled by totalitarian visions rather than democratic struggles. By defining agency through such a limited (and, curiously Republican Party) notion of choice, *Fight Club* reinscribes freedom as an individual desire rather than the "testing of boundaries and limits as part of a communal, collective process."[15] In the end, *Fight Club* removes choice as a "public demand and duty"[16] and in doing so restricts the public spaces people are allowed to inhabit as well as the range of subject positions they are allowed to take up. Those spaces of debate, dialogue, and resistance such as union halls, democratic social movements, clubs, and other educational/ political sites simply disappear in this film. Hence, it is no wonder that *Fight Club* is marked by an absence of working men and women who embody a sense of agency and empowerment, focusing instead, on largely middle-class heterosexual white men who are suffering from a blocked hypermasculinity.

Consumerism in *Fight Club* is criticized primarily as an ideological force and existential experience that weakens and domesticates men, robbing them of their primary role as producers whose bodies affirm and legitimate their sense of agency and control. The importance of agency is not lost on director David Fincher, but it is restricted to a narrowly defined notion of masculinity that is as self-absorbed as it is patriarchal.[17] Fincher is less interested in fighting oppressive forms of power than he is in exploring how men yield to it. Freedom in *Fight Club* is not simply preoccupied within the depoliticized self; it also lacks a language for translating private troubles into public rage, and as such succumbs to the cult of immediate sensations in which freedom degenerates into collective impotence. Given Fincher's suggestion that men have no enduring qualities outside of their physicality, resistance and affirmation are primarily taken up as part of a politics of embodiment that has little concern for critical consciousness, social critique, or democratic social relations of resistance. In *Fight Club*, the body is no longer the privileged space of social citizenship or political agency, but becomes "the location of violence, crime, and [aggression]."[18] What changes in *Fight Club* is the context enabling men to assault each other, but the outside world remains the same, unaffected by the celebration of a hypermasculinity and violence that provides the only basis for solidarity.[19]

Fight Club's critique of consumerism suffers from a number of absences that need to be addressed. First, the film depicts capitalism and the ideology of consumerism as sutured, impenetrable, and totalizing, offering few if any possibilities for resistance or struggle, except by the heroic few. There is no sense of how people critically mediate the power of capitalism and the logic of consumerism, turn it against itself, and in doing so offer up daily possibilities for resistance, survival, and democratic struggles.[20] No space exists within *Fight Club* for appropriations that might offer critical engagements, political understanding, and enlightened forms of social change. Moreover, consumerism, for David Fincher, can only function within the libidinal economy of repression, particularly as it rearticulates the male body away from the visceral experiences of pain, coercion, and violence to the more "feminized" notions of empathy, compassion, and trust. Hence, masculinity is defined in opposition to both femininity and consumerism, while simultaneously refusing to take up either in a dialectical and critical way.

Second, *Fight Club* functions less as a critique of capitalism than as a defense of a highly stereotypical and limited sense of masculinity that is seen as wedded to the immediacy of pleasure sustained through violence and abuse. Once again, *Fight Club* becomes complicitous with the very system of commodification it denounces since both rely upon a notion of agency largely constructed within the immediacy of pleasure, the cult of hypercompetitiveness, and the market-driven desire of winning and exercising power over others. Third, *Fight Club* resurrects a notion of freedom tied to a Hobbesian world in which cynicism replaces hope, and the ideology of the "survival of the fittest" becomes literalized in the form of a clarion call for the legitimation of dehumanizing forms of violence as a source of pleasure and sociality. Pleasure in this context has less to do with justice, equality, and freedom than with hypermodes of competition mediated through the fantasy of violence. More specifically, this particular rendering of pleasure is predicated on legitimating the relationship between oppression and misogyny, and masculinity gains its force through a celebration of both brutality and the denigration of the feminine. Hence, *Fight Club* appears to have no understanding of its own articulation with the very forces of capitalism it appears to be attacking and this is most evident in its linking of violence, masculinity, and gender. In other words, *Fight Club*'s vision of liberation and politics relies on gendered and sexist hierarchies that flow directly from the consumer culture it claims to be criticizing.

Violence and the Politics of Masculinity

Unlike a number of Hollywood films in which violence is largely formulaic and superficially visceral, designed primarily to shock, titillate, and celebrate the sensational, *Fight Club* uses violence as both a form of voyeuristic identification and a pedagogical tool. Although *Fight Club* offers up a gruesome and relentless spectacle of bare-knuckled brutality, bloodcurdling and stylistic gore, violence becomes more than ritualistic kitsch: it also provides audiences with an ideologically loaded context and mode of articulation for legitimating a particular understanding of masculinity and its relationship to important issues regarding moral and civic agency, gender, and politics. Violence in *Fight Club* is treated as a sport, a crucial component that lets men connect with each other through the overcoming of fear, pain, and fatigue, while reveling in the illusions of a paramilitary culture. For example, in one vivid scene, Tyler initiates Jack into the higher reaches of homoerotically charged sadism by pouring corrosive lye on his hand, watching as the skin bubbles and curls. Violence in this instance signals its crucial function in both affirming the natural "fierceness" of men and in providing them with a concrete experience that allows them to connect at some primal level. As grotesque as this act appears, Fincher does not engage it – or similar representations in the film – as expressions of pathology.[21] On the contrary, such senseless brutality becomes crucial to a form of male bonding, glorified for its cathartic and cleansing properties.[22] By maximizing the pleasures of bodies, pain, and violence, *Fight Club* comes dangerously close to giving violence a glamorous and fascist edge.[23] In many respects, *Fight Club* mimics fascism's militarization and masculinization of the public sphere with its exultation of violence "as a space in which men can know themselves better and love one another legitimately in the absence of the feminine."[24] As a packaged representation of masculine crisis, *Fight Club* reduces the body to a receptacle for pain parading as pleasure, and in doing so fails to understand how the very society it attempts to critique uses an affirmative notion of the body and its pleasures to create consuming subjects. Terry Eagleton captures this sentiment:

> Sensation in such conditions becomes a matter of commodified shock-value regardless of content: everything can now become pleasure, just as the desensitized morphine addict will grab indiscriminately at any drug. To posit the body and its pleasures as an unquestionably affirmative category is a dangerous illusion in a social order which reifies and regulates corporeal pleasure for its own ends just as relentlessly as it colonizes the mind."[25]

But the violence portrayed in *Fight Club* is not only reductionistic in its affirmation of physical aggression as a crucial element of male bonding; it also fails to make problematic those forms of violence that individuals, dissidents, and various marginalized groups experience as sheer acts of oppression deployed by the state, racist and homophobic individuals, and a multitude of other oppressive social forces. What are the limits of romanticizing violence in the face of those ongoing instances of abuse and violence that people involuntarily experience every day because of their sexual orientation, the color of their skin, their gender, or their class status?[26] There is no sense in *Fight Club* of the complex connections between the operations of power, agency, and violence, or how some forms of violence function to oppress, infantalize, and demean human life.[27] Nor is there any incentive— given the way violence is sutured to primal masculinity – to consider how violence can be resisted, alleviated, and challenged through alternative institutional forms and social practices. It is this lack of discrimination among diverse forms of violence and the conditions for their emergence, use, and consequences, coupled with a moral indifference to how violence produces human suffering, that positions *Fight Club* as a morally bankrupt and politically reactionary film.[28] Representations of violence, masculinity, and gender in *Fight Club* seem all too willing to mirror the pathology of individual and institutional violence that informs the American landscape, extending from all manner of hate crimes to the far right's celebration of paramilitary and protofascist subcultures.

Fight Club does not rupture conventional ways of thinking about violence in a world in which casual violence and hip nihilism increasingly pose a threat to human life and democracy itself. Violence in this film functions largely through a politics of denial, insulation, and disinterest and is unable to criticize with any self-consciousness the very violence that it gleefully represents and celebrates. *Fight Club* portrays a society in which public space collapses and is filled by middle-class white men – disoriented in the pandemonium of conflicting social forces – who end up with a lot of opportunities for violence and little, perhaps none at all, for argument and social engagement.[29] Macho ebullience in *Fight Club* is directly linked to the foreclosure of dialogue and critical analysis and moves all too quickly into an absolutist rhetoric which easily lends itself to a geography of violence in which there are no ethical discriminations that matter, no collective forces to engage or stop the numbing brutality and rising tide of aggression. While Jack renounces Tyler's militia-like terrorism at the end of *Fight Club*, it appears as a meaningless gesture of resistance, as all he can do is stand by and watch as various buildings explode all around him. The message here is entirely consistent with the cynical politics that inform the film – violence is the ultimate language, referent, and state of affairs through which to understand all human events and there is no way of stopping it. This ideology becomes even more disheartening given the film's attempt to homogenize violence under the mutually determining forces of pleasure and masculine identity formation, as it strategically restricts not only our understanding of the complexity of violence, but also, as Susan Sontag has suggested in another context, "dissolves politics into pathology."[30]

The pathology at issue, and one which is central to *Fight Club*, is its intensely misogynist representation of women, and its intimation that violence is the only means through which men can be cleansed of the dire affect women have on the shaping of their identities. From the first scene of *Fight Club* to the last, women are cast as the binary opposite of masculinity. Women are both the other and a form of pathology. Jack begins his narrative by claiming that Marla is the cause of all of his problems. Tyler consistently tells Jack that men have lost their manhood because they have been feminized; they are a generation raised by women. And the critical commentary on consumerism presented throughout the film is really not a serious critique of capitalism as much as it is a criticism of the feminization and domestication of men in a society driven by relations of buying and selling. Consumerism is criticized because it is womanish stuff. Moreover, the only primary female character, Marla, appears to exist to simultaneously make men unhappy and to service their sexual needs. Marla has no identity outside of the needs of the warrior mentality, the chest-beating impulses of men who revel in patriarchy and enact all of the violence associated with such traditional, hyper-masculine stereotypes.[31]

But representations of masculinity in *Fight Club* do more than reinscribe forms of male identity within a warrior mentality and space of patriarchical relations. They also work to legitimate unequal relations of power and oppression while condoning a view of masculinity predicated on the need to wage violence against all that is feminine both within and outside of their lives.[32] Masculinity in this film is directly linked to male violence against women by virtue of the way in which it both ignores and thus sanctions hierarchical gendered divisions and a masculinist psychic economy. By constructing masculinity on an imaginary terrain in which women are foregrounded as the other, the flight from the feminine becomes synonymous with sanctioning violence against women as it works simultaneously to eliminate different and opposing definitions of masculinity. Male violence offers men a performative basis on which to construct masculine identity, and it provides the basis for abusing and battering an increasing number of women. According to the National Center for Victims of Crime, an estimated six million women are assaulted by a male partner each year in the United States and of these, 1.8 million are severely assaulted.[33] Affirming stereotypical notions of male violence, while remaining silent about how such violence works to serve male power in subordinating and abusing women, both legitimates and creates the pedagogical conditions for such violence to occur. *Fight Club* provides no understanding of how gendered hierarchies mediated by a misogynist psychic economy encourages male violence against women. In short, male violence in this film appears directly linked to fostering those ideological conditions that justify abuse towards women by linking masculinity exclusively to expressions of violence and defining male identity against everything that is feminine.

Fight Club as Public Pedagogy

> There is a link between epistemology and morality: between how we get to know what we know (through various, including electronic, media) and the moral life we aspire to lead. . . . Terrible things, by continuing to be shown, begin to appear matter-of-fact, a natural rather than man-made catastrophe. Zygmunt Bauman has labeled this the "production of moral indifference."[34]

While *Fight Club* generated a number of critical commentaries, few reviewers addressed the misogynistic nature of the film or the warrior mythology of the 1980s that it so closely resembles ideologically and politically.[35] In some cases, high profile critics such as Janet Maslin, writing in the *New York Times*, not only defended the film as a serious attempt to examine the "lure of violence" in a "dangerously regimented, dehumanized culture," she also condemned as mindless those critics who might view the film as a nihilistic "all-out assault on society."[36] Oddly enough, Twentieth Century Fox, the studio that produced *Fight Club*, viewed such criticism as dangerous rather than simply mindless, and proceeded to withdraw all of its movie advertising in the trade paper *The Hollywood Reporter* because it had published two critical reviews of the film. But while such politics are not new to Hollywood, the overt attempts by a major studio to censor the voices of dissent – because some critical reviews speak to the willing use of political power by corporate institutions in the cultural sphere to close down democratic relationships, denigrate women, and celebrate mindless violence – should nevertheless elicit public outrage. Certainly, Twentieth Century Fox has little to fear from "progressive" critics who largely praised the film. For example, Amy Taubin writing for *Sight and Sound* extolled the film for "screwing around with your bio-rhythms" and for expressing some "right-on-the *zeitgeist* ideas about masculinity."[37] Taubin, it seems, was also bowled over with Brad Pitt's new-found masculinity, and claims that "Pitt has never been as exquisite as he is with a broken nose and blood streaming down his cut body."[38] Susan Faludi made the remarkable statement in *Newsweek* that *Fight Club* is a *feminist film.*[39]

It seems that the connection between *Fight Club*'s underlying misogynist premises and its similarity to a number of recent Hollywood films that offer denigrating images of women has been lost on critics such as Maslin, Taubin, and feminist backlash expert Faludi. It gets worse. On-line journal, *Slate*, argued that veteran rock video director, Fincher, had transformed cinema with his hip digital editing style and that the most "thrilling thing about *Fight Club* isn't *what it says* but how . . . Fincher pulls you into its narrator's head and simulates his adrenalin rushes" (my emphasis).[40] Gary Crowdus, reviewing the video release of *Fight Club*, praises it as a "pitch-black comedy, an over-the-top, consciously outrageous social satire, characterized by excess and satire."[41] The violence in this film for Crowdus is merely an expression of comic fun and for those critics who missed it, each scene of violence "simply provided a comic or dramatic context for every fight, with each bout functioning in terms of character development or to signal a key turning point in the plot."[42] Largely formalist in nature, Crowdus's praise of the film completely ignores how it might be taken up as a form of public pedagogy or public transcript. There is no sense of how *Fight Club* resonates and functions through its refusal to rupture dominant codes within a much larger discursive arena in which violence, masculinity, and sexism are being presented by the right-wing and dominant media. Crowdus makes the mistake of treating this text as if it were merely hermetic and in doing so he appears unable to engage it through a language of articulation that addresses *Fight Club* in the context of contemporary representations and politics, particularly around the inter-relationship among gender, violence, and masculinity.

Fight Club's overall success with a large number of critics was also buoyed by an ongoing series of interviews with its stars Edward Norton, Brad Pitt, and Helena Bonham Carter, as well as a number of well-placed interviews with the film's director David Fincher.[43] Norton, for example, argues that the film is about young men having a problem defining their manhood and that it has little to do with fighting: "The fight club is not about fighting; it is a manifestation of a desire to strip away everything and rediscover yourself."[44] Norton goes so far as to claim that *Fight Club* is really a comedy similar to the classic coming-of-age film, *The Graduate*.

One of the more incredible, if not entirely inane, comments comes from Helena Bonham Carter who defends the film by claiming that Fincher is a feminist. In describing why she took on the role of Marla, she claims "The script was awfully dark, and in bad hands it could have been immature or possibly even irresponsible. But after meeting him, I could tell that it wasn't going to be a concern. He's not just an all-out testost package. He's got a healthy feminist streak."[45]

Fincher appeared at times to be caught on the defensive in having to provide some theoretical explanation and ethical justification for the film. Claiming that *Fight Club* was a film "that's downloaded in front of you. It doesn't wait for you," he seemed to suggest that many critics were tripping over themselves trying to understand the film. He has also argued that while the film is a coming-of-age narrative, he doesn't "purport for a second to know what a film should be, what entertainment should be, how much it should teach, how much it should titillate. I am just trying to make a good, funny movie."[46] And, of course, the implication is that neither should his audience. Fincher's comments are more than disingenuous; they represent, at the very least, an apologetic discourse for the increasing merger of over-the-top violence, hypermasculinity, and sexist inscriptions of women in Hollywood films.[47]

All of these comments exhibit a cavalier indifference to the ways in which films operate as public pedagogies within a broader set of articulations. That is, they ignore how such films function as public discourses that address or at least resonate with broader issues in the historical and sociopolitical context in which they are situated. There is no sense of how *Fight Club* – or films in general – bridge the gap between public and private discourses, playing an important role in placing particular ideologies and values into public conversation while offering a pedagogical space for addressing specific views of how everyday lives are intertwined with politics, social relations, and existing institutional formations. For instance, Fincher seems completely unaware of how his portrayal of violence and hypermasculinity resonates with the reactionary mythology of warrior culture that reached its heyday during Ronald Reagan's presidency and found its cultural embodiment in figures such as John Wayne, Oliver North, and a host of Hollywood movies celebrating rogue warriors such as *Lethal Weapon*, *Missing in Action*, *Robocop*, and *Rambo*.[48]

Given the enormous violence, misogyny, aggression, and political indifference that permeates contemporary daily life, it is crucial to understand how representations of male violence, scorn for everything that is feminine, and a protofascist politics in a film such as *Fight Club* resonate with a broader assemblage of historical and contemporary forces to reproduce, rather than challenge, some of the more oppressive forces in American society. Clearly, many critics of *Fight Club* as well as Fincher and the film's stars, appear completely indifferent to the kind of ideological work *Fight Club* performs in linking masculinity, violence, and politics at a historical moment when public politics is collapsing into privatized discourses and pleasures, and the crisis of masculinity is widely perceived as the most important manifestation of changing economic conditions. While it would be easy to dismiss the comments by Fincher, Norton, and Bonham Carter as nothing more than self-serving publicity – or simply idiotic in light of the representational politics of the film – such comments exemplify a period in which, as Hannah Arendt has pointed out in another context, violence might best be understood less by connecting it to people who are "cold-blooded enough to 'think the unthinkable,' [than to the fact] that they do not think."[49] Against the emergence of films such as *Fight Club* and the refusal on the part of critics and others to link the violence in the film to the violence directed against women, public life, and democracy itself, progressives and others need to question not only the conditions for the production of such films, but also how they work to construct particular definitions of agency. Such questions are crucial if progressives are going to rightfully explore what tools are needed to resist such romanticized notions of violence and masculinity.

Equally important is the need to understand *Fight Club* within both the heritage and the growing re-emergence of fascist cultural formations.[50] Paul Gilroy argues convincingly that contemporary formations are organized around "the special investment that fascist movements have made in the ideal of fraternity. The comprehensive masculinization of the public sphere and the militaristic style with which this has been accomplished in many different settings . . . [as well as] the strongly masculinist character derived principally from the exultation of war. . . ."[51] *Fight Club* emulates elements of what Gilroy calls a generic fascism, partially rehabilitating certain fascist ideas and principles that debase civic culture, and it does so by allowing an "armed and militarized political subject . . . to know itself"[52] through the aestheticization of politics in which libidinal pleasure, paramilitary rituals, and authoritarian rule intersect to authenticate "proto-fascistic, fascistic, and pseudo-fascistic forms of political culture."[53] Home-grown fascism may be easy to spot in the growing presence and violence of neo-Nazi organizations and other hate groups such as the National Association for the Advancement of White People, but it is less obvious in those popular modes of representations and image making – including films such as *Fight Club* – that feature excessive doses of paramilitary spectacle, appeal to the logic-defying patterns of conspiracy theory, and mobilize forms of identification around the temptations of fascist investments in militarized forms of male bonding and solidarity. Gilroy rightly argues that militarization was and remains the center of fascist style and aesthetic values and increasingly finds its most persuasive expressions in the pedagogical space that links entertainment with politics. Fincher's film reminds us that "The heritage of fascist rule survives inside democracy as well as outside it."[54]

In opposition to films such as *Fight Club*, progressives need to consider developing pedagogies of disruption that unsettle the commonsensical assumptions and ways of thinking that inform films and other cultural texts, particularly those that construct and legitimate certain subject positions, identities, values, and social relations that both celebrate pathologizing violence and render hypermasculinity as a space in which to reinscribe the hierarchies of gender, race, sexuality, and politics. James Snead is right in arguing that

> Mass culture in America today consists of an entirely new set of artifacts – mass visual productions. These new artifacts require new ways of seeing and new ways of thinking about what we are seeing . . . . We have to be ready, as film-goers, not only to see films, but also to see through them; we have to be willing to figure out what the film is claiming to portray, and also to scrutinize what the film is actually showing. Finally, we need to ask from whose social vantage point any film becomes credible or comforting, and ask why?[55]

But this should not suggest that educators, progressives and others simply need to teach students and others the skills of critical literacy in order to demythologize representations of violence, or to engage gendered representations, for instance, in radically new ways. This is an important but inadequate strategy. We need to go beyond questions of literacy and critique to issues of politics, power, and social transformation.

At the very least, the emergence of films such as *Fight Club* suggests that progressives need a new civic language and vocabulary to address the relevance of culture, politics, and pedagogy in order to understand not just how to read texts critically, but also to comprehend how knowledge circulates through various circuits of power in order to put into place images, experiences, representations, and discourses that objectify others and create the ideological conditions for individuals to become indifferent to how violence in its diverse expressions promotes human suffering. This suggests developing forms of public pedagogy that not only critically engage how language, images, sounds, codes, and representations work to structure basic assumptions about freedom, citizenship, public memory, and history, but also becoming attentive to how the material relations of power that produce and circulate forms of common sense can be challenged and transformed on both a national and transnational level. In this instance, public pedagogy links knowledge to power in an effort to understand how to affect social change. At stake here is both recognizing and developing a new vision of what we want the future to be, and struggling to acknowledge that the fundamental nature of cultural politics and knowledge production has not only changed dramatically in the last 50 years but that the culture industries and visual culture have become the primary pedagogical/political forces/spaces in shaping consciousness and legitimating dominating social practices. This is not meant to suggest that culture exists in opposition to what some have called a material politics as much as it points to the necessity of recognizing the pedagogical nature of any attempt to both unlearn and to relearn what it might mean to challenge those commonsense assumptions and institutional forms that shape oppressive relations, regardless of how and where they manifest themselves.

Films such as *Fight Club* become important as public pedagogies because they play a powerful role in mobilizing meaning, pleasures, and identifications. They produce and reflect important considerations of how human beings should live, engage with others, define themselves, and address how a society should take up questions fundamental to its survival. At the same time, if we are to read films such as *Fight Club* as social and political allegories articulating deeply rooted fears, desires, and visions, they have to be understood within a broader network of cultural spheres and institutional formations rather than as isolated texts. The pedagogical and political character of such films resides in the ways in which they align with broader social, sexual, economic, class, and institutional configurations.

Needless to say, *Fight Club*, as well as any other cultural text, can be read differently by different audiences, and this suggests the necessity to take up such texts in the specificity of the contexts in which they are received. But at the same time, educators, social critics, and others can shed critical light on how such texts work pedagogically to legitimate some meanings, invite particular desires, and exclude others. Acknowledging the educational role of such films requires that educators and others find ways to make the political more pedagogical. One approach would be to develop a pedagogy of disruption that would attempt to make students and others more attentive to visual and popular culture as an important site of political and pedagogical struggle. Such a pedagogy would raise questions regarding how certain meanings under particular historical conditions become more legitimate as representations of the real than others, or how certain meanings take on the force of commonsense assumptions and go relatively unchallenged in shaping a broader set of discourses and social configurations. Such a pedagogy would raise questions about how *Fight Club*, for instance, resonates with the ongoing social locations and conditions of fear, uncertainty, sexism, and political despair through which many people now live their lives. More specifically, a pedagogy of disruption would engage a film's attempts to shift the discourse of politics away from issues of justice and equality to a focus on violence and individual freedom as part of a broader neoliberal backlash against equity, social citizenship, and human rights. Such an approach would not only critically engage the dominant ideologies of masculinity, violence, and sexism that give *Fight Club* so much power in the public imagination, but also work to expose the ideological contradictions and political absences that characterize the film by challenging it as symptomatic of the growing reaction against feminism, the right-wing assault on the welfare state, and the increasing use of violence to keep in check marginalized groups such as young black males who are now viewed as a threat to order and stability.

Any attempt to critically address *Fight Club* and the implications its presence suggests for the changing nature of representational politics must also acknowledge that power is never totalizing, and that even within an increasingly corporatized social landscape there are always cracks, openings, and spaces for resistance. *Fight Club* reminds us of the need to reclaim the discourses of ethics, politics, and critical agency as important categories in the struggle against the rising tide of violence, human suffering, and the specter of fascism that threatens all vestiges of democratic public life. Precisely because of its ideological implications, *Fight Club* posits an important challenge to anyone concerned about the promise of democracy, and what it might mean for critical intellectuals and others to take a stand against the dominant media, while providing opportunities to develop what

Paul Gilroy calls in another context, "minimal ethical principles."[56] At the heart of such an engagement is the need to accentuate the tension between the growing threat to public life and the promise of a democracy that both remembers the history of human suffering and works to prevent its reoccurrence. The political limits of *Fight Club*'s attack on capitalism and consumerism should point to the need for a more sustained and systematic critique of the dire conditions of contemporary social life, especially as such conditions encourage a critique of neoliberalism that does not confuse it with fascism but at the same time points to those elements within global capitalism that remind us of what makes fascism possible.

Notes

1. Two versions of this essay appeared in *JAC (in press)* and *New Art Examiner* (Dec/Jan 2000/1): 32–7, 60–1.

2. Fredric Jameson, *The Seeds of Time* (New York: Columbia University Press, 1994), p. xii.

3. Theodor W. Adorno, *Critical Models* (New York: Columbia University Press, 1993), p. 290.

4. See, for example, Janet Maslin, "Such a Very Long Way from Duvets to Danger." *The New York Times* (October 15, 1999): B14; Amy Taubin, "So Good It Hurts." *Sight and Sound* (November, 1999): 16; Gary Crowdus, "Getting Exercised Over *Fight Club*." *Cineaste* 25.4 (2000): 46–8.

5. This genre was an outgrowth of a number of films, beginning with Quentin Tarantino's *Reservoir Dogs*. James Wolcott has labeled this genre as "scuzz cinema.... which earns its name from the pervasive, in-your-face, foulmouthed scuzziness of its low-life characters, situations, and atmosphere, all of which convey the bottom falling out of civilization." See James Wolcott, "Live Fast, Die Young, and Leave a Big Stain." *Vanity Fair* (April, 1998): 148. The latter infatuation with violence, cynicism, glitz, and shoot-outs in diners got a remake by adding a more updated gesture towards social relevance, i.e., critique of suburban life, consumerism, etc.

6. Eleanor Byrne and Martin McQuillan, *Deconstructing Disney* (London: Pluto Press, 1999), pp. 3–4.

7. Rustom Bharacuha, "Around Aydohya: Aberrations, Enigmas, and Moments of Violence." *Third Text* 24 (Autumn, 1993): 56.

8. Needless to say, feminist and gay theorists have been analyzing the politics of masculinity for quite some time. For an important series of theoretical analyses on the changing nature of masculinity in Hollywood cinema that draws on many of these traditions, see Stevan Cohan and Ina Rae Hark (eds.), *Screening the Male: Exploring Masculinities in Hollywood Cinema* (New York: Routledge, 1993).

9. Homi Bhabha, "Are You a Man or a Mouse," in Maurice Berger, Brian Wallis, and Simon Watson (eds.), *Constructing Masculinity* (New York: Routledge, 1995), pp. 57–65.

10. Susan Faludi, *Stiffed* (New York : W. Morrow, 1999).

11. Tom Peters adds a new twist in applying the logic of the market to everyday life by arguing that everyone should define themselves as a saleable item, a commodity. Specifically, Mr. Peters argues that everyone should come to see and treat themselves as brands. According to Peters, the one sure way of being successful in life is to market yourself as a brand name. Or, as Mr. Peters puts it, "It's this simple. You are a brand. You are in charge of your brand. There is no single path to success. And there is no one right way to create a brand called You. Except this: Start today. Or Else" Tom Peters, "The Brand Called You." *Fast Company* (August/September, 1997): 94.

12. This paragraph on Operation Mayhem is taken from Henry A. Giroux and Imre Szeman, "IKEA Boy and the Politics of Male Bonding: *Fight Club*, Consumerism, and Violence." *New Art Examiner* (December/January 2000/2001): 60.

13. Bill Readings, *The University in Ruins* (Cambridge, MA: Harvard University Press, 1996), p. 48.

14. Homi K. Bhabha, "The Enchantment of Art," in Carol Becker and Ann Wiens (eds.), *The Artist in Society* (Chicago: New Art Examiner, 1994), p. 33.

15. Ibid.

16. Ibid.

17. For some excellent commentaries on the politics of masculinity, see R.W. Connell, *Masculinities* (Berkeley: University of California Press, 1995); Maurice Berger, Brian Wallis, and Simon Watson (eds.), *Constructing Masculinity*, Paul Smith op. cit. (ed.), *Boys : Masculinities in Contemporary Culture* (Boulder, CO: Westview Press, 1996).

18. Paul Gilroy, "'After the Love Has Gone': Bio-Politics and Ethepoetics in the Black Public Sphere," *Public Culture* 7.1 (1994): 58.

19. For an interesting commentary on the way in which dominant forms of masculinity work to reproduce particular notions of racism, see Robin D. G. Kelley, "Confessions of a Nice Negro, or Why I Shaved My Head,"

in Don Belton (ed.), *(Speak My Name): Black Men On Masculinity and the American Dream* (Boston: Beacon Press, 1997), pp. 15–28.

20. For an interesting analysis of what might be called the dialectic of consumerism, see Robert Miklitsch, *From Hegel to Madonna: Towards a General Economy of "Commodity Fetishism"* (Albany, NY: SUNY Press, 1998).

21. Susan Bordo offers a number of critical insights around the relationship between art and its growing tendency to celebrate and "become more sympathetic of the pathologies of our culture than of exposing them." See Susan Bordo, *Twilight Zones: The Hidden Life of Cultural Images* (Berkeley: University of California Press, 1999), p. 27.

22. Dr. Nadine Hoover is on target in arguing "There is something terribly wrong with our society when abuse becomes a means of bonding." Cited in Andrew Jacobs, "Violent Cast of High School Hazing Mirrors Society, Experts Say." *New York Times* (March 5, 2000): NE 27–8.

23. The classic work on the relationship between fascism, male violence, and hatred of women is Klaus Theweleit, *Male Fantasies vols. 1 and 2* (Minneapolis: University of Minnesota Press, 1987, 1989).

24. Paul Gilroy, *Against Race* (Cambridge, MA: Harvard University Press, 2000), p. 146.

25. Terry Eagleton, *The Ideology of the Aesthetic* (Cambridge, MA: Blackwell, 1990), p. 344.

26. One wonders how Fincher would retheorize the relationship between misogyny and the celebration of violence in *Fight Club* in light of the recent attack by mobs of young men against a number of women in Central Park after the Puerto Rican Day parade in New York City during the summer of 2000. Of course, it would be fatuous to claim that utterly misogynist films such as *Fight Club* are directly responsible for the recent incident in which 56 women were attacked by roving bands of young men who doused them with water, groped them, and ripped off their clothes. But I don't think it would be unreasonable to argue that misogynist films such as *Fight Club* help to legitimate such acts, because they exercise a pedagogical force shaped largely by a dominant politics of sexist representations that contributes to an increasing climate of hatred and objectification of women.

27. Commenting on the kinds of violence that is often ignored in films such as *Fight Club*, Holly Sklar writes "Imagine [films such as *Fight Club* giving] sustained national attention to the violence waged on the mind, body, and spirit of crumbling schools, [or to] low teacher expectations, employment and housing discrimination, racist dragnets, and everyday looks of hate by people finding you guilty by suspicion." Holly Sklar, "Young and Guilty by Stereotype." *Z Magazine* (July/August, 1993): 53.

28. For a masterful analysis of the complexities of theorizing violence as well as a critique of its romanticization, see John Keane, *Reflections on Violence* (London: Verso, 1996).

29. This theme is take up in a number of recent books: see Jeffrey C. Goldfarb, *The Cynical Society: The Culture of Politics and the Politics of Culture in American Life* (Chicago: University of Chicago Press, 1991); Joseph N. Capella and Kathleen Hall Jamieson, *Spiral of Cynicism: The Press and the Public Good* (New York: Oxford University Press, 1997); Russell Jacoby, *The End of Utopia* (New York: Basic Books, 1999); William Chaloupka, *Everybody Knows: Cynicism in America* (Minneapolis: University of Minnesota Press, 1999); Zygmunt Bauman, *In Search of Politics* (Stanford CA: Stanford University Press, 1999); Carl Boggs, *The End of Politics: Corporate Power and the Decline of the Public Sphere* (New York: Guilford Press, 2000).

30. Cited in Carol Becker, "The Art of Testimony." *Sculpture* (March, 1997): 28.

31. For one of the most popular celebrations of this warrior mentality, see Robert Bly, *Iron John : A Book About Men* (Reading, MA: Addison-Wesley, 1990). For a sustained critique of this position, see James William Gibson, *Warrior Dreams: Paramilitary Culture in Post-Vietnam America* (New York: Hill and Wang, 1994).

32. This theme is explored in Tania Modleski, *Feminism Without Women* (New York: Routledge, 1991).

33. Cited from the National Center For Victims of Crime website. See: http://207.222.132.10/index%7E1.htm.

34. Geoffrey Hartman, "Public Memory and its Discontents." *Raritan* 8.4 (Spring, 1994): 28, 26.

35. On the cult of the warrior mythology and its relationship to male violence, see the exceptionally important work done on this subject by James William Gibson, *Warrior Dreams*, op. cit.

36. Janet Maslin, "Such a Very Long Way from Duvets to Danger," op. cit.

37. Amy Taubin, "So Good It Hurts," op. cit., p. 16.

38. Ibid., p. 17.

39. Susan Faludi, "It's 'Thelma and Louise' for Guys." *Newsweek* (October 25, 1999): 89.

40. David Edelstein, "Boys Do Bleed." *www.Slate.com* (October 15, 1999): 4.

41. Crowdus, "Getting Exercised Over *Fight Club*," op. cit. p. 46.

42. Ibid., p. 47.

43. See, for example, Bob Strauss, "Actors Defend Ultra Violent Film." *The Arizona Republic* (October 15, 1999): D1; Gavin Smith, "Inside-Out-on-One With David Fincher." *Film Comment* (Sept/October, 1999): 58–67.

44. Edward Norton cited in Barry Koltnow, "Club's Call to Arms is Not Call to Violence." *Centre Daily Times* (October 19, 1999): 11C.
45. Cited in Benjamin Svtkey, "Blood Sweat and Fears." *Entertainment Weekly* (October 15, 1999): 28.
46. Both quotes come from Svtkey, ibid., pp. 26, 31.
47. I take up this issue in Henry A. Giroux, *Fugitive Cultures* (New York: Routledge, 1996), and in Henry A. Giroux, *Channel Surfing: Racism, the Media and the Destruction of Today's Youth* (New York: St. Martin's Press, 1998).
48. This issue is taken up brilliantly in Susan Jeffords, *Hard Bodies: Hollywood Masculinity in the Reagan Era* (New York: Rutgers University Press, 1994). Of course, this type of representation is ongoing and can be found in recent films such as *Saving Private Ryan, The Thin Red Line,* and *Three Kings.*
49. Hannah Arendt, "On Violence," in *Crisis of the Republic* (New York: A Harvest Book, 1969), p. 108.
50. See for example, Martin A. Lee, *The Beast Reawakens: Fascism's Resurgence From Hitler's Spymasters to Today's Neo-Nazi Groups and Right-Wing Extremists* (New York: Routledge, 2000).
51. Paul Gilroy, *Against Race* (Cambridge, MA: Harvard University Press, 2000), p. 146.
52. Ibid., p. 150.
53. Ibid., p. 158.
54. Ibid., p. 152
55. James Snead, *White Screens/Black Images* (New York: Routledge, 1994), pp. 131, 142.
56. Gilroy, *Against Race*, op. cit., p.5.

Index

INDEX

INDEX

INDEX

INDEX

INDEX

INDEX

INDEX

Lightning Source UK Ltd.
Milton Keynes UK
UKOW06f0728050216

267799UK00001B/126/P